AF587796

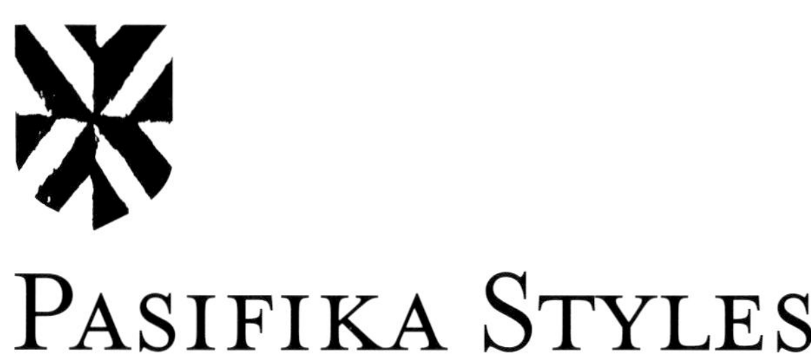

Pasifika Styles

Artists inside the museum

Edited by Rosanna Raymond and Amiria Salmond

University of Cambridge Museum of Archaeology
and Anthropology, Cambridge
in association with
Otago University Press

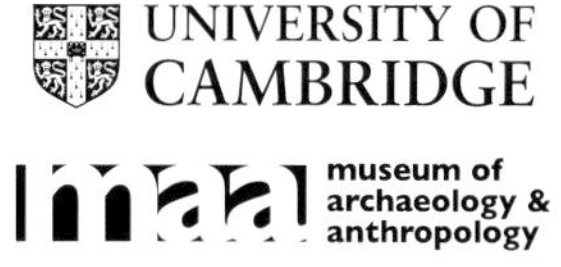

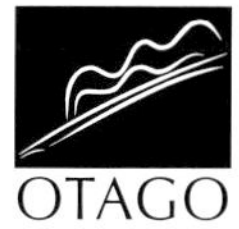

This book is dedicated to Karlos Quartez

First published 2008 to accompany the exhibition *Pasifika Styles*
5 May 2006 to 23 February 2008
by the University of Cambridge Museum of Archaeology and Anthropology
Downing Street, Cambridge, UK CB2 3DZ
www.maa-cambridge.org

In association with

Otago University Press
PO Box 56, Dunedin, New Zealand
Fax: 64 3 479 8385 or www.otago.ac.nz/press

Front cover image: *he tautoko* (2006). Artist: Lisa Reihana. Photographer: Kerry Brown.
Back cover image: *Whakaruruhau* (2005). Artist: Louise Potiki-Bryant.

ISBN 978-1-877372-60-5 (Otago)
ISBN 978-0-947595-17-3 (Cambridge)
A catalogue record of this book is available from the British Library

Designed by Delete
Photography by Josh Bell, Kerry Brown, Carine Durand, Jocelyne Dudding, Ani O'Neill, Gwil Owen, Rosanna Raymond, Sherry Roberts, Amiria Salmond, Mike Weston.

Printed through Condor Production Ltd, Hong Kong

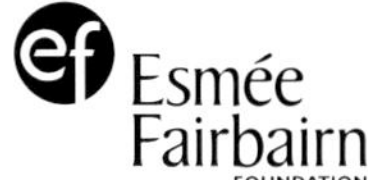

The Leverhulme Trust

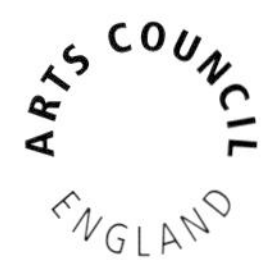

Contents

PREFACE

Nicholas Thomas
Director, University of Cambridge Museum of Archaeology and Anthropology

In 1990, during a family holiday, my first visit to New Zealand, I wandered into the Sarjeant Gallery in Wanganui, a town on the North Island's west coast, and encountered *Te Moemoea no Iotefa – the Dream of Joseph*, subtitled 'a celebration of Pacific art and taonga'. I walked around the exhibition with a sense of mounting excitement: here was an extraordinary combination of historic museum objects, contemporary islands craft, drawings, paintings, and sculptures by young Polynesian migrant artists, colonial photographs, and works by white New Zealand artists that responded in one way or another to Pacific culture. The show seemed at a stroke to subvert or disregard all the old hierarchies and distinctions, crossing ethnic boundaries, presenting past and present, 'craft' and 'art', together. *Te Moemoea*, curated by Rangihiroa Panoho, was in fact a life-changing inspiration: in due course I began research on art in Aotearoa New Zealand, and would spend much of the subsequent decade talking to artists and others, hanging out on the sidelines as exhibitions such as Jim Vivieaere's *Bottled Ocean* came together, and looking, often critically, at museums from the outside in. I never imagined that 15 years later I'd be appointed the director of one, and would again witness a sparkling staging of 'Pacific art and *taonga*', in Cambridge (UK) of all places.

Amiria Salmond and Rosanna Raymond have collaborated to produce a landmark exhibition, that capitalizes on the diverse, witty, sexy and serious body of art, fashion, exhibition and performance that grew and evolved in Aotearoa over the 1990s and subsequently. But their collaboration was in fact on a project and a process, a set of voyages and encounters, not just the production of a display. The exhibition incorporates the work of several senior artists, notably Maureen Lander and Lisa Reihana, others such as John Ioane and Michel Tuffery whose early exhibitions include Panoho's 1990 show, and many younger practitioners in various media. But what makes it a challenging and distinguished successor to shows such as *Te Moemoea* and *Bottled Ocean* is neither in bringing the field up to date – 'where Aotearoa went next', as it were – nor in being the first major show of this body of work in the UK, though both these accomplishments are important. Not least, because a point that has become obvious to Aotearoa audiences remains less evident to European ones: that the great cultures of the Pacific are not past but present, neither dead nor degraded but very much alive, and culturally productive in ways that can't be pigeonholed. The *Pasifika Styles* Performing Arts Festival, an integral aspect of the project, did much to underscore this.

But *Pasifika Styles* has a more distinctive significance in the space between art and museology. A number of Pacific, Maori, and Pakeha artists in New Zealand had been moved by, and moved to respond to, collected objects and museum environments in their work. How could they not? Those *taonga* or ancestral treasures were among the most present and powerful expressions of cultural tradition; their institutionalization in museums, let's face it, what had been and maybe still were white settler museums, indexed loss and dispossession, even as it made cultural resources available, or potentially available, to communities and artists today. Yet, if this emerged as an issue and a theme in practice within New Zealand, it was never the focus. *Pasifika Styles* turned what might otherwise have appeared the unsuitability of the host institution – a university museum far from New Zealand, an ethnographic collection, not a contemporary art space – to advantage, I think quite brilliantly, by fomenting a process of engagement between contemporary practitioners and historic artefacts.

To do so was to acknowledge one process of expatriation by staging another. The importance of MAA's Pacific collections is quite out of proportion to the size and visibility of the museum. Hardly well-known among the general public outside Cambridge, the collections include unique pieces deriving from the voyages of Cook and Vancouver to the Pacific, the single most important collections in the world from Fiji and the Torres Strait Islands, gathered during the researches of early curators Anatole von Hügel and Alfred Haddon respectively, and hundreds of other outstanding carved, woven, painted and assembled objects, ranging from canoes and house-posts through masks to ornaments and fish-hooks, representing hundreds of cultural groups from New Guinea to Hawaii and Rapanui. The bulk of these objects were brought to Britain between the late eighteenth and early twentieth centuries, the collections sometimes an afterthought, sometimes an aim of exploratory and anthropological expeditions, of missionary work, of trade and colonization, and even tourism.

The preservation of great collections of cultural objects, remote from their communities of origin, people who in many cases hold no comparable collections themselves, has needless to say been seen as problematic, if not simply as an ongoing colonial wrong that should be redressed through repatriation. While it is often assumed by educated people in the UK and elsewhere that museum collections consist largely of imperial loot that ought to be returned, in fact both processes of acquisition, and contemporary attitudes among those who were collected from, are more various than these perceptions suggest. Many articles were obtained through what, so far as can be established historically, was understood as fair dealing by parties on both sides; if some objects certainly were illegitimately appropriated, or were traded in invidious circumstances, there are many others that were not removed from ordinary or community use, but were actually produced on commission for fieldworkers or travellers, or that people explicitly wished to be taken back to a traveller's home country, for whatever reasons of their own.

These manifold interests at the scene of collecting seem mirrored in recent and contemporary responses to collections among Maori, Pacific Islanders, and other native peoples. Certainly some, particularly those struggling with ongoing settler-colonialism, effectively see expatriated collections as a sphere for contestation over sovereignty, and feel deeply that they ought to be brought home, irrespective of the specific circumstances of their collection. Others are in contrast affirmative, seeing the export of great works as a strategy of empowerment on the part of their ancestors, or, at any rate consider these objects now as cultural ambassadors.

The substance of this book is effectively concerned with the creative and diverse responses of the artists who participated in *Pasifika Styles* to this issue, to the Cambridge collections in general, and in some cases to specific objects associated with their own *whakapapa* (genealogy). Though the exhibition, the associated events, and this book are interesting on many levels, I see the central accomplishment of the project as a whole in reframing this problematic, and bringing it to a new level of sophistication. There is a certain kind of heritage-speak around various government and international agencies, which presumes people have an organic attachment to material objects associated with their past. This might broadly reflect the profound attachment that many Maori and Pacific Islanders may have to *taonga*, to historic treasures, but is quite inadequate in reflecting the diversity of attachments (and non-attachments), as well as the sorts of ambivalence and even estrangement engendered by historic processes. It is important to recall that some Islanders are fundamentalist Christians, suspicious of art forms associated with the pagan past, and would not welcome engagement with historic collections; in contrast those who participated in *Pasifika Styles* have broadly welcomed engagement, but have done so in notably diverse ways, some ultimately more reserved or sceptical, others more positively affirmative, of what the museum could offer.

Out of the voyages and encounters that Amiria and Rosanna have curated, with imagination, *aroha* (love) and endless hard work, the Museum of Archaeology and Anthropology takes away a renewed sense of our commitment to engagement, to work with people with historic links to our collections. We tend, in museum statements, to refer to a commitment to 'collaborate with originating communities', which is a slightly anodyne, even misleading way of putting it. Certainly, we do work with local organizations and groups – and currently are doing this with Inuit, Zuni, and Torres Strait Islanders among others. But this is not a formal diplomatic process, intended simply to supplement information, to do our duty, to tick boxes. Rather, it has the unpredictability of people coming together, and, as *Pasifika Styles* has revealed and exemplified, the ideas and works that emerge from such encounters are not necessarily present in the people, the objects, or the institution beforehand. The voyages – of colonial explorers, indigenous people, and curators alike – lead to discoveries of all sorts. The business of discovery is contentious. But – *Pasifika Styles* suggests – it is a pleasure too.

Nicholas Thomas
September 2007

Acknowledgments

The *Pasifika Styles* project was made possible by the combined efforts of a broad and diverse community, encompassing Britain, New Zealand, and many points between and beyond. We are extremely grateful to all those who donated their support and advice to the project, and particularly to the many people who gave freely of their time, energy and experience, putting their shoulders to the paddle in order to make it happen.

Special thanks go to the exhibiting artists, who brought their works (listed at the back of this volume) and, where possible, themselves, to Cambridge: Donna Campbell, Chris Charteris, Jeanine Clarkin, Kewana Duncan, Bethany Edmunds, Jason Hall, Niki Hastings-McFall, Lonnie Hutchinson, Shigeyuki Kihara, Maureen Lander, Nick McFarlane, Hemi Macgregor, Mark McClean, George Nuku, Ani O'Neill, Reuben Paterson, James Pinker, Louise Potiki-Bryant, Rachel Rakena, Lisa Reihana, Natalie Robertson, Mandrika Rupa, Greg Semu, Suzanne Tamaki, Lisa Taouma, Dan Taulapapa-McMullin, Tracey Tawhiao, Filipe Tohi, Michel Tuffery, Sheyne Tuffery, Francis Upritchard, Che Wilson, and Wayne Youle. Also to Kahu Te Kanawa.

Thanks and praise to the *Pasifika Styles* team, who built a strong platform on which the artists could present their work, while at the same time orchestrating a warm welcome for them in Cambridge: Mark Elliott (Installation Co-ordinator), Sandi Goodwin (Festival Production Manager), Sarah-Jane Harknett (Workshop and Publicity Co-ordinator), Anita Herle (Senior Curatorial Advisor), Carl Hogsden (Technical Consultant), Alexander Leiffheidt (Festival Director), Billie Lythberg (New Zealand Project Liaison), Brenda Railey (Artists' Auction Coordinator), Aroha Rangi (London Launch Coordinator), Sarah Robins (Producer and Interviewer, *Kōrero Mai* audio project), Georgia Tsouni (Festival Marketing Director and Assistant to the Festival Director), Wonu Veys (Curatorial Assistant and Gala Opening Co-ordinator), Mike Weston (Sponsorship Agent), Rebecca Wilson (Catalogue-brochure Editor), Wendy Brown (Museum Administrator), Matt Buckley and Marcus Miller (Workshop), Sam McGrath-Thompson (Head Museum Attendant) and Carine Durand, Rachel Feinmark, Alice Rogalla von Bieberstein, Melanie Rouse and Rebecca Taylor (student volunteers). Also to workshop partner organizations Manaia Maori Performing Arts, Escape Artists, and Toi Hauiti.

Our warm gratitude to those who offered their support in words and in kind to *Pasifika Styles*, by giving their names and backing, acting as referees for funding applications, and gifting their skills, expertise and aroha to the project: Chris Adams, Gerrard Albert, Dominic Alessio, Mark Amery, Claire Anholt, Cushla Aston, Atamira Dance Company, Penelope Barr, Matt Barron, Alison Bartley, Beats of Polynesia, Natasha Beckman, Suzanne Blumhardt, Lui Brame, Rachel Broadmore, Deidre Brown, Jason Brown, Kerry Brown, Ron Brownson, Asha Burchett, Karl and Kateia Burrows, Suzanne Campbell-Jones, Anna Cameron, Anton Carter, Garth Cartwright, Bronwyn Chang, Stephen Chard, Daniel Clarke, Neville Clifton,

Brent Clough, Zac Cole, Jeremy Coote, Elizabeth Cory-Pearce, Amanda Cropper, Paul Cullin, Alice Curtis Rose, Rachel Dawick, Anne D'Alleva, Geoff Devereux, Luke Dixon, Chaz Doherty, Kamalu Du Preez, Jasper Edwards, Simone Ellis, Sefa Enari, Chris Evans, Mary Fenwick, Fatu Feu`u, Kylie Fife, Neil Finn, Tim Finn, Kathleen Fogarty, Mere Forbes, Dianna Fuemana, Mhari Gallagher, Virginia Garlick, Fenn Gordon, Peter Gordon, Stuart Gray, James Hadley, Liz Hancock, Brent Hansen, Kat Harrington, Chili Hawes, Rachel Helyer Donaldson, Mark and Manuka Henare and whanau, Amanda Hereaka, Abigail Hinton, Carla Hofler, Steve Hooper, Grace Houet, Esther Hudson, Jonathan Hunt, Sarah Hunter, Susan Huria, Erolia Ifopo, Will Ilolahia, John Ioane, Carol Ivory, Jeff, Esther and Maia Jessop, Pare Keiha, Bev Kerr, Rachael Kinley, Marilyn Kohlhase, Mark Kopua, Georgina Langdale, Jeremy Leeming, Karl Leonard, Huttson Lo, Innes Logan, Mere Lomaloma Eliot, Ema and Vea Mafile`o, Kolokesa Uafa Mahina, Ole Maiava, Sean Mallon, Manaia Maori Performing Arts, Damon Mangos, Levi Mapina Lalamasina, Jenny Marshall, Russell Marshall, Marques Marzan, John McDavitt, Michael McGrath, Ben Morris, Andrew Moutu, Darcy Nicholas, Gary Nicholas, Ngahuia Ngata, Sarah Ngata, Wayne Ngata, Tony Panayiotou, James Peace, Merimeri Penfold, Giles Peterson, Lemi Ponifasio, Richard Purkiss, Teremoana Rapley, Kayne Raymond, Ulric Raymond, Flicky Riddell, Neil Robinson, Anne and Jeremy Salmond, Veronica Sekules, Derek Smail, Natasha Smith, Rewai Solomon, Pauline de Souza, Mary Strang, Marilyn Strathern, Linda and Mua Strickson-Pua, Awhina Tamarapa, Megan Tamati-Quennell, Katie Taney, Ann Taylor, Anne Taylor, Ngahuia Te Awekotuku, Haniko Te Kurupa, Linda Te Puni, Thea Thomson, Philip Thwaites, Ben Tippett, Nicholas Thomas, Sarah Todd, Suzan Tokcan, Colleen Toomey, Peter Tovey, Makerita Urale, Karen Van Oostrum, Caroline Vercoe, Donna Vose, Ralph Walker, Fiona Wall, Frances Walsh, Emere and Wharehoka Wano, Chantelle Whaiapu, Suzanne White, Leafa Wilson, Kitty Wishart and Angharad Wynne-Jones.

We are grateful to the following people for their advice, critique and encouragement in the development stages: Marjorie Allthorpe-Guyton, Matiu Baker, David Booth, Aaron Brown, Elizabeth Caldwell, Venu Dhupa, Jolene Douglas, Elizabeth Ellis, Ngarino Ellis, Otis Frizzel, Rob Garrett, Lil Grey, Arapata Hakiwai, Catherine Hamilton, Sam Hauwaho, Vilsoni Hereniko, Celia Hunt, Bryn Hyacinth, Buddy Mikaere, Glen Mills, Robert Leonard, Jonathan Mane-Wheoki, Ngahiraka Mason, Anna Miles, Cath Nesus, Graeme Osborne, Pacific Arts Centre, Rangi Panoho, Nicola Railton, Leilani Salesa, Huhana Smith, Mike Spedding, Paul Tapsell, Katerina and Teresia Teaiwa, Diggeress Te Kawana, James Te Puni, Jo Torr, Jim Vivieaere and Tim Walker.

Last but by no means least, our thanks to the funding bodies and other organisations which provided the resources necessary to launch *Pasifika Styles* and keep it (and its participants) going for the duration of the project. For financial support we are grateful to the Esmée Fairbairn Foundation, Arts Council England, The Leverhulme Trust, the Arts and Humanities Research Council, Littoral Arts Trust, The University of Cambridge's Crowther Beynon and Smuts funds, Te Waka Toi, The Pacific Arts Committee of Creative New Zealand and the Artists' Auction Fund. For in-kind support and sponsorship we would like to thank *Art Asia Pacific* magazine, Bass FM, Cambridge Apartments, CAT Scaffolding, Curious Films, Delete, Delmaine Fine Foods, Kim Crawford Wines, Loop Recordings, the New Zealand High Commission London, *New Zealand Inspired* magazine, *New Zealand News UK*, Ngati Ranana, Objectspace Gallery, October Gallery, PandIS, PicPac, PISUKI, The Providores and Tapa Room, Sacred Cafe, Spacific (UK), *Spasifik* magazine (NZ), the Tautai Trust, Tohu Wines, Transmit and Waimata Cheese.

George Nuku would like to add the following dedication and acknowledgments for his work, *Outer Space Marae* (2006): *Ki nga tamaiki katoa o te ao* – the work is dedicated to the divine ones on earth; in particular Kahuti Te Heu Heu Tamihana, Naboua Ta`akoi Te Rangikoianake, and Te Aonehe Xavier Puruhi. My acknowledgements to the following; Shigeyuki Kihara, Te Waka Toi, Dan Willdridge and Omeka Takiari – *Nga mihi nui kia koutou*.

Pasifika Styles, a waiata

Che Wilson
Pūkōrero/Kaitito (Orator and Composer)
Pasifika Styles Artist and Tikanga (Maori Protocol) Advisor

This *waiata* was composed to support the opening of the *Pasifika Styles* exhibition. The words of the *waiata* embrace a range of Polynesian languages to acknowledge the common ancestry of *tagata Pasifika* (Pacific peoples). This artform was also adopted to remind people to acknowledge great events in the form of song.

Nō Tahiti nui, Nō Kahiki loa
Nō Tawhiti pāmamao![1]

We are the people of the Great Tahiti, the Long Kahiki, the Distant Tawhiti.
Noble and great, we ARE *divine.*

Whakawhiti te Moananui-ā-Kiwa
Ki whenua tauhou, mātao e.
Mokemoke kau ana mo te wā roa
Hari koa i te wā iti nei
Hari koa i te wā iti nei

We crossed the Great Ocean of Kiwa
To land, new and cold.
A long solitude in foreign hands
We celebrate this special day
An expression of life!

(Tū mai)
Tū mai e Sina (Hina)[2] hei rama i te pō

Sina (the Moon Goddess) stands as a beam of light in darkness

(Arahi)
Arahi i ngā uri ki te whenua nei

Guiding YOU, our descendants to this land to celebrate this day.

(Karanga)
Kia kā mai te ora, te mana e
Kia kā mai te ora, te mana e

You re-energise and stimulate the life in us, YOUR ancestral and modern taonga.

Whakawhetai (Fa`afetai)[3] atu ki te rangi
He rā hari koa, aroha e

Thanks to the heavens above
For this celebration, as you,

E hono nei ngā tai o te moana
Te Moananui-ā-Kiwa e
Te Moananui-ā-Kiwa e

(Tū mai)
Tū mai e Sina (Hina) hei rama i te pō
(Arahi)
Arahi i ngā uri ki te whenua nei
(Karanga)
Kia kā mai te ora, te mana e
Kia kā mai te ora, te mana e, te mana e, te mana e!

Nō Tahiti nui, Nō Kahiki loa, Nō Tawhiti pāmamao. Hi!

Our descendants, have come together
To celebrate our collective descent,
OUR divinity!

Sina (the Moon Goddess) stands as a beam of light in darkness

Guiding YOU, our descendants to this land to celebrate this day.

You re-energise and stimulate the life in us, YOUR ancestral and modern taonga.

We are the people of the Great Tahiti, the Long Kahiki, the Distant Tāwhiti. Noble and great, we ARE divine.

Che Wilson, March 2006

Notes

1 These are the Tahitian, Hawaiian and Maori names of the Homeland of Hawaiki.
2 This is a reference to the Samoan and Maori name for the Goddess of the Moon.
3 Depending on the language of the singer they can use any Pacific variation of the word '*whakawhetai*' (to give thanks) and/or Sina (Moon Goddess).

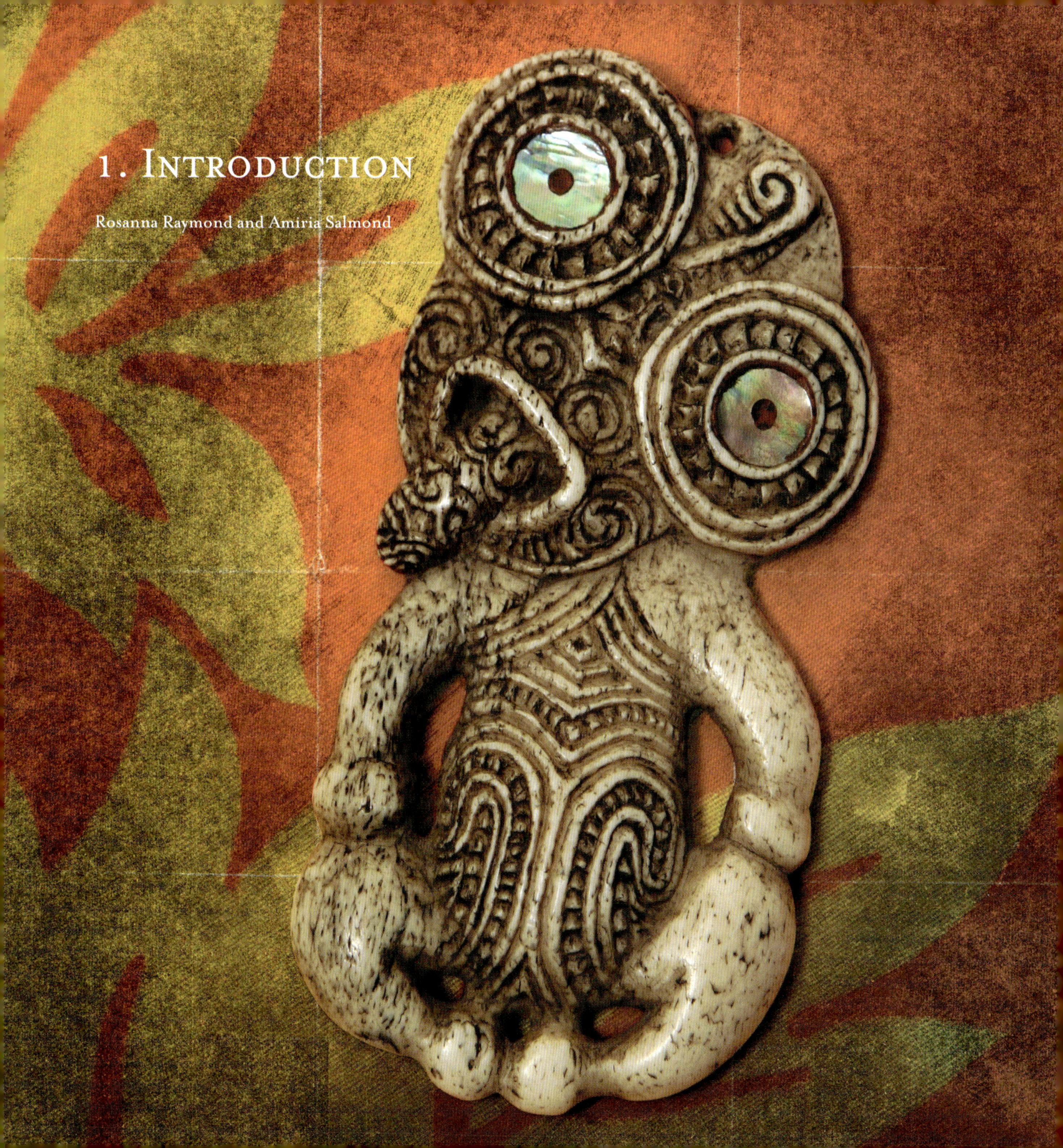

1. Introduction

Rosanna Raymond and Amiria Salmond

Carved bone *hei tiki* from MAA's collections (Z 6458), photographed in *The Living Room* (2006), an installation by Ani O'Neill and Tracey Tawhiao. Photograph: Kerry Brown.

1. Introduction

Rosanna Raymond and Amiria Salmond

Opening night

The visitors made their way up the stone staircase of the Museum as the glass-topped roof of the gallery resonated with the volume of singing voices, drums drumming and feet beating on the mezzanine floor. Everything was alive, from the faces of people as they first saw the artworks, to the sunshine glancing off shiny plastic and sweaty brows, to the feathered adornments vibrating on old and new gods as their relatives took over the room.

The *Pasifika Styles* project at the University of Cambridge produced a major exhibition of contemporary artworks at the Museum of Archaeology and Anthropology, a festival of performing arts in venues around the city, and numerous other public and artistic activities and events. This was the first time the Museum had undertaken such a large-scale collaboration with artists, and the first time most of the artists had chosen to exhibit their work in a museum. Many of the pieces on show were by people of New Zealand Maori and Pacific Island descent, but the scope of the project was not ethnically defined – the idea was to emphasise the global impact of cultural trajectories emerging from Polynesia, which have moved far beyond lines of descent. More than twenty New Zealand- and London-based artists visited Cambridge to take part in performances, to study the museum's Oceanic collections, and to run public workshops and drop-in sessions that drew people into the museum from around the UK and beyond. Several were also able to participate in an international conference on Pacific art, offering their views on a variety of issues to those who write from a distance about their work. Their presence in the museum had a major impact on staff, students, scholars and members of the public who visited the exhibition, some of whom recorded their surprise and interest in the vitality of contemporary artistic practice in the Pacific.

> [I was] surprised to see contemporary Pacific work... fantastic and especially after the colonial gathering of downstairs (Michelle, a visitor from Australia).

> [What I liked most was] the humour of the contemporary references and the feeling that it is 'living' art not an artefact in a museum (respondent to the visitor survey).

One of the main objectives of *Pasifika Styles* from the institutional side was to literally enliven the Museum, demonstrating the present-day relevance of its collections by inviting to Cambridge some of the people to whom they are most important. Beginning as a small-scale collaborative venture between an artist – Rosanna Raymond – and an anthropologist curator – Amiria Salmond – *Pasifika Styles* soon expanded through the efforts of a dedicated international team of supporters including UK-based Maori and Pacific Islander groups, museum staff and students, the Far Cry Theatre company and members of the New Zealand arts community. From the idea of a modest temporary show tucked into a corner of the gallery, *Pasifika Styles* came to encompass a two-year exhibition occupying the Museum's entire top floor, an extensive visiting artists and workshop programme, a website, a travelling satellite exhibition and a privately managed theatre festival.

Written by those closely involved in the project, whether as participants or commentators, this publication both records what was achieved through the combined efforts of the project team and its extended network, and describes the processes through which *Pasifika Styles* was realised. Although collaborative programmes between museums and artists and between ethnographic museums and originating communities are increasingly widespread (Corrin 1994; Kent 1999; Peers and Brown 2003; Stanhope 1999) *Pasifika Styles* was unusual in the extent to which it relied on the active support and initiative of the collaborating group. Artists were involved from the very beginning of the project, establishing its rationale and objectives, influencing the course of its development, and directing the final presentation of their work. With the help of supporters and their broader communities, for example, they organised a fund-raising auction to help those who were not awarded funding from New Zealand to travel to Cambridge. Leading up to the opening night of the exhibition, they worked alongside the curators and museum staff on the gallery floor, doing everything from sewing aprons for the volunteer serving staff to installing artefacts from the museum's collections alongside their own artworks.

Yet this sense of shared purpose and momentum took time to build, and the project's development was not without its challenges and controversies. A long process of research and relationship building, described in the second part of this introduction and in other contributions, was essential to its realisation. Questions arose early about how the artworks would be positioned within the loaded context of an ethnographic museum, resulting in set-backs at the fundraising stage and inspiring sometimes heated discussions among the artists and between the artists and the curators about the project's name, publicity and branding (see Lythberg, this volume). Disciplinary boundaries both within and outside the Museum generated practical and theoretical challenges, and the exhibition's unorthodox curatorial strategy unleashed uncertainties and whispered, as well as openly voiced, reservations. In the end, however, those who chose to support and participate in *Pasifika Styles* threw their collective weight behind it, and this international community effort is what enabled it to happen. The project came to serve the interests and desires of many different people, and in this sense it succeeded in transcending – if not resolving – many of these tensions.

Most importantly, perhaps, *Pasifika Styles* established and consolidated relationships that will long outlive its more attention-grabbing 'outputs'. In enabling artists and museum professionals to meet and deal together with art works and artefacts, new and unexpected insights emerged and opportunities opened up for future development. Some artists were inspired by their encounters with the Museum and its collections, leading to new collaborations and novel directions in their artistic practice and research. Through contacts made in the course of the project, several went on to residencies in other UK and European institutions (Cartwright 2007: 37, 40) some of which in turn chose to purchase pieces of their work. For academics and museum professionals involved in *Pasifika Styles*, the project was similarly instrumental and revealing. International interest in its innovative methodology led to invitations for the curators to speak in forums from Vilnius to Honolulu, Lyon, New York and Oslo. Graduate students have studied the planning, execution and reception of the exhibition (e.g. Durand, this volume), and for those schooled in current orthodoxies about indigenous people and museums, the complexity and variety of artists' responses was a revelation. Others involved in the project were touched by the depth of feeling generated by these encounters, encouraging them to rethink assumptions from the purpose of museums and their collections to the very nature of people and things.

This book at once describes and instantiates some of the legacy of *Pasifika Styles*, for the museum, for the people involved in the project, and for those interested in the relationship and curation of art and ethnography in general. True to the nature and *kaupapa* (guiding strategy) of the project, the process of its realisation is described in diverse ways from a range of perspectives, including those of artists and museum professionals as well as commentators and supporters. Some contributors provide extended analyses that situate the exhibition in a broader cultural, historical or processual context, while others offer more concise and personal reflections. Just as the path was opened at the beginning of each key stage by experts in *tikanga Māori* or Maori cultural practice, the book begins with the *waiata* composed by Che Wilson to inaugurate the exhibition and record its flowering in an oral historical art form. The *waiata*, like the exhibition, weaves together strands from the divergent but ultimately connected descent lines of different Polynesian islands, among the first inhabitants of Te Moana-nui-a-Kiwa (the Maori name for the Pacific Ocean). Whilst incorporated into a unified *kaupapa* (a word which also means the body of a cloak), each thread maintains its own distinctive integrity; this is not a melting-pot but a network of relations held in creative tension.

Why Maori protocol should play such a prominent role in *Pasifika Styles* (and why Maori terminology features strongly in this publication) is illuminated by the first contribution to follow the Introduction. Deidre Brown, a contemporary art curator and historian of Maori art at the University of Auckland, describes the emergence of 'Pasifika' art within the broader context of Maori and Pacific art practice. She foregrounds the capacity of collections to bring otherwise distant people together, citing curator Rosanna Raymond's vision of museums as 'arenas for cultural exchange', and posits 'a philosophical divide between indigenous people who believe that their treasures should be repatriated and those who think that they can achieve another life in foreign locations and collections'. Brown's contribution articulates the diversity of reactions to working within the museum on the part of the *Pasifika Styles* artists, many of whom have a history of thoughtful engagement with ethnographic forms, from writing to photography to museum display and collecting. It also situates the artists' work in 'a continuum of innovative Pacific art practice' dating back several centuries, implicitly challenging the idea that colonisation caused a catastrophic rupture in Polynesian art-making traditions. In contrast to those who would regard the process of mining museums for artistic inspiration as an inauthentic mode of cultural invention, Brown echoes artist Maureen Lander's assertion (cited in Herle) that 'what is traditional [is] to be innovative'.

In an interview with the *Pasifika Styles* curators, Lisa Taouma, a New Zealand-Samoan writer and broadcaster, paints a vivid picture of the cross-cultural context in which much of the work on display in the exhibition and performed in the festival was created. Describing the vitality and complexity of artistic trajectories which she groups, like Brown, under the rubric 'Pasifika' (a Polynesian language rendering of 'Pacific') Taouma outlines the rise of a distinctive 'Kiwi Pacific Islander' identity and its influence on mainstream New Zealand, as well as its familial but ambiguous relationship to the indigenous Maori people. Focusing on recent artistic developments, she describes how 'Pasifika styles' – much more than a superficial trend – have become an integral aspect of the country's cultural and visual landscape over the last decade, and how Pacific people are struggling to retain control of elements of their artwork and identity as these same elements are co-opted by commercial interests and a post-colonial politics of identity.

New Zealand-based art historian and project lynchpin Billie Lythberg reminds us that although *Pasifika Styles* was the first major exhibition of contemporary Pacific art in the United Kingdom, it belongs to a series of curatorial outings of similar work in New Zealand and abroad which may be linked in certain ways to *Te Maori*, the much-cited 'blockbuster' show of historic Maori art that toured the US and New Zealand in the early 1980s. Tracing a lineage of innovative curatorial strategies applied to the display of both contemporary art and historic *taonga* (see also Thomas's preface to this volume) Lythberg teases out common threads between these exhibitions in order to reveal the collaborative process that made *Pasifika Styles* special. Recounting how elements of the project's methodology set 'a standard for all future collaborative shows to follow', she describes in detail her personal role as a 'living face' for the curators in New Zealand, a job which included not only practical tasks such as coordinating the packing and transportation of much of the artwork, but also dealing with controversies arising from the challenges of long-distance communication. Her contribution articulates some of the points of contention that arose between the artists, the curators and the museum, and how these were addressed so that the project was finally able to bring 'the people and the song back to the Oceanic collections in Cambridge'.

Artist Lisa Reihana offers a short personal account of her involvement in *Pasifika Styles*, culminating in a description of two of her three works included in the exhibition, notably *he tautoko* (2006), the result of two periods of research and art-making in Cambridge as a participant in the project's Visiting Artists programme funded by Arts Council England (see also Matthews 2007). Describing *Pasifika Styles* as 'an exciting model that progressive museums can use to re-invigorate their collections', Reihana outlines how working with the museum yielded artistic inspiration. Her piece is followed by an extended discussion of the exhibition as a whole by Anita Herle, a Senior Curator at MAA, who further details Reihana's work (part of which has been purchased by the museum) as well as that of many of the other artists on display. Herle's contribution positions *Pasifika Styles* within current debates in museums about cultural properties and their restitution, emphasising how, in line with recent theoretical developments, the project 'helps shift the focus on utterly fixed objects unambiguously owned by individuals, communities and institutions, to a more relational understanding of the dynamic links between people and things'. Her fine-grained analysis details the diversity of ways in which the artists responded to the museum and its collections, and includes many direct quotations from them, selected as labels for their work. Herle also decribes the gala opening night, during which historical items from the museum's stores were deployed by artists in the rituals and performances that inaugurated the exhibition, emphasising how this and the exhibition itself were 'facilitated by museum staff relinquishing strict authority over the collections and methods of presentation'.

Doctoral candidate and project volunteer Carine Durand recounts her experiences as a participant-observer in *Pasifika Styles*, a role she undertook as part of her ethnographic fieldwork as a student in the University's Department of Social Anthropology. Interested in how museums are developing relationships with artists and indigenous groups in response to long-standing critiques of their position as hegemonic, colonial institutions, Durand describes how her research methodology was challenged and reconfigured during her fieldwork, much of which took place quite literally 'in a glass case' as she assisted the artists with their installations. Her analysis engages with the growing literature on dialogues between anthropology and art (Schneider and Wright 2006), and draws insightful analogies, as well as direct connections, between her own work and that of the artists she worked with, which appeared to her as a form of ethnography. Durand's contribution thus offers original insights into the social dynamics of museum-based collaborations, and suggests 'new possibilities for creative exchange between art and anthropology'.

Artist Reuben Paterson emphasises the importance of museums involving the contemporary descendants of the people who made the objects in their collections in their presentation, noting that: 'Representing ourselves is our own responsibility; only we can ensure the honesty and truth of the cultural image a museum or gallery will present of us'. The *Pasifika Styles* project was ground-breaking, he asserts, in that it invited the participation of artists from the beginning of the project, when the *kaupapa* was still being worked out, and not simply to provide decorative elements, or to sanction the project superficially, toward the end. Whilst supportive of such collaborative endeavours, Paterson also challenges museums to think deeply about their reasons for holding onto other peoples' cultural treasures, asking them to 'consider if, in this age of international travel, you truly need these objects in the same way we do'.

As the person in charge of the actual construction of the exhibition, a process involving some fifteen visiting artists participating in the mounting of their own work, Mark Elliott, now a Curator in the Museum, was at the front line of a dynamically creative yet often nerve-wracking collaborative process. Elliott's personal account of the installation reveals, with refreshing honesty, some of the tensions that can arise when different cultural and professional worlds come together. Like Paterson, Elliott is approving of the current enthusiasm on the part of museums to develop relationships with 'source communities', but he also lays down certain qualifications. These include the need for institutions to be aware of the level of personal commitment and resources required to manage different working styles among the collaborating parties, and the importance of clear communication. The emphasis of his piece though is on the positive emotional and intellectual impact of bringing people and *taonga* together, an effect which he personally found 'profoundly moving' and which encouraged Elliott and others in the museum to reconsider their role in relation to the collections.

Museum Outreach Organiser Sarah-Jane Harknett offers some reflections on the *Pasifika Styles* workshop programme, a series of artist-led public activities and events that she co-ordinated together with the curators. Echoing Elliott, she outlines some of the practical as well as philosophical issues that arose in planning and executing the workshops, as well as how these were productively resolved. Her account emphasises the importance of the ritual proceedings surrounding the exhibition opening, which she feels created a sense of unity and shared purpose among all those involved. In his own contribution, Che Wilson, who officiated at these gatherings together with his *tuakana* or senior relative Gerrard Albert, then gives the background of his involvement as both artist and *tikanga* (Maori protocol) expert. Wilson explains the purpose of the blessing in Maori terms, emphasising the importance of keeping some things away from the public eye so that they are not mistaken as 'a performance for the benefit of anthropologists'. He describes how the precedent set by the museum in allowing *taonga* to be used by ritual experts and performers on these occasions has had both spiritual and practical effects, opening doors in museums around the world.

Fanny Wonu Veys offers a glimpse 'behind the scenes at the museum' with an account of her experiences as a curatorial assistant, facilitating artists' encounters with *taonga* in the museum's stores. Her piece exemplifies the way in which such engagements between people and things can be revealing for artist and museum professional alike: the artists were taken with the details, beauty and skilled execution of particular items, as well as being overwhelmed by the sheer volume of what was in the store; for Veys the often emotional way in which objects were greeted, handled and addressed suggested a whole new way of regarding and dealing with the artefacts in her care.

That *Pasifika Styles* inspired and enabled a variety of creative 'spin-offs' is highlighted by Sarah Robins, whose *Korero mai* audio project arose out of the early stages of exhibition planning and was supported by funds raised for the larger venture. Robins recounts how long-standing relationships sometimes yield unexpected fruit – plans to collaborate with Raymond had been on hold due to the tyranny of distance (the two met in New York; Robins is now based in Melbourne, Australia, Raymond in London), but were re-activated when she heard about *Pasifika Styles.* The project became a springboard for her initiative, and she was able to conduct interviews with nearly all the artists, adding a whole new dimension to the exhibition; extracts were used as labels for some artist's work, and the audio tracks included in a purpose-built sound station in the gallery. The interviews remain available to listen to online through the *Pasifika Styles* website (www.pasifikastyles.org.uk).

The power of artworks and artefacts to re-connect people over long distances is also a theme of the penultimate essay in this volume, by artist Niki Hastings-McFall. In her piece, *Dad's Chair*, the title of her work in the exhibition, the artist describes her family connections to both Samoa and England, and how creating the work and exhibiting it in Cambridge has helped her to strengthen ties with English family, who will become its *kaitiaki* (guardians or caretakers) following the exhibition's closing. *Dad's Chair* (2006) belongs to Hastings-McFall's *Polynisation* series, which explores the coming together of Pacific and white New Zealand cultures described in Taouma's earlier contribution. The final work in the volume is photographer Kerry Brown's evocation of the changing moods of the exhibition in the form of a visual essay, a rich and personal account picking out details and moments in the life of Pasifika Styles.

Collectively, the various contributions to this volume identify *Pasifika Styles* as a pioneering project. Not only did it stage a major exhibition of contemporary Pacific art for the first time in Britain,[1] it did so through the combined and collaborative efforts of a diverse and geographically dispersed group of people. The decision to take such a collaborative approach was partly a result of necessity, in that the resources needed to launch the project and move it on from one stage to the next were not always available when required, meaning that the active and often voluntary support of team members, their families and communities was indispensable. Crucially, however, collaboration was also built into the *kaupapa*, the guiding strategy of *Pasifika Styles*, from the start. Whereas many – perhaps most – such projects are initiated by a museum, often as part of larger research or public outreach programmes designed primarily with institutional objectives in mind, *Pasifika Styles* was planned at least as much by and for those involved in the project as it was geared to the priorities of the museum. In developing their curatorial strategy, the curators used the analogy of a *waka* or Polynesian voyaging canoe to convey their situation to prospective participants in the project. The remainder of this introduction describes the journey of *Pasifika Styles* from the perspectives of its two curators, Amiria Salmond and Rosanna Raymond.

Launching the waka

AS: *At the wānanga or planning meeting we held in Auckland in June 2005 to recruit artists to the project, we talked of how we saw* Pasifika Styles *as a voyaging* waka, *one far too large for the two of us to paddle all the way back to England alone. We were preparing as much as we could for the journey, and to welcome people when they arrived, but we needed strong arms to help carry everyone and their works to Cambridge. Rosanna had a good slogan which she repeated over the course of the workshop – that whatever people expected from Cambridge, the situation was currently one of 'all* mana, *no money', as all our big funding applications were still pending.*

RR: *Amiria and I had built the framework of the* waka *– defining the structure of how the exhibition space within the museum might flow – but we left many elements open so as to truly incorporate the voices of the artists and how* *they wanted to their work to be presented. We deliberately did not follow a conventional curatorial approach of selecting particular works and dictating how they would be exhibited, as we wanted them to be able to react to the space on their own terms. We weren't afraid to highlight potential difficulties the project might encounter. Having already made contact with several funding bodies and arts organisations, we had received mixed feedback to the* kaupapa *we were developing. I was also aware, from attending other international exhibitions of Polynesian art, how audiences who have no real experience of the Pacific lack the context from which to approach the artwork, so that sometimes the very cultural stereotypes the work tries to challenge end up getting reinforced instead. At the same time we wanted* Pasifika Styles *to be a show in which the artists' work was allowed space to breathe, not be boxed in by academic analysis and long explanatory texts.*

The seeds of the project had been sown in a series of conversations that took place over several years between the Museum and some of the artists who would go on to play important roles in *Pasifika Styles.* This long lead-in time was important for building and strengthening the relationships that were key to the project's success. Rosanna Raymond first visited MAA in 2001, together with fellow artist George Nuku, where they met Senior Curator Anita Herle and studied some of the Museum's Maori and Pacific collections.

RR: *Moving over to England from New Zealand profoundly changed my way of working as an artist. For the first time I had no immediate artistic community to rely on for inspiration and guidance, so I turned to the next best thing for me – the* taonga *in museums – to try and bridge that physical distance. I knew England had vast quantities of imperial booty in museum collections and I wanted to meet and greet as much of it as I could. Through the* taonga, *the past became present and I felt connected to my people once more as they inspired me to keep creating and producing new works. These encounters also brought me closer to the academic world in which they had been hibernating. I started to attend some of the conferences that focused on Polynesian arts and culture, and to get involved with art historians and anthropologists. I was curious to hear what scholars had to say and found that I could add my own voice to theirs. All of a sudden the museum became a live space to me, not one dedicated only to the past but a space that could also nurture the future.*

Over the following months, Raymond recommended the Museum to many of her acquaintances from Ngati Ranana, the London Maori Club.[2] Through this connection, MAA received many Maori visitors who were welcomed as researchers and invited to look at and handle *taonga* (treasured ancestral objects) from the Museum's stores. Although research visitors often come to examine items from the collections, this was the first time the museum had received such a steady stream of people whose interest was principally inspired by ancestral and cultural ties to the artefacts.

Raymond met her *Pasifika Styles* co-curator Amiria Salmond when she helped curate an exhibition of works by Maori artists living in London, mounted at the New Zealand High Commission in Haymarket.[3] Salmond attended the opening, and the two began a series of conversations that extended over the following months, covering topics from the role of museums in relation to people whose ancestors produced the artefacts in their collections, to the changing reception and influence of contemporary Maori and Pacific Island art. At the time Raymond was becoming involved in a number of academic research projects as a participating artist, so discussion often turned to how Pacific cultures were being written about by scholars, particularly in the discipline of social anthropology.

AS: *I was reading a lot of articles about the 'invention' of tradition, which attempted to analyse recent cultural developments in the Pacific. Anthropologists were gaining intellectual mileage from the way in which Maori and Pacific Islanders were 'self-consciously reviving' or 'creatively re-imagining' their cultures, particularly in urban contexts, and even authors who asserted their sympathies with Polynesian aims seemed to take great delight in exposing the recent and apparently 'European-inspired' pedigree of certain claims about the past and the present. Rosanna and I exchanged articles and discussed the theories of various authors, some of whom mentioned her work. I found her analysis of what was happening much more persuasive than a lot of the anthropological scholarship, and it began to influence my own theoretical work.*

RR: *My first impressions of the world of academia and anthropology were somewhat negative, being based on various academic articles I read which analysed the Pacific from a distance, written by professionals with supposedly impartial views. It seemed a strange world filled with experts who used long words, discourses and diatribes, commentating on our culture behind closed doors, publishing books about us but not for us. Often our involvement as practitioners was welcomed, but our analysis of what we were up to was not. We were asked to provide art works, performances and to contribute to research, but our accounts of the process were seemingly not valued unless validated by an 'educated' expert. Among and within*

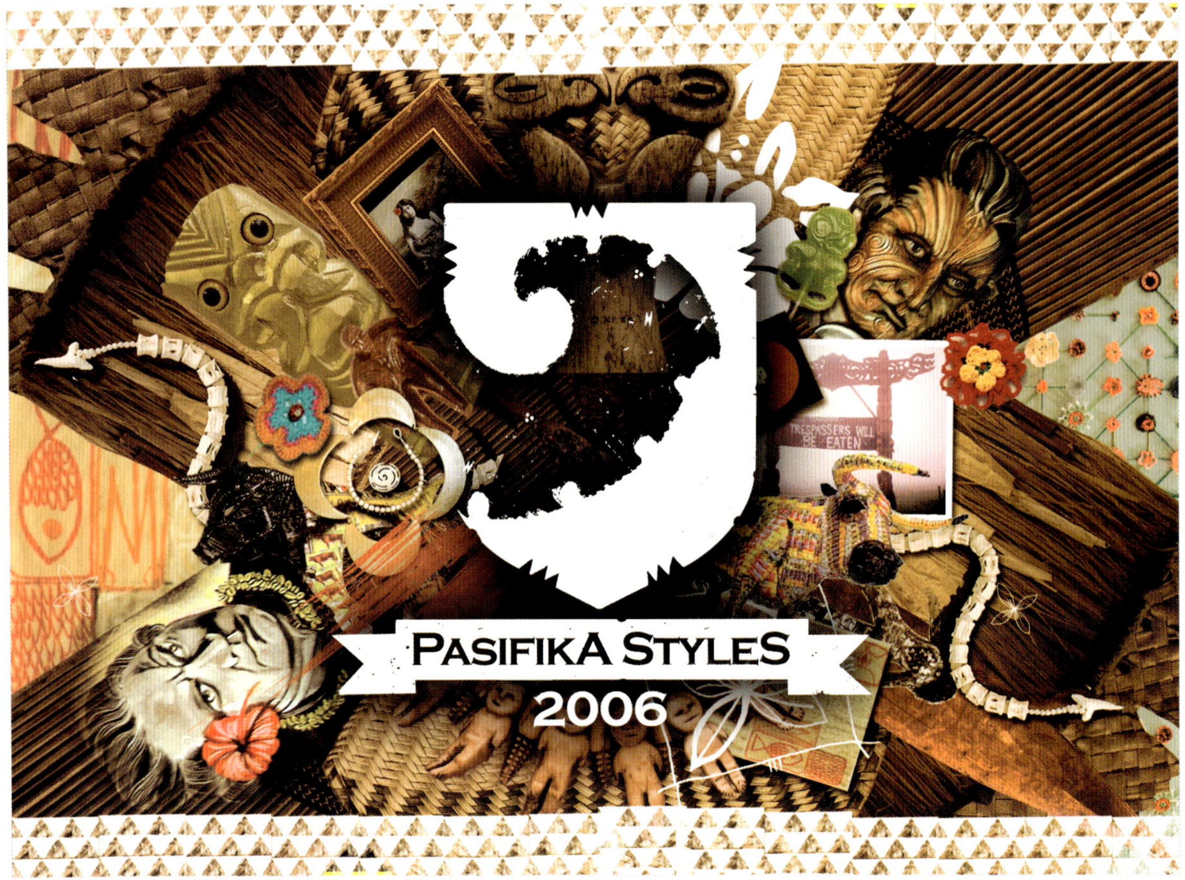

FIG. 1: POSTCARD USED TO PROMOTE THE *PASIFIKA STYLES* PROJECT DURING THE DEVELOPMENT PHASE, DESIGNED BY DELETE.

Polynesian communities we were having our own debates on issues such as authenticity, hybridity, and contemporaneity, but it was in the galleries and in the streets that they were articulated, using the arts to convey our own theories and issues about being Maori and Pacific Islanders in the twenty-first century.

Out of these discussions came the idea for a small temporary exhibition that would showcase the distinctiveness and vitality of artistic and cultural developments now emerging from Polynesia. As New Zealand is home to some of the largest concentrations of Maori and Pacific Island peoples (and had shaped the curators' own experiences) it was resolved to focus on the particular trajectories that were developing there, which had come to influence the 'mainstream' European-oriented settler culture. Some of the curators' ideas were presented in the form of a joint paper and performance at the Tate Modern in 2003,[4] and a draft exhibition outline was produced. The Museum supported the proposal, and began to commit small amounts of seed funding to the project as well as employing Raymond as a part-time Research Associate. These funds also enabled her to represent the museum at a conference convened by Decibel, then the division of Arts Council England charged with promoting ethnic diversity in the arts.[5]

RR: *The Decibel conference was held at the British Museum, and I attended two days of lectures, contributing to open debates on arts and culture in the UK. While it was exciting to be there, I soon realised that the Decibel version of 'diversity' was focused on four main target groups – African, Afro-Carribean, Asian, and Chinese minorities. I was trying to find a way for the voice of the Pacific to be present and accounted for, especially as we all shared a British colonial legacy. It surprised me that the whole gathering was structured according to a western framework. I was used to New Zealand, where indigenous Maori protocols are typically woven into the fabric of such meetings. And while many of the themes of the conference were familiar, it was strange for me to feel like an outsider at a gathering designed to promote the inclusion of cultural minorities. I managed to create a space, asking if there was room for other cultural groups present in the UK with links to the English colonial past to access funding, and my comments stimulated a lively debate on the definition of diversity.*

Raymond's remarks also drew the attention of senior people in Arts Council England who were keen to broaden the concept of 'diversity' they were charged with promoting to include a wider range of interest groups. As it turned out, the connections forged at this conference would provide the bulk of resources necessary to launch *Pasifika Styles* as a viable project, and helped to transform it from a modest temporary exhibition into a two-year multifaceted programme.

Over the following months the curators began to contact artists whose work they felt related to the emergent themes of the exhibition, and to recruit support from UK-based Maori and Pacific Island groups. A well-attended presentation for members of these communities was held in London, hosted by Ngati Ranana, where the curators gained feedback and received many indications of support. Further meetings with the Arts Council were held involving Museum curatorial and outreach staff and initial funding applications were drafted, proposing a visiting artists programme tied to a large exhibition and a week-long festival of music, theatre and dance. During this phase, Alexander Leiffheidt, director of Far Cry Theatre, joined the team when he offered to produce the *Pasifika Styles* festival. Submissions to Arts Council England yielded sufficient seed-funding to begin to develop the project in earnest, enabling a visual identity to be developed (fig. 1) and allowing the curators and Leiffheidt to travel to New Zealand to recruit participating artists and drum up local interest and support.

Voyaging

In January 2005 Raymond arrived in Auckland to conduct research interviews for the project, funded by a personal grant from the British Arts and Humanities Research Council (supplemented by funds from Arts Council England). There she met up with Salmond, who was already there conducting fieldwork while on sabbatical leave from the museum, and they began to canvas the New Zealand arts community about their proposed exhibition.

RR: *After months of cyber communication I could finally reconnect with the artistic community I had left behind in 1999. Email had helped me to keep in contact but in my heart I knew that* kanohi ki te kanohi *(face to face) meetings were crucial in bringing the project to life. At first Amiria was concerned that her presence as an anthropologist at the interviews would produce different or negative reactions, but I insisted that she be present as we were working together. We started on a road trip across the North Island of New Zealand – the great fish of Maui – meeting and discussing the project with hundreds of people from all parts of the country's creative community.*

Heading down to the capital Wellington, Raymond and Salmond had a series of meetings with artists, curators and scholars of Maori and Pacific art, as well as representatives of Creative New Zealand, the national arts council. The road trip continued as they made their way north, staying with family and friends around the North Island.

AS: *Talking to all these people, we started to get a feeling for how* Pasifika Styles *might be received in New Zealand. A lot of those we spoke to were supportive and enthusiastic, seeing this as an opportunity to promote some of the country's leading and emerging artists, but others were more reserved, even suspicious of what these 'expatriate' curators were going to say about 'their' art. The fact that there was (at that time) no one with an art historical background involved in the project was evidently problematic*

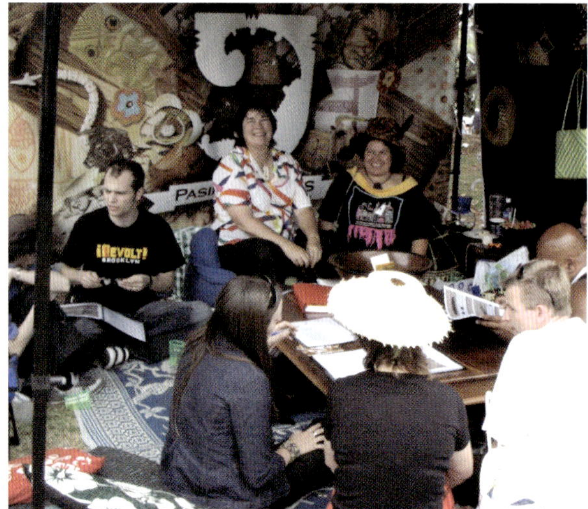

FIG. 2: THE *PASIFIKA STYLES* STALL AT THE PASIFIKA FESTIVAL, WESTERN SPRINGS, AUCKLAND, MARCH 2005. PHOTOGRAPH: ROSANNA RAYMOND.

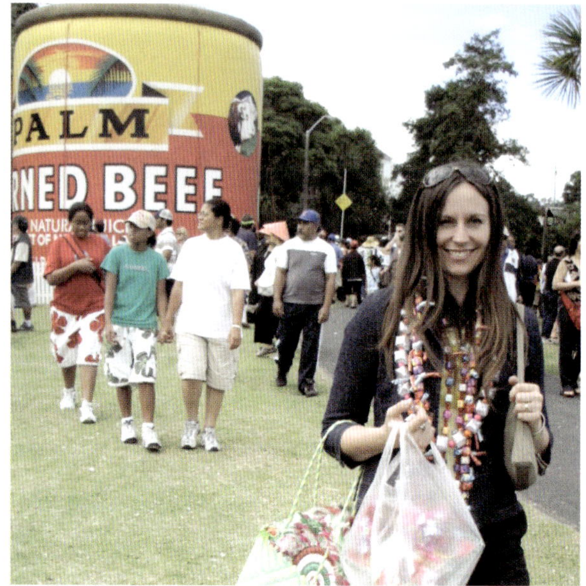

FIG. 3: COLLECTING FOR THE MUSEUM AT THE PASIFIKA FESTIVAL. PHOTOGRAPH: ROSANNA RAYMOND.

for some in the fine arts community, where disciplinary boundaries seemed to be assiduously maintained. Local impressions of the anthropology of art did not seem favourable – it was associated in many people's minds with primitivist and ethnically oriented understandings. Despite our explanations, some remained convinced that this was just another exhibition of Maori and Pacific Island artists which, mounted in a museum, could not avoid reducing the work of the artists to the marginal status of 'ethnic art'.

RR: *What surprised me were the concerns some of the gatekeepers of the art world had about the emphasis I was placing on the role of the artist in collaborating with museums and directing the presentation of their work. I had experienced first hand in the UK how institutions were developing new modes of practice to incorporate and acknowledge artists' voices, even recruiting their help to facilitate new forms of knowledge, but this process had not yet taken off in New Zealand, or at least artists' voices didn't seem to be valued as much as in the UK.*

The video-recorded interviews with artists confirmed that there was much interest in working within the space of the museum. A diversity of views were expressed about what the museum represented and how it might inform different people's art practice, but what united those the curators spoke to was their enthusiasm for engaging with the *taonga* in the collections:

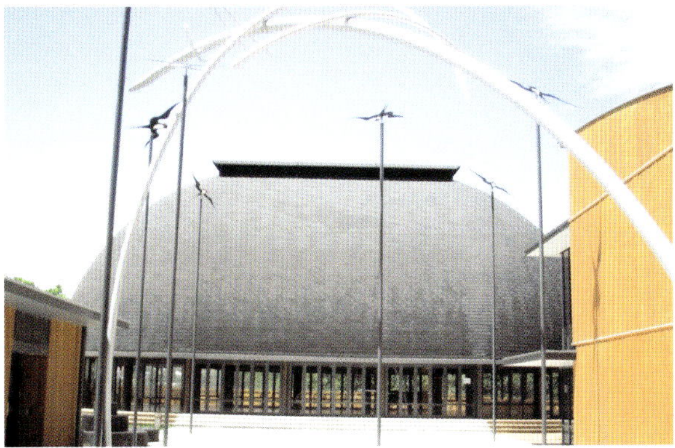

FIG. 4: THE FALE PASIFIKA, UNIVERSITY OF AUCKLAND. PHOTOGRAPH: ROSANNA RAYMOND.

There's such a lot of valuable material and inspiration [in museums]... [W]hen I go and see those collections you know you're kind of looking at your future as well as the past (Chris Charteris).

If we build [up a] relationship [with museums] at least we know that [our *taonga* are] there rather than having to wait for our *tupuna* [ancestors] that are locked up in those cupboards and boxes to call out to us (Che Wilson).

If I had the opportunity to go and visit these works it would be of tremendous value... because for me it's about not only going to have a look at these sort of archival materials to see how it was made... but it's about paying tribute back to my ancestors. That is very important, [that] we actually get our hands on it, that we actually have a *kōrero* [talk] with our ancestors through revisiting these works (Shigeyuki Kihara).

Back up in Auckland, the curators continued to meet artists and academics in the lead-up to the Pasifika Festival. This annual event, a signature point in New Zealand's cultural calendar, attracts contributors from all over the Pacific as well as several hundred thousand visitors each year, and a stall was booked to promote the project. Flip-books containing photographs of Oceanic items in the museum's collections were prepared for members of the public to examine, with a comments book for them to share their views on the *taonga* and what they were doing in a UK museum. A marquee was borrowed along with cushions and mats on which people could come and sit to take time out from the bustle of the festival. Many people visited the *Pasifika Styles* tent on the day (fig. 2) including several artists. The curators received much positive feedback from members of the Maori and Pacific Island communities, and were able to take turns walking around all the different 'villages',[6] purchasing contemporary craft works to display in the

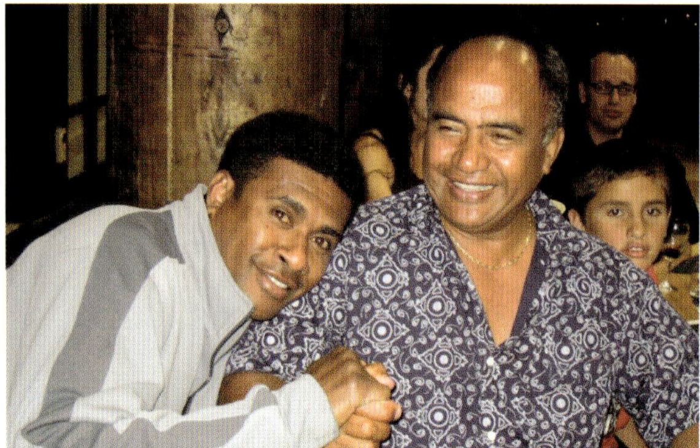

FIG. 5: LEVANI VALOSI (LEFT) AND FATU FEU` U AT THE *PASIFIKA STYLES* PROJECT LAUNCH, AUCKLAND, MARCH 2005. PHOTOGRAPH: ROSANNA RAYMOND.

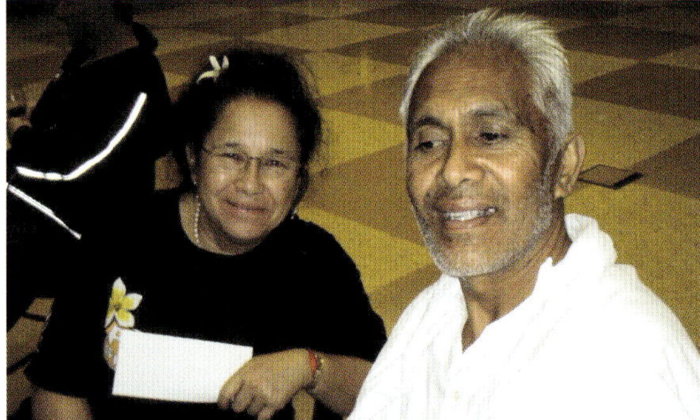

FIG. 6: MARILYN KOHLHASE (LEFT) AND JIM VIVIEAERE. PHOTOGRAPH: ROSANNA RAYMOND.

show and for the museum's permanent collections (fig. 3).

This first research trip gave the curators and the festival director a sense of what some of the artists hoped to get out of such a project, as well as how the exhibition and associated events might be perceived by different people in New Zealand. They were encouraged by the enthusiasm of the majority of those they spoke to, and heeded the warnings of those concerned about the different ways in which the exhibition might be misconstrued. Word of *Pasifika Styles* was spreading around all the various networks with which they had made contact. It was time to thank all the people that had agreed to speak with them, and who had supported the project in various ways, from providing introductions, to lending their equipment, time and labour in support, to hosting the curators during their travels.

AS: *We wanted Rosanna's time in New Zealand to end with a bang – a big event designed to draw attention to the project. She insisted that any such event should also be a way of thanking everyone who had helped us so far, in the proper Polynesian way – by providing* manākitanga *or hospitality to all actual and potential supporters. As we only had a very limited budget, our families and friends pitched in to help us to put on a good show. The Fale Pasifika at the University of Auckland* (fig. 4) *was booked by a relative with University connections. One friend brought and installed a sound system for a nominal charge, Rosanna's brother, who is a chef, served up a spit roast, and other family members made salads, washed dishes and laid food out on tables. We invited everyone we had spoken to as well as some of the people we still wanted to meet.*

The Auckland launch of *Pasifika Styles* (figs. 5 & 6) was designed to act as a focal point – if only fleetingly – for all the geographically dispersed conversations that had gone into building up the project network. It succeeded in demonstrating to potential participants, sceptics and supporters alike, that the project had *mana* and backing; that it was something more than just talk. While Raymond and Leiffheidt returned to the UK soon after, Salmond stayed on in New Zealand, maintaining a presence by attending gallery openings and continuing to meet and discuss the project with a wide range of people. Formal invitations to participate were sent out to many of the artists, and funding applications submitted to a variety of bodies in New Zealand and the UK. A number of these were successful, enabling Raymond to return for a second time to New Zealand. This also allowed the curators to invite many of the artists to Auckland for a weekend workshop or *wānanga* to give further substance to *Pasifika Styles* (see also Lythberg, this volume).

AS: *Maureen Lander, one of the artists and my former teacher, let us use her workshop area in the Maori Studies department at the University of Auckland for two days during our* hui *with the artists. The aims of this gathering were to work up the* kaupapa *of the project, discuss the exhibition and develop ideas for the outreach and workshop programme that was part of what we called the 'living heart'. At the meeting, Rosanna and I presented our ideas for the arrangement of spaces within the gallery into zones characterised by different modes of display – 'Gallery', 'Museum', 'Living Room' and 'Streets' – and showed images and plans of the space. The artists were then able to respond to our concepts as well as the nature of the museum, raising their own issues and enthusiasms for working in such a context.*

RR: *The* wānanga *showed the artists we were serious about involving them right throughout the exhibition process. The living heart requires people, and people need to be looked after, so a lot of the emphasis was on* manākitanga. *To quote George Nuku:* 'Manāki*'s an amazing word:* mana *– your total self,* aki *– to give your power, to host, to be made welcome ... to be made to feel at home' (artist's interview,* Pasifika Styles *website). We wanted to* manāki *the artists in Cambridge, to make them feel welcome and at home in the Museum. By bringing them in I wanted to help develop more opportunities for them to create their own context and to present or represent themselves as much as possible. We described how the aim of the project was to provide a platform so that the voices of scholarship and those of artists could enhance each other, instead of artists just providing fuel for academics to discuss amongst themselves. If I had not spent so much time on the ground listening to the artists and to the community that produces the work which finds it ways into galleries and museums, the exhibition would have been a very different beast – it could have been curated out of existence by high art rhetoric. Despite various setbacks, the support for our* kaupapa *from the artists is what made us persevere.*

Approach

Both curators were back in the UK by September 2005, preparing for the count-down to installation.

AS: *Our fundraising schedule made the lead-in to the exhibition opening more than a little bit hair-raising. One of the biggest applications – to the Esmée Fairbairn Foundation – meant the difference between a small in-house production (involving the re-lining of a few glass cases) and a full-gallery re-fit complete with sound stations, flat screen digital displays and a professionally built audio-visual suite. Luckily we were awarded the full amount we applied for – but didn't find out until the end of November, just six months before we were due to open! In the scheme of international shows, let alone one as complicated as this (involving so many lenders based about as far as it is possible to get from the United Kingdom) this was an exceptionally short timeframe for such an ambitious exhibition.*

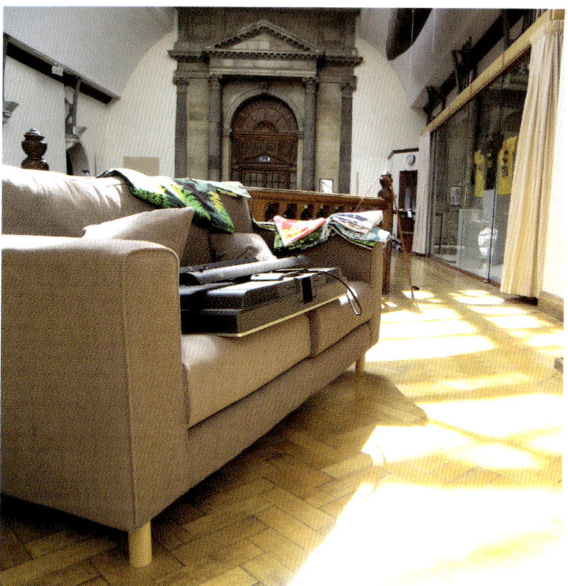

FIG. 7: THE ANDREWS GALLERY CLEARED IN PREPARATION FOR THE INSTALLATION OF *PASIFIKA STYLES*, MARCH 2006. PHOTOGRAPH: CARINE DURAND.

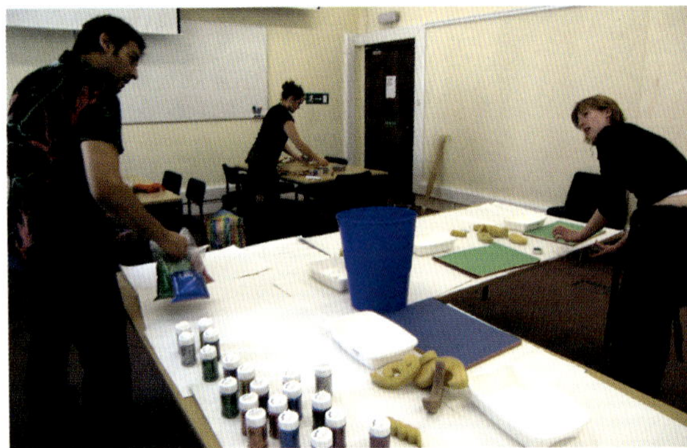

FIG. 8: Artists Reuben Paterson (left) and Ani O'Neill (centre), preparing for workshops at the Museum, April 2006. Photograph: Carine Durand.

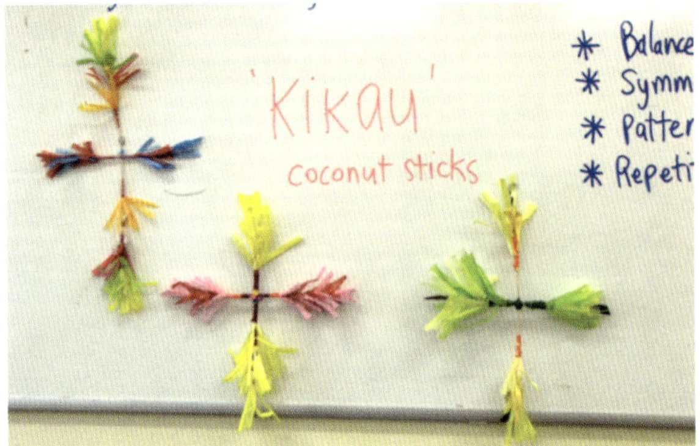

FIG. 9: 'Little stars' (*'etu iti*) by Ani O'Neill. Photograph: Carine Durand.

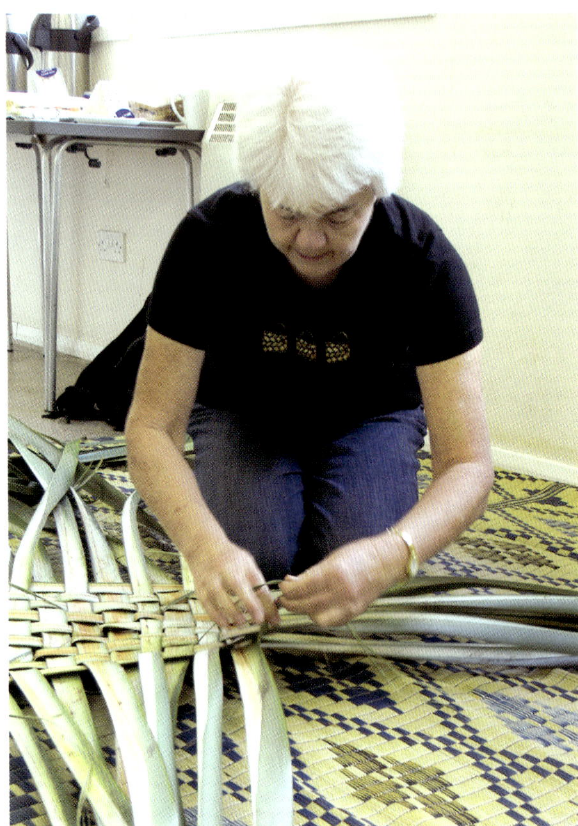

FIG. 10: Artist Maureen Lander demonstrating Maori *raranga* weaving during her workshop at the University Botanic Garden, May 2006. Photograph: Carine Durand.

Following news of this award, the project team swung into action, holding weekly meetings to discuss progress and identify what had been done and what still needed doing. Team meetings involved museum staff as well as key volunteer project supporters and students taking the museum's MPhil in Social Anthropology and Museums, who were participating in *Pasifika Styles* as the practical component of their course. Although the museum had undertaken several major research and exhibition projects in the past, there were no precedents for much of what the team was doing, particularly in the areas of marketing and publicity, cultivating commercial sponsors, organising artists' accommodation and managing the innumerable strings of correspondence generated by the inclusive project methodology.

AS: *In hindsight, we probably should have pulled the plug on* Pasifika Styles *when we failed to get funding for a Project Administrator. This meant that, in addition to developing the project conceptually and doing all the things involved in actually curating the exhibition, Rosanna and I were*

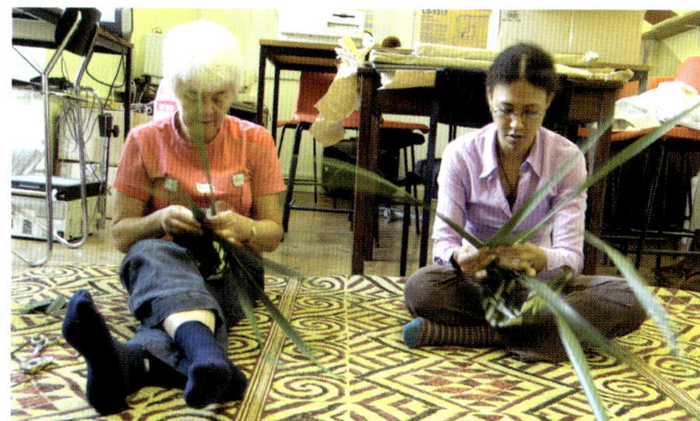

FIG. 11: MAUREEN LANDER AND CURATORIAL ASSISTANT WONU VEYS PRACTISING *RARANGA* WEAVING AT THE MUSEUM, MAY 2006. PHOTOGRAPH: CARINE DURAND.

spending hours brokering sponsorship deals, doing basic accounting and responding to what seemed like a tidal wave of email correspondence. In the end, though we didn't keep everyone happy all of the time, we just about managed to keep on top of it, but only by investing nearly all of our personal and professional time and energy in the project.

RR: *Working in the museum brought about different challenges and considerations from those of a commercial gallery accustomed to constant change.* Pasifika Styles *was about to truly test the infrastructure of the institution. Small things like the availability of petty cash, which fuel productions in the commercial world, were non-existent in the museum, so we had to create new ways of working within the university infrastructure. This put pressure on many of the staff, all of whom play a variety of roles in the faculty as a whole.*[7] *Lack of full-time workshop staff, health and safety regulations and the mechanics of purchasing materials were just some of the issues we had to address to get the exhibition ready. At the same time I felt a sense of freedom working within the museum context, since art within a gallery space is basically a commodity, and this approach could not have encompassed the variety of art practises we wanted to assemble.*

The displays previously occupying the top floor of the museum were cleared out by March as the re-fit of the Andrew's Gallery began to unfold.

RR: *I was getting used to the echo of my footsteps as I walked around the gallery. Walls and surfaces had been prepped, and the smell of fresh paint and sawdust filled the air. The skeleton was laid out before us, awaiting new flesh. We could only prepare up to a point as many of the works were site-specific installations, and while this was exciting, it did make for nervy times. I had the advantage of knowing the capabilities of many of the artists; indeed, their multi-faceted skills were part of why we wanted them to get involved in the project in the first place. The do-it-yourself ethic is strong in New Zealand and we knew this would be needed — we had already asked the installation artists to come prepared, as MAA did not have the staff to help everyone at the same time. Most of the other works had arrived in the country by ship, but we were holding our breath to see how long Customs would take to release them. So far we had one lone and naked couch* (fig. 7)*, a big flat screen TV still in its box, and a schedule that seemed to get longer by the day. Now it was time for me to become an artist again and install my own work before the onslaught of visiting artists descended upon us* (see Durand, this volume).

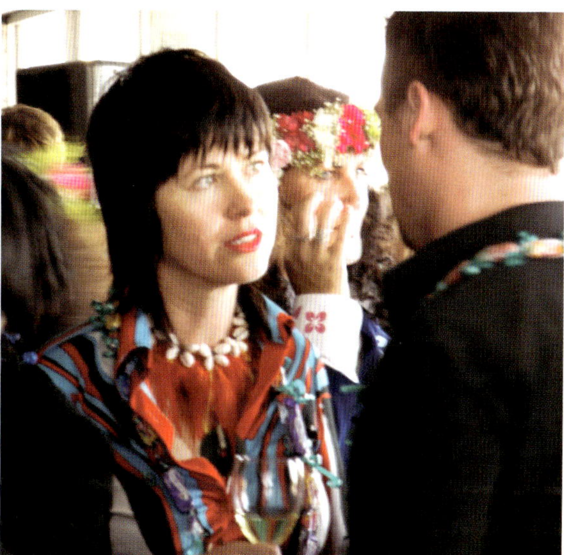

FIG. 12: ARTIST NATALIE ROBERTSON AT THE *PASIFIKA STYLES* LONDON LAUNCH, APRIL 2006. PHOTOGRAPH: CARINE DURAND.

Arrival

The first visiting artists arrived on 17 April to conduct research on the museum's collections, and were soon followed by others keen to begin work on their installations. Ani O'Neill, Maureen Lander and Reuben Paterson came early to teach practical sessions on Maori and Pacific art in local Cambridge primary schools, at the University Botanic Garden and at the museum (figs. 8 to 10), Ani using the results of her workshops in her *`etu iti* (2006) installation (see also Harknett, this volume).

RR: *For me the Visiting Artists programme was a crucial part of the project. It demonstrated the diversity of living art forms in Aotearoa today and the way they are woven together in Polynesian cultures, sometimes so tightly they cannot easily be teased apart. Some aspects of our art practice can fall between the cracks of funding body criteria because they overlap several categories normally considered separate, and it has been a struggle to get these forms acknowledged – is it visual media, theatre, dance or performance art? This is what happened with our Performing Arts Festival, originally conceived as involving a wide spectrum of dance, music and theatre performances in the courtyard of the museum. Because of how funding bodies set their criteria and make their decisions, these elements of the project got bracketed out and the Festival moved into theatres. Other aspects of our art, including some of the principles integral to artistic practice (as to Polynesian life in general) such as* manākitanga *(see above), are not considered relevant to 'Art' in the Western system, so are often not eligible for funding. We wanted to provide a platform to encourage people to understand these relationships by reaching out to audiences unfamiliar with the culture, and we were fortunate to be supported in this by Arts Council England. The workshops were particularly important here as they allowed artists to engage directly with people who often had no experience and very little knowledge of the Pacific. Through their presence in Cambridge, the artists created the dynamic needed to bring the collections alive for others, offering new narratives and establishing new ties with people whose culture has been collecting and housing our* taonga *for more than two centuries.*

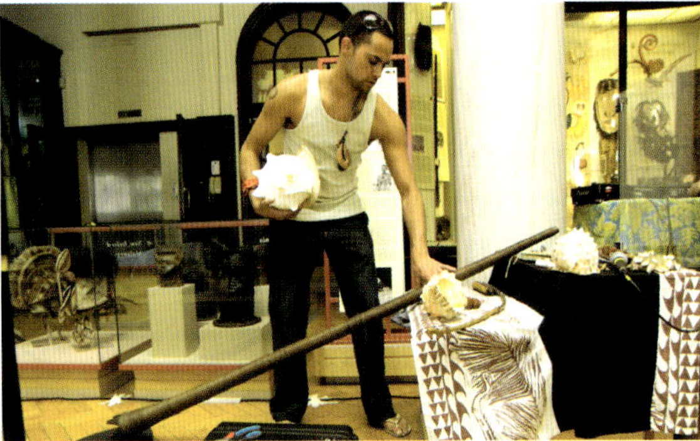

FIG. 13: Jerome Kavanagh setting up *taonga pūoro* (Maori musical instruments) for his performance at the exhibition opening. Photograph: Carine Durand.

Other artists soon arrived, along with a television documentary crew from New Zealand, who were making a feature on the project for the nationwide network Maori Television.[8]

AS: *There was intense excitement (as well as relief) as the shipped works finally arrived at the museum, just ten days before the opening of the exhibition. It felt like Christmas, unwrapping all those meticulously packed treasures after their long journey from New Zealand. By that stage we were being followed around the gallery by Jonathan the cameraman, who recorded everything going on. His presence was welcome, but made me slightly nervous, as we were all under so much pressure. The artists that had arrived to install their work were amazing – they had heeded our warnings about limited resources and come prepared – some even brought their own tools to help with the installation! There were some difficult moments as well. Museum staff were run off their feet trying to get the exhibition up, offering hospitality to the artists, organising the big gala opening and preparing for the Pacific Arts Association conference the following week. Tensions emerged as some people were unable to get the assistance they wanted or needed, but these were mainly swiftly defused in the impetus to achieve our common goal.*

For some there was a brief respite a week before the opening in the form of the project's London launch, a reception hosted by the New Zealand High Commission at New Zealand House and coordinated by arts project manager Aroha Rangi, who showed her support for the project by offering her professional skills free of charge. This event was attended by a number of the artists and by members of UK-based Polynesian communities, who played important roles alongside museum staff and volunteers in creating the ambience that made the event a success (fig. 12).[9] The next day, it was back to work on the exhibition.

RR: *Everyone was working hard on the installation – the galleries became a hive of activity, as new works unfolded in front of our eyes. Artists and museum people were working together, old friends among the artists were reunited, and new friendships were being formed. The* taonga *had brought us all together and there was a special energy building, a vibrant atmosphere you don't often get to experience as a visitor to a museum.*

The marathon efforts and steadily building momentum of the past few months reached a crescendo on 5 May with the gala opening of the exhibition (see Herle, Elliott, Wilson and Veys, this volume).

AS: *For me the day of the opening passed in a blur of tension followed by release, triumph and exhaustion. It was a good feeling, being able to hand over to Che, Gerrard, Ngati Ranana, and others who would pilot* Pasifika Styles *safely into harbour on this new phase of its voyage. At the opening party you could barely squeeze through the crowd, the museum was so packed. Music playing in the galleries, Pasifika food provided as a* koha *(gift) by project supporters The Providores and wine from Tohu Wines – I had never seen the place so full of laughter and light as we* manāki*'ed our* manuhiri *(visitors) in grand style. Rosanna and Jerome Kavanagh's performances, using* taonga *from the museum's collections* (fig. 13)*, took us back to the heart of the matter, the old voices of the* pūkāea *and greenstone* mere *used as a gong recalling the deeper significance of our efforts as they answered the calls of the living.*

New horizons

Just as artist George Nuku challenged guests at the exhibition opening with his spine-tingling *wero* (described in Herle, this volume) *Pasifika Styles* calls for a new openness in dialogues between Pacific art and anthropology. Instead of reinscribing hierarchies that privilege academic discourse over artistic practice and commentary, it asks those engaged in a scholarly way with Pacific artwork, both from the past and of the present, to show their hand; to be up front about their assumptions and prepared to defend them in person, not just from the safe distance of conferences and journals. At the same time it places a similar onus on artists to reconsider whatever they might think about anthropology and museums, and to engage in new conversations.

Some of these discussions have already begun. One week after the opening of the *Pasifika Styles* exhibition, MAA jointly hosted the annual meeting of the Pacific Arts Association Europe (PAA-E) together with the Sainsbury Centre for Visual Arts at the University of East Anglia.[10] Included in a programme dominated by scholarly papers on a variety of historical and contemporary themes was an 'Artists' Forum', where *Pasifika Styles* artists were invited to raise issues for discussion.

RR: *When we heard the PAA-E was to be held in Cambridge I was excited, as here was a chance for the voices of the artists to be heard alongside those of scholars. We organised the session so they could speak back to those who write about their work and help reorient the terms of the debate. The forum was chaired by Pauline de Souza of the University of East London (and director of the UK's Diversity Art Forum) who steered us into lively discussion. I'm not sure how well the format worked – some of the delegates might not have been prepared for dealing with a large number of vociferous and articulate artists; a few found it quite confrontational, and others just didn't turn up, which to me highlighted the divisions between connoisseurs interested only in historical material and those prepared to engage with the living faces of Polynesian art. Looking back, it might have been better to integrate artists' contributions throughout the conference programme, rather than treating them like an island in the Pacific – out in the margins and easy to ignore. We would then be forced to listen to each other, which is how I have learned and benefited from the scholarly world.*

After the events surrounding the opening of the exhibition in May 2006, *Pasifika Styles* has continued to spark debate and act as a source of learning and inspiration as its legacy unfolds. A satellite exhibition, *Northern Skies Southern Stars*, containing digital images by *Pasifika Styles* artists, was curated by student Carine Durand and Rosanna Raymond and has been exhibited in Cambridge, London and Le Havre, spreading word and visual imagery of the project further afield. The workshop programme continued into the summer and beyond, bringing more visiting artists to Cambridge and encouraging an ever-wider community to engage with Pacific arts and culture (see Harknett, this volume). The curators and other members of the exhibition team have given numerous gallery talks and tours to student groups, and have been invited to speak about the project at scholarly and artistic gatherings around the world.

The second high point of the project, the *Pasifika Styles* Festival, took place over a week in May 2007, one year later than originally envisaged, a delay caused by the exigencies of funding. Three plays by Maori and Pacific Island playwrights were shown for the first time in the UK in Cambridge venues, and short film screenings were held at the Museum, together with an Activities Day led by Pacific artists. Produced by Alexander Leiffheidt of Far Cry Theatre in association with the museum, the Festival once again brought the living faces of contemporary Pacific art to Cambridge. It demonstrated the vitality and cosmopolitan nature of these artforms, showcasing once again the global reach of artistic trajectories emerging from Polynesia.

Notes

1 Coincidentally, the opening of *Pasifika Styles* was closely surrounded by several other more or less substantial exhibitions in the UK featuring contemporary Pacific art, including *Mana: ornament and adornment from the Pacific* at the Cuming Museum, Southwark, London (28 February to 15 July 2006); and *Red Wave Collective: contemporary paintings from Fiji, Solomon Islands, Tonga, Samoa* at the October Gallery, London (11 May to 24 June 2006). See Weeks 2006: 50-51.

2 Ngati Ranana was founded as the London Maori Club in the late 1950s and today has a membership of around fifty people (Ngati Ranana website).

3 *A Matau Pakiwaitara*, in 2001.

4 This was at the conference *Fieldworks: Dialogues between art and anthropology*, 26-28 September 2003.

5 The meeting was called *A Free State*, and took place on 18-19 March 2004.

6 The Pasifika Festival is grouped into geographically-defined clusters or 'villages' – 'Samoa', 'Tonga', 'Niue' etc.

7 The Museum of Archaeology and Anthropology is an embedded institution in the University's Faculty of Archaeology and Anthropology. Academic staff teach in their respective departments, and others have responsibilities that extend across the Faculty.

8 *Toi Maori on the Map: an artistic invasion of the colonial heartland* was directed by Megan Douglas and produced by Scottie Douglas Productions with funding from Te Waka Toi (the Maori committee of the New Zealand arts council Creative New Zealand). It was broadcast on Maori Television Wednesday 1 November 2006, 8:30pm, and Wednesday 27 June 2007, 8:30pm.

9 Whilst the London launch succeeded in drawing the attention of UK-based communities and media with a special interest in the Pacific, who subsequently responded very positively to the exhibition, it did not manage to generate interest among the notoriously selective British art press (a problem faced similarly by other major exhibitions of Polynesian art on at the same time) (See Cartwright 2007: 37, 40).

10 The Sainsbury Centre opened its exhibition *Pacific Encounters: Art and Divinity in Polynesia 1760-1860* later that month, but arranged a special preview for PAA-E delegates. Several of the *Pasifika Styles* artists went on to residencies attached to this exhibition and many were involved in its blessing and opening.

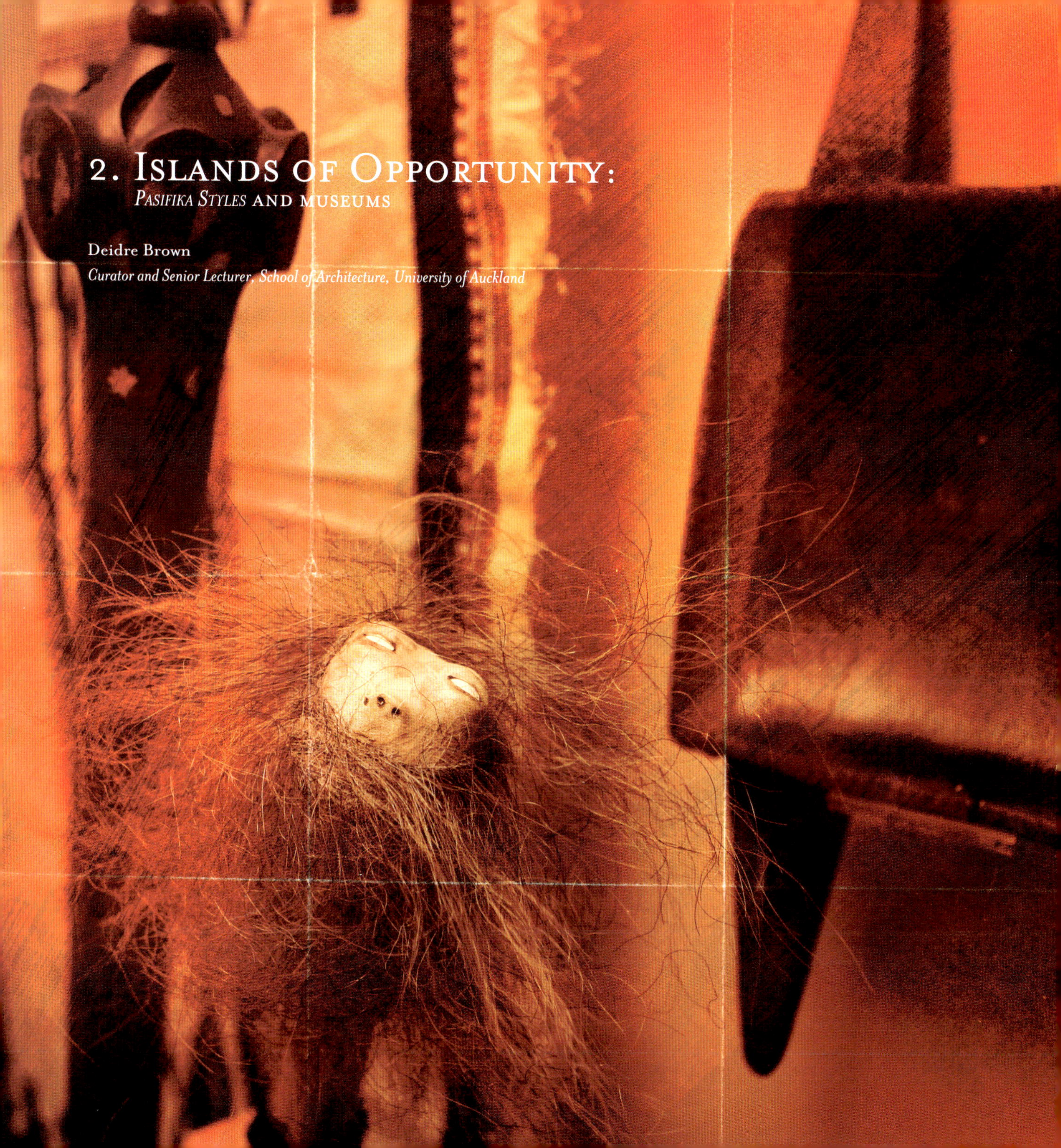

2. Islands of Opportunity: *Pasifika Styles* and Museums

Deidre Brown

Curator and Senior Lecturer, School of Architecture, University of Auckland

A piece from Francis Upritchard's work *Sports Heads* (2005) in the Fijian case, Anthropology gallery, MAA. Photograph: Kerry Brown.

2. Islands of Opportunity:
Pasifika Styles and museums

Deidre Brown

Curator and Senior Lecturer, School of Architecture, University of Auckland

At the closing session of the 2007 Pacific Arts Association conference in Paris, Rosanna Raymond, a London-based artist and curator of the *Pasifika Styles* exhibition, made the interesting statement that she was sure her Pacific ancestors had given their *taonga* (treasures) to foreign collectors because they knew their descendants would, in time, join them overseas.[1] Her opinion presents a new perspective on *taonga* in international museums and how they might be accessed and activated by their communities. It may also indicate a philosophical divide between indigenous people who believe that their treasures

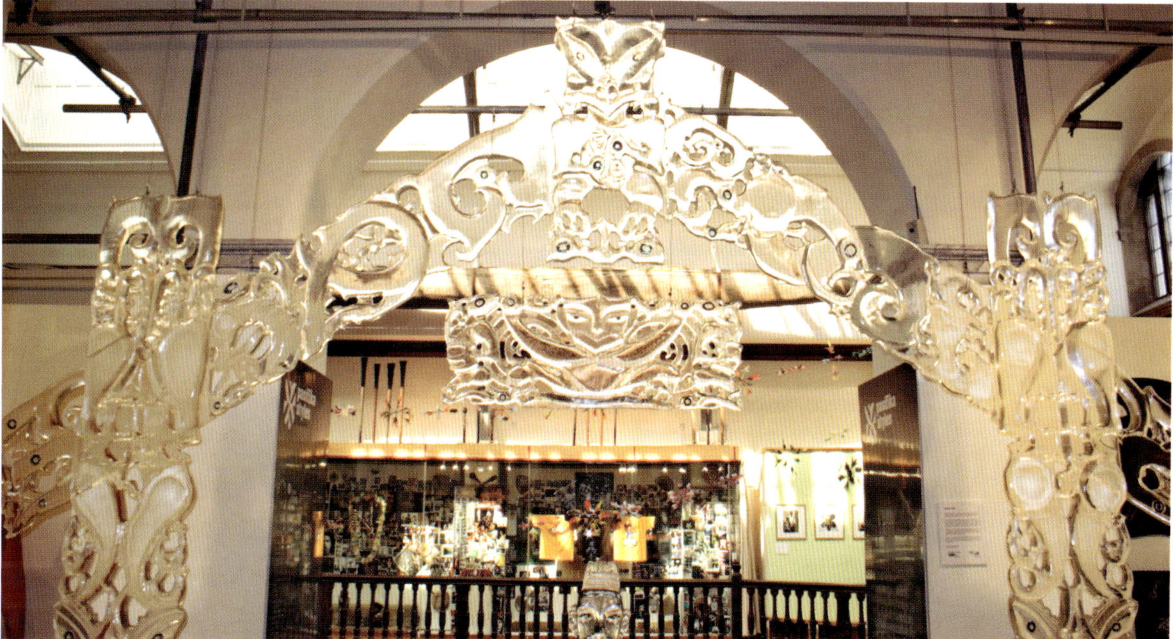

Fig. 14: George Nuku's Outer Space Marae (2006) at the entrance to the exhibition. Photograph: Kerry Brown.

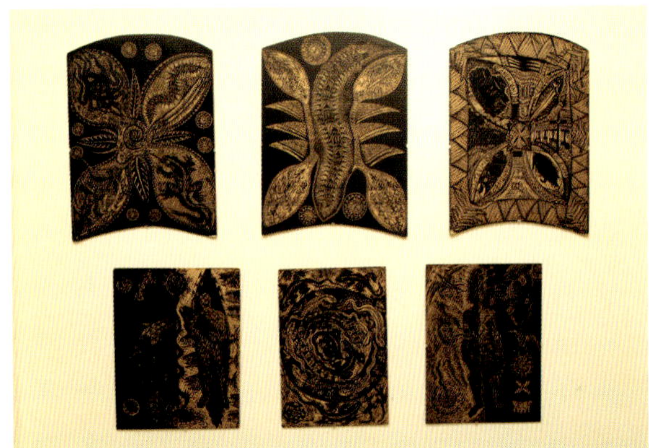

FIG. 15: WOODCUTS BY MICHEL TUFFERY. PHOTOGRAPH: KERRY BROWN.

should be repatriated and those who think that they can achieve another life in foreign locations and collections. *Pasifika Styles* is one of the first exhibitions to address these issues and the role that international museums and museum collections play in informing and inspiring contemporary Pasifika art practice.

Some of the artists in *Pasifika Styles* would be in agreement with Raymond, whilst others have attempted to give 'voices' to *taonga* that they perceive to be isolated in a museum context. According to George Nuku, whose astounding *Outer Space Marae* (2006) creates a floating and translucent *waharoa* (carved entrance) to the exhibition (fig. 14), repatriation is not a means by which Maori will regain *tino rangatiratanga* (self-sovereignty) over their identity and art (*Pasifika Styles* label text).[2] Indeed, *Outer Space Marae*, in its sheer size and its appropriation of Perspex as a material of *whakairo rakau* (Maori wood carving), demonstrates that contemporary Pacific people can engage with the world in a significant way that enhances indigenous culture. He observes of the collected *taonga* that surround his *waharoa*, 'do you honestly think a lock and key and maybe a reinforced door is going to contain the power that those things represent? It's like trying to bottle air, mate, it's impossible' (ibid.).

Nuku's description of an affecting spiritual power, retained by *taonga* within museum collections, is reiterated by other artists exhibiting in *Pasifika Styles*. Michel Tuffery (fig. 15) likens the museum to a *marae* (open air forum) or church in the way in which the space encourages the visitor to interpret objects according to their own understandings. 'It's mainly what the object does to you', he notes, 'It's actually up to the individual to come up with their own way of bringing it alive' (*Pasifika Styles* label text).[3] If Nuku and Tuffery's comments are taken together, then the *taonga* and viewer are in a reciprocal relationship and a conversation where one affects the other – a situation not too different from that when the *taonga* was in its original context. However, the *taonga*'s dislocation – physically, temporally and culturally – from its Pacific context can also be disturbing for many indigenous people, and is a response demonstrated in other work made for *Pasifika Styles*.

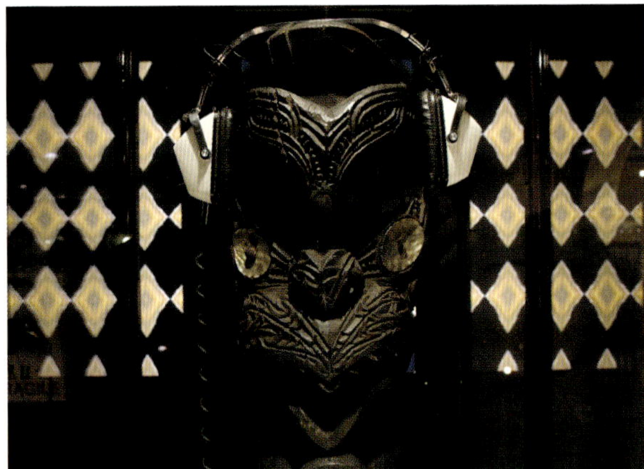

FIG. 16: *HE TAUTOKO* (2006) BY LISA REIHANA (DETAIL). PHOTOGRAPH: KERRY BROWN.

Like Nuku and Tuffery, Lisa Reihana believes that *taonga* can retain their power and identity in a museum setting. However her *he tautoko* (2006) installation (see also Reihana and Herle, this volume) suggests that the *taonga* are dislocated by attempting to offer support (the literal translation of *tautoko*)

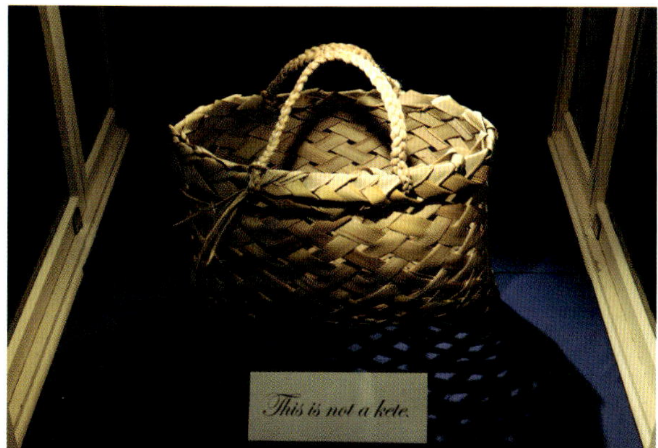

FIG. 17: *This is not a kete* (2006) by Maureen Lander. Photograph: Kerry Brown.

to selected Maori collection items from the museum. In order to catch up on life at home, she has provided one nineteenth-century male Maori *tekoteko* (house gable figure) from the Museum's collection with a set of headphones, and surrounded him with video footage of Aotearoa-New Zealand skies and *tukutuku* (geometric fibre patterns) formed by digitising footage taken around the museum (fig. 16). The figure is both informed by the installation and displayed in a context sympathetic to his original architectural purpose.

The concept of rejuvenation is also important in the work of Maori fibre artist Maureen Lander. She was one of the first contemporary Maori artists to create interpretive works based on *taonga* held in national and international museums. Her 1994 installation (reworked in 2006 for *Pasifika Styles* (fig. 17)) *This is not a kete*, presented *kete* (plaited New Zealand flax bags) in cabinets in order to draw attention to the loss of utilitarian characteristics when museums display such *taonga* as art objects (see also Dunn 2002: 145). In the ten years following the opening of the 1984 *Te Maori* exhibition in New York, there were a number of exhibitions of customary Maori art that had emphasised the formal qualities of *taonga*, for the purpose of recontextualising

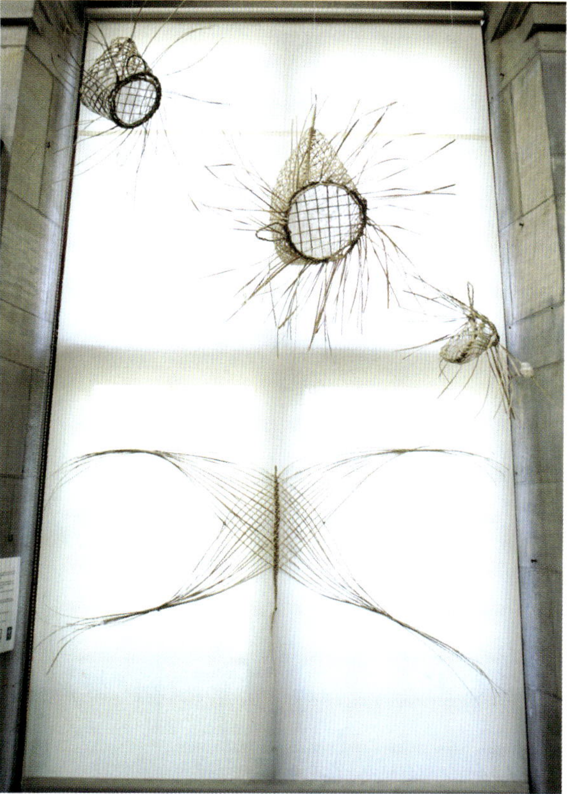

FIG. 18: Maureen Lander's *Airy-Theory Artefacts* (2006). Photograph: Kerry Brown.

the work as art through its display and appreciation in fine art gallery settings.[4] For many practitioners, such as Lander, the consequential loss of purpose remains a problematic aspect of contemporary art museum displays of *taonga*. One of her earliest international site-specific installations examining this issue was *Mrs Cook's Kete*, a 2002 collaboration with sculptor Christine Hellyar using the collections and spaces of the Pitt Rivers Museum at Oxford University. Pieces made for this work were subsequently purchased by the Cambridge museum, and Lander has presented some of them as part of the display of

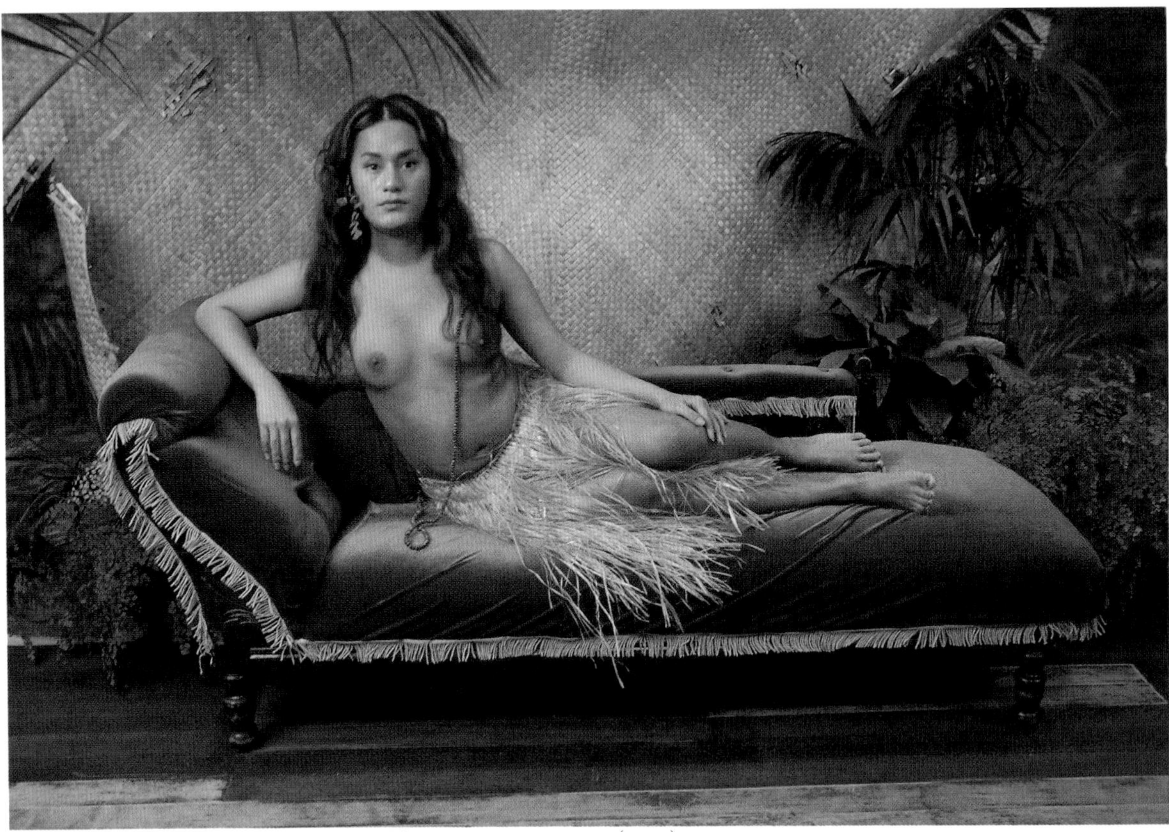

FIG. 19: PART I OF SHIGEYUKI KIHARA'S TRIPTYCH *FA'A FAFINE: IN A MANNER OF A WOMAN* (2005).

her work in *Pasifika Styles*. Lander's artwork explores the spatial relationships and new meanings created when museums display indigenous objects, and she attempts to give a presence to other *taonga* that are kept in storage. She notes: 'Discovering them is like meeting old friends for the first time – a sense of recognition and sadness, and an urge to bring them back into the light and give them new life through referencing them in my art-making process' (*Pasifika Styles* web-log).

The rediscovery of kin through pictorial collections has presented another opportunity for Pasifika[5] artists to bring their people out of a colonial context and into a new light. Ethnographic photography, which has reinforced Western stereotypes of Pacific people through its pseudo-'documentary' nature, informs Shigeyuki Kihara's contribution of photographic self-portraits to *Pasifika Styles*. As a *fa'a fafine*,[6] she has been able to undermine the fixed gender roles contrived by Western studio photographers working in the late nineteenth- to mid twentieth-century Pacific. Her work in the exhibition (fig. 19) shows her in archetypal ethnographic poses: sepia-toned, alternatively alluring and staunch and, from a Western

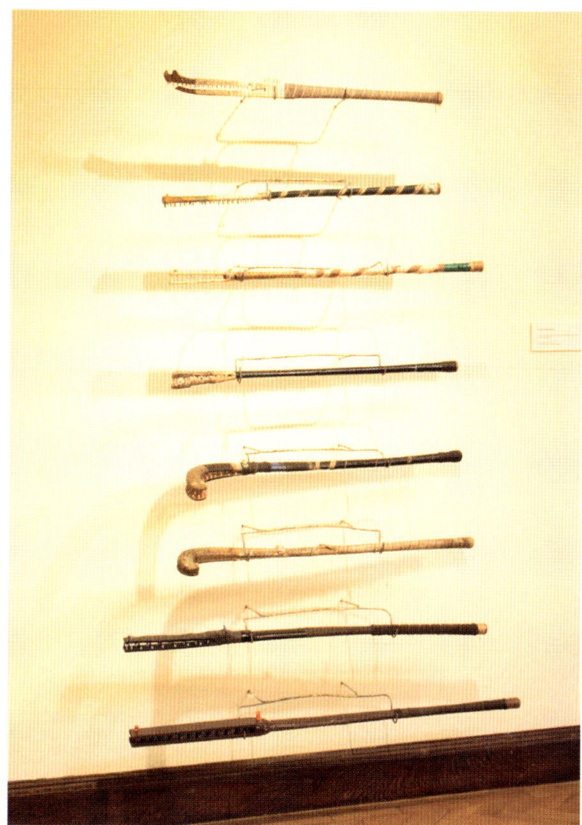

FIG. 20: *Jealous Saboteurs* (2005) by Francis Upritchard. Photograph: Museum of Archaeology and Anthropology.

perspective, semi-clothed. As a person of Asian and Samoan descent, her self-portraits introduce ambiguity into some of the racial attitudes that this type of studio photography once promoted. The power between photographer and subject, and West and its native 'other', is reversed as a consequence, and the relationship is further complicated by Kihara's role as artist and model. By counter-appropriating the media, technologies and concepts of ethnographic photography, Kihara is reclaiming the *mana* (prestige, status, standing) of her ancestors.

Artists such as Nuku, Tuffery, Reihana, Lander, and Kihara view their work as part of a continuum of innovative Pacific art practice. Pacific peoples have always demonstrated an inventive approach to new technologies, materials and ideas, possibly because they have had to adapt to local resources as they migrated from island to island, moving from large forested land masses to exposed atolls and sometimes back again. Considerable skill was applied to the embellishment of clay, bone, stone and wood, depending on its availability, and also skin, with evolving design patterns and concepts being readily transferred across media. Polynesian fibre artists were also particularly adept in experimenting with the malleability, resilience, texture and colour of new plants, skins and fur, and they not only developed fashions associated with status, but also quickly made functional items to facilitate the tasks of everyday life (Toi Maihi, in Brown and Ellis 2007: 77-96). European arrival heralded some dramatic changes in Maori and Pacific Island art, particularly in colonial situations. Early 'contact' changes were technological, as makers saw advantages in replacing stone tools with metal, and fibre with cotton and wool. The next developments were conceptual, as artists became aware of themselves as individuals and as indigenous peoples, distinct from each other at a tribal level and ethnically distinct from other cultures. In these times of questioning, Christianity offered an explanation for these differences, although the missions were often superseded by indigenous converts themselves in spreading the new religion. As a consequence, the subject matter of Polynesian art changed to include self-portraiture and to embrace Christian iconography. The post-World War Two Pacific diaspora, which led to the development of migrant Pacific communities in rim countries such as Australia, Aotearoa-New Zealand, and North America, has created an Oceanic cultural 'melting-pot' out of which has emerged a collective body of work known as 'Pasifika' art. In the last fifty years, Pasifika art has shifted aesthetically, sometimes with associated technological and conceptual changes, as Pacific people have participated in western education, and particularly tertiary art education, systems. While European influence has changed Pasifika art aesthetically, it has not changed it conceptually. Indeed, western media, art practices and technologies have often been employed by Pacific artists to perpetuate Pacific concepts. In keeping with their heritage, artists like Nuku, Tuffery, Reihana, Lander, and Kihara, choose to innovate and validate their practice as Maori and Pacific art. Seen in this light, Pasifika artists working in new media are not disconnected from custom, but are rather continuing a tradition of innovation and change in their work, viewing the global landscape – with its new technologies, materials and ideas – as yet another 'island' of opportunity.

The perspectives of Palangi/Pakeha (European-descended) artists, like London-based New Zealander Francis Upritchard, are also represented in *Pasifika Styles*. Spatial, temporal and cultural relationships created by museum displays of objects, particularly those derived from a colonial context, have been a central theme in Upritchard's installations for some years. In 2003, as a reverse commentary about the objectification of *taonga*, she made resin Pakeha (New Zealand European) *upoko toi* (preserved human heads), amongst other faux artifacts. The following year she fabricated other *taonga*, such as *patu* (Maori cleavers), in resin and plastic, as part of a wider exploration of the West's often superfluous attempts to hold on to the past through objects. *Jealous Saboteurs* (2005), the first of Upritchard's works featured in *Pasifika Styles* (fig. 20),[7] is an installation of 'Pacific-esque' crocodile carvings fashioned from hockey sticks, themselves acquired from a charity shop. The carvings are mounted and displayed in a stacked installation reminiscent of museum displays of such *taonga*. Upritchard's use of found objects and their fabrication into new objects with different meanings is itself a practice similar to the collecting of indigenous *taonga* and their recontextualisation, with new constructed meanings, in museum displays. When compared to that of Maori and Pacific Island artists, her work is clearly different in its focus on the grotesque, the gaze and the uncanny as motivations for colonial collecting and display.

When asked about her personal response, as an artist and a Maori person, to museum collections of *taonga*, Lander remarks that museums play a different role than that of the community in the continuum of Pasifika art. Museums, she notes, conserve art and, when certain art practices have declined or been replaced, have offered artist-scholars like her the opportunity to learn from old *taonga* through understanding their materials, making and purpose.[8] Raymond has spoken of the frustration and pain of 'looking at a [museum-held] *taonga*... that is so familiar, yet separated from its original place and purpose', but has also said that 'meeting' them in the museum opens up a 'direct line ... with my cultural heritage' so that 'the past becomes present' (*Pasifika Styles* label text).[9] She recommends that Pacific people work with museum collections to reduce the distance that has developed between source communities and their *taonga* over the past two centuries. In the future, she believes, museums could become 'arenas for cultural exchange, going outside the boundary of the space into everyday life'. Exhibitions like *Pasifika Styles* are one of the most important steps in this process, and in this instance it has allowed Pacific people, of Maori, Pacific Island and European descent, to interrogate the relationship between collected and collector, indigenous and colonial, customary and contemporary, and local and foreign. More significantly, mounted in a non-Pacific venue, it has articulated the vision of Pasifika artists, working internationally, who believe that the distance between *taonga* and their original communities can be bridged conceptually.

Notes

1. Rosanna Raymond, artists' panel with Charmaine Iliau, Shigeyuki Kihara, and Karamia Muller, Pacific Arts Association Conference, Musee du Quai Branly, Paris, 7 July 2007.
2. See also George Nuku, artist statement, *Pasifika Styles* web-log.
3. See also Michael Tuffery, artist statement, *Pasifika Styles* web-log.
4. It should be noted that *Te Maori* did not include any fibre art work, a controversial exclusion that subsequent exhibitions – such as *Taonga Maori: Treasures of the New Zealand Maori People* (1989), *Whatu Aho Rua: A weaving together of traditional and contemporary pieces of taonga* (1989), and *Kohia ko Taikaka Anake: Artists construct new directions* (1990) – sought to rectify (see Mane-Wheoki 1995: 1-2).
5. 'Pasifika' is a term coined by Pacific Island peoples in New Zealand to describe themselves collectively.
6. *Fa'a fafine* is a Samoan term that can be translated as 'in a manner of a woman' and describes people who possess both male and female qualities.
7. Two works from Upritchard were displayed in the exhibition. The first, *Jealous Saboteurs* (2005), was purchased by Auckland Art Gallery after the artist was awarded the 2006 Walters Prize, and was replaced by *Sports Heads* (2005).
8. Maureen Lander, in an interview with Sarah Robins, January 2006 (audio file, *Pasifika Styles* website).
9. See also Rosanna Raymond, *Pasifika Styles* web-log.

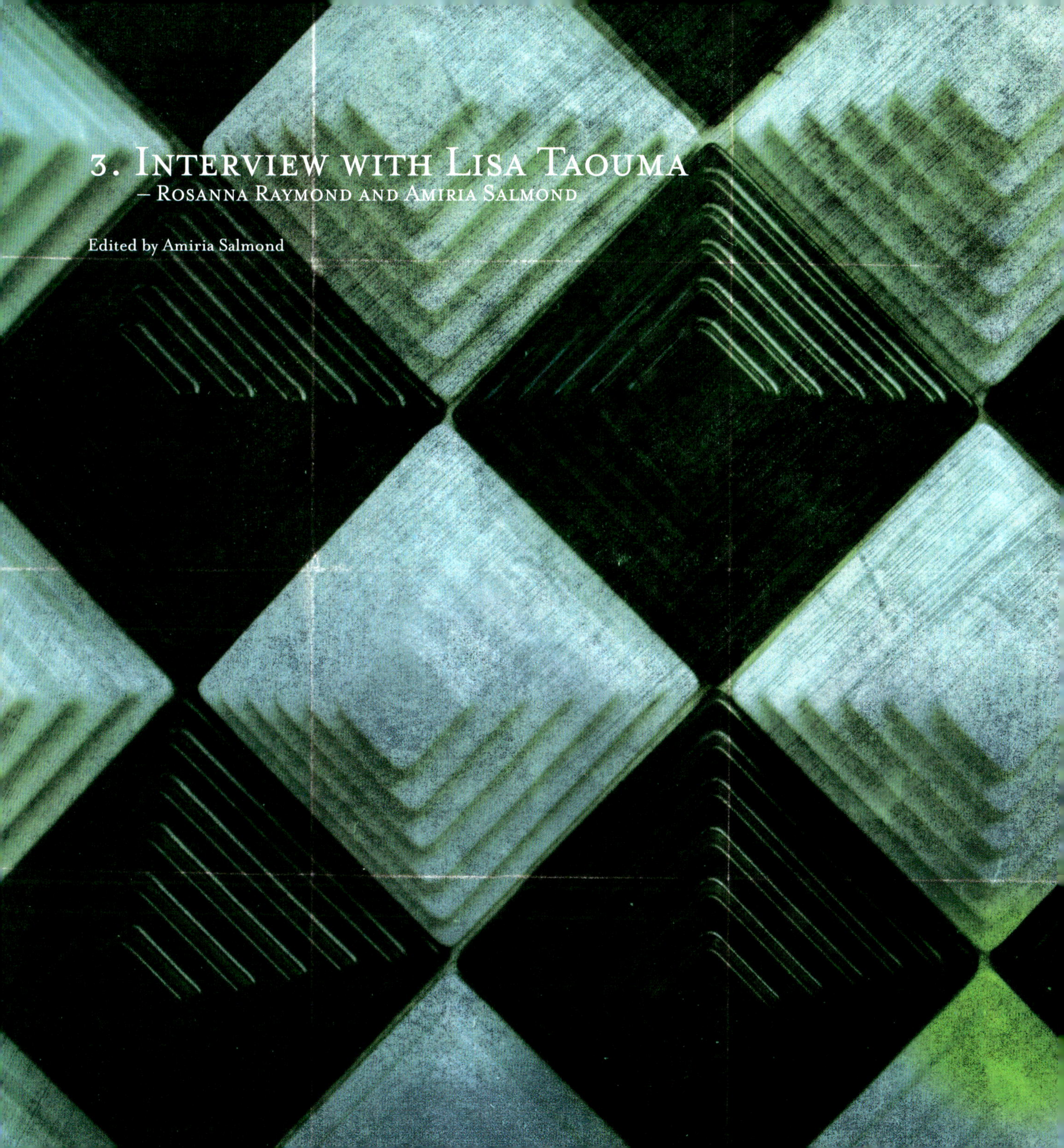

3. Interview with Lisa Taouma

– Rosanna Raymond and Amiria Salmond

Edited by Amiria Salmond

Detail from Filipe Tohi's work *Tupu`anga* (ancestor, origin or source) (2005). Photograph: Kerry Brown.

3. Interview with Lisa Taouma
– Rosanna Raymond and Amiria Salmond

Edited by Amiria Salmond

Lisa Taouma is a scholar, journalist and broadcaster specialising in contemporary Pacific art and culture, particularly in New Zealand. She produced the Represent *documentary on contemporary New Zealand-based Pacific art and culture for display in the* Pasifika Styles *exhibition.*

LT: *One of the really interesting things about Pacific Islanders in New Zealand is that in recent years there's been a huge resurgence of art-making focused around the idea of a New Zealand Pacific identity, which has parallels with similar movements among other migrant cultures with a diasporic history. New Zealand's Pacific identity has just started to assert itself in the last ten years and it's being realised across the broad spectrum of the arts. What I find most interesting is that the identity now is really different from how the Pacific has been traditionally perceived by 'mainstream' New Zealand. Also, we're not seeing the same sort of work that a lot of the original migrant artists from the Islands were doing because there are now New Zealand-born Pacific Islanders that have completely new issues and forms of expressing their identity. The frangipanis and the frigate birds and the literal island references are giving way to things like ironic slang used on t-shirts. We're seeing a really Kiwi Pacific feel and a strong statement that Kiwi Pacific Islanders are different to the generation before them, to the people who migrated from the Islands.*

RR: *How does Pacific Islander art relate to Maori culture, the* tāngata whenua *[indigenous people] of New Zealand? Have you seen much 'cross-polynisation' or lessons learned from each other that have affected the artists and their work?*

LT: *One of the things that comes to mind with Maori-Pacific crossovers is the work of the* tatau *(Samoan tattoo) artist Paolo Suluape. He did a really interesting but very controversial thing in the late 1980s, when he* tatau*'ed a Maori carver who wanted to get into doing* tā moko *(Maori tattoo). At that time there were no Maori* tā moko *artists working with traditional tools – it was all needle work – and so he came to Paolo and Paolo gave him a* pe`a *(thigh and buttock tattoo) and a* tatau. *(There was some talk about him in turn giving Paolo a* moko *but that didn't happen in the end). The work was done on a marae in a beautiful meeting house and they had all the Samoans there and all the Maoris there and and they were doing Maori and Samoan singing as part of the* tatau *process. It sounds beautiful, and I think it's a really good example of an art form that came to fruition through cross-pollenisation between Maori and Pacific communities. Perhaps though there are more parallels between the Pacific communities' issues here in New Zealand and those of other migrant groups, like the Asian communities. There are of course Maori and Pacific works based around similar political issues, like land and sovereignty – Maori and Hawaiian artists, for example, have taken similar stances on land and related issues. But I think people want to find parallels between Pacific and Maori issues here, and they're actually really different because we're a migrant community and Maori are an indigenous community and I think especially the new generation of Pacific artists have different kinds of issues. At the same time there are connections – the Pacific Island kids who are making all the t-shirts with clever slogans* (Fig. 21) *also cater to a big Maori market in South Auckland, so they've expanded their FOB* *slogans and thrown Maori references in there too.*[1] *Also with things like the national Pacific Island radio network Niu FM, they have a huge Maori audience because it's a brown radio station that's nationwide. But in terms of political issues I don't know that there's the same united focus now that there may have been 10 or 20 years ago, with things like the Pacific involvement in the protests against the Springbok Tour.*[2]

RR: *What about some of the tensions which recently resulted in some Maori groups pulling out of various Pacific-focused events?*

LT: *It's interesting actually because the Polynesian Festival ('Polyfest'), which is the big annual Pacific Island secondary school kids festival — they have 100,000 kids participating — is a traditional dance festival. The teams are divided into five Island groups, including the Maori stage. What has happened in the past is that the Maoris have wanted to have their own festival and at some point they organised a breakaway festival just for the Maoris, but they've worked that out that and now they're part of Polyfest again. So that's one event that brings Maori and Pacific Islanders together under the Polynesian umbrella. Those tensions are still there in other ways, though. When I'm working as a journalist, I notice that there's often a kind of separation of the Maori and the Polynesian with the terminology used. Polyfest, for example, used to be called the Maori and Polynesian Festival. And there are really interesting issues around the word 'Pacific' as well. It's a word that's bandied around a lot in New Zealand because of our geographical location, and people are finally realising that there's a big commercial value in the term Pacific. So we're seeing* tapa *tablecloths on Shortland Street [a popular soap opera] and there's a very strong Pacific theme evident in advertising — brown faces are now very cool and are being used to advertise a lot of youth product. That's probably the only time you see a lot of brown kids on TV! Aside from that there's not a strong visual presence — brown faces aren't used to sell 'quality' or high end product. Culture is used because it's 'cool' — but this in itself means that Pasifika has become a commercially viable flavour. And that's reflected in a lot of mainstream art as well. A lot of Palagi (white) artists from New Zealand that travel overseas have developed a distinctly Polynesian flavour in their work that they may not have had in New Zealand because it's a unique selling point overseas.*

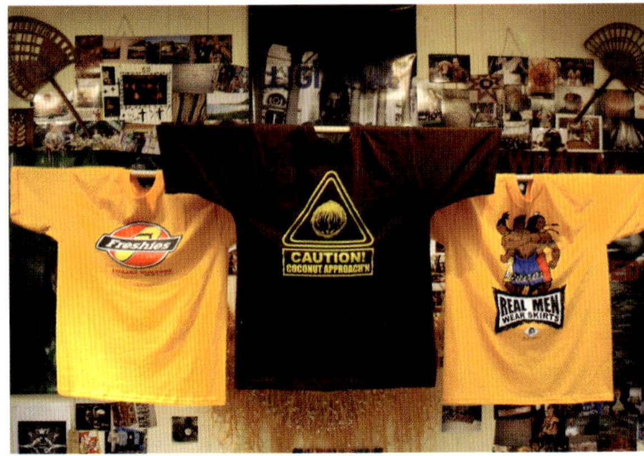

FIG. 21: T-SHIRTS PURCHASED BY THE CURATORS AT OTARA MARKET, ON DISPLAY IN ROSANNA RAYMOND'S INSTALLATION *EYE LAND PART II: WELCOME 2 DA K'LUB* (2006). PHOTOGRAPH: KERRY BROWN.

RR: *Do you think this has been detrimental to the arts and cultural movements because it aestheticises our cultural heritage?*

LT: *Yes. As with a lot of art in the Islands, we've got to be really clear about definitions of what is tourist or souvenir art. There are all these mainstream artists who are making postcards with frangipanis and hibiscuses because they want to sell New Zealand as part of the South Pacific, because of course geographically we're here in this part of the world and nobody can copyright the frangipani and hibiscus — they've become common motifs. But some Pacific artists have taken issue with people using the frangipani for example. I think there was actually a court case about the appropriation of a particular artist's work which used these motifs and it became an intellectual property issue, trying to copyright the use of what has become an iconic Pacific motif.*[3] *Do we own these things, especially the patterns used in* siapo *and* tapa *making?*[4] *These images have been used in the mainstream for commercial purposes and for the tourist market, and maybe that's what has caused the friction — that there's revenue being made off these motifs and it's an ongoing argument. Those are issues I've come across a lot as a journalist, with particular artists who are really upset about traditional Pacific motifs being used in that way.*

AS: What's your take on the idea put forward by some academics that when people are worrying about issues of property and copyright, that's a mark of their Westernisation?

LT: Well it's an interesting deflection – it's not addressing the central issue. For me it's a defensive reaction to the discussion that's going on and not to the problem itself I think. The cultural sensitivities people have about things like the pe`a, they're very passionate and emotional issues, and they're issues that involve a wide spectrum of belief systems. Saying that they're just playing the Palagi game is just part of the whole power dynamic involving the colonised body – who's got power, and who's powerless.

RR: That brings us to how the community values these things in a very different way to the market, which affects the artists and the people who need to earn a living.

LT: Community awareness and consumption of the work is a very topical thing because, after a long time, these spaces are finally being opened up to Pacific communities. We never used to see brown faces in theatre, for example; there was no concept of brown dollars for tickets in that industry, even ten years ago, and now we are seeing performances that are actually being made for a brown audience. Before there were a lot of Pacific plays, but they were targeted at our mainstream theatre-going audience; it was seen as a foreign medium for Pacific Islanders. One of the first Pacific plays that drew a Pacific crowd was Think of the Garden, back in the early 90s. They deliberately targeted the Pacific market so that's when you first saw that movement into the theatres. And so the community is becoming more conscious of these Pacific artists, and you're getting these spaces in art galleries, theatres and things where people are realising that it's not a big freaky thing and it's quite accessible. You go to openings now and there are all these Pacific community people there and it has become a regular thing to go to these museums and galleries. So there's a lot more community involvement now and awareness of what's being portrayed in the arts. And because there are more and more performances and art being made specifically for a brown audience, people are aware of how things are being presented to a mainstream audience as well, and the differences between them; 'who's telling the story and who's it being told to' has become a real issue with a lot of the community now because they're recognising that this might be being made to speak to them whereas that's for a mainstream audience.

AS: Does that community seal of approval add to the value of the art?

LT: Yes. The community value of a work is important because it affects the way the work's written up, the way it's seen and talked about. Having that community voice and support is just as important as the selling of it in some ways. There's more scope now for people to be vocal about art, either positively or negatively, and because of that people want to have community backing. It also validates their work – it comes back to that sense of work being made for brown people now; that becomes your target audience in a lot of ways, even if it may be bought by white people, the voice is speaking to a brown audience.

AS: And does the need for that seal of approval ever create problems? Do people have to struggle to get it?

LT: Yes, that's the flipside. There's a lot of work that's seen as really high-brow and perhaps inaccessible, self indulgent or pretentious, and it's missing that audience. In the spectrum of art making there's room for everybody, but it's not all one big cosy happy Pacific environment. It must be difficult to produce work that's not necessarily accessible to a Pacific audience if at the same time you want that approval – it's a big issue. It's a question of boundaries and what you can and can't do within a certain community. The problem with the community focus is that if you're making work that's transgressive or breaking traditional boundaries you risk being inaccessible. You're also going to get much more of a reaction now than you would have in the past because people are so much more aware of what's going on in the arts. One of the growing areas of contention is the build up of right-wing Christian groups in the Pacific community. These groups have a particular agenda and a particular moral code and they're very vocal about that. There's a big reaction to art making coming from those groups which was never there before

RR: *One of my questions was about the traditional – why is this considered traditional or that authentic culture? Does the issue of authenticity affect art practice, as well as the commentaries that are written about artists by others?*

LT: *Absolutely, and that ties in again with the idea of a Kiwi Pacific identity. (Samoan author) Albert Wendt has written about it a lot, for example about tourist culture; people coming to the Pacific Islands and expecting to see what they consider authentically 'primitive' artwork, as well as drums and hula girls. A lot of work has been in reaction to that, in a way, to what people expect to see when they see the Pacific and to what the traditional signifiers and iconography of the Pacific have been. Much of this work is deliberately 'anti-authentic' in that it says 'we're authentic because we're Islanders and that should be enough'. Lily Laita did a big oil painting piece, for example, called* Death to the Frangipani. *Those are issues that came up in the early 1990s, though, and I think a lot of younger artists now have new concerns; we've found a place to sit between Fa`a Samoa and F`apalagi*[5] *and I think kids are now aware that they're one of thousands of Kiwi-born Pacific people who have their own issues and completely different experiences from their parents, which are nonetheless just as valid. The forging of that identity has been a major breakthrough, and it's been because of a new confidence about being a Pacific person here, and letting go of all those feelings of inadequacy about not being Pacific enough in that in that sort of authentic sense.*

March 2005

Notes

1 FOB stands for 'fresh off the boat', an originally pejorative term for recent immigrants to New Zealand from the Pacific Islands, which has more recently been reclaimed as a positive identity by Pacific Island youth culture.

2 Vigorous and often violent nationwide demonstrations were sparked in 1981 by the South African Springbok rugby team's tour of New Zealand. Whilst a primary focus of protest was South Africa's apartheid regime, the tour also brought to the surface issues surrounding institutionalised racism in New Zealand, particularly toward Maori and Pacific Island people.

3 Taouma was referring here to the threatened suit by Samoan artist Fatu Feu`u against New York-based *pākeha* artist Max Gimblett, which never actually proceeded. The skirmish is briefly discussed in Shand 2002: 55.

4 *Siapo* and *tapa* are names for bark cloth, often decorated with distinctive motifs.

5 'The Samoan Way' and 'the European way' respectively.

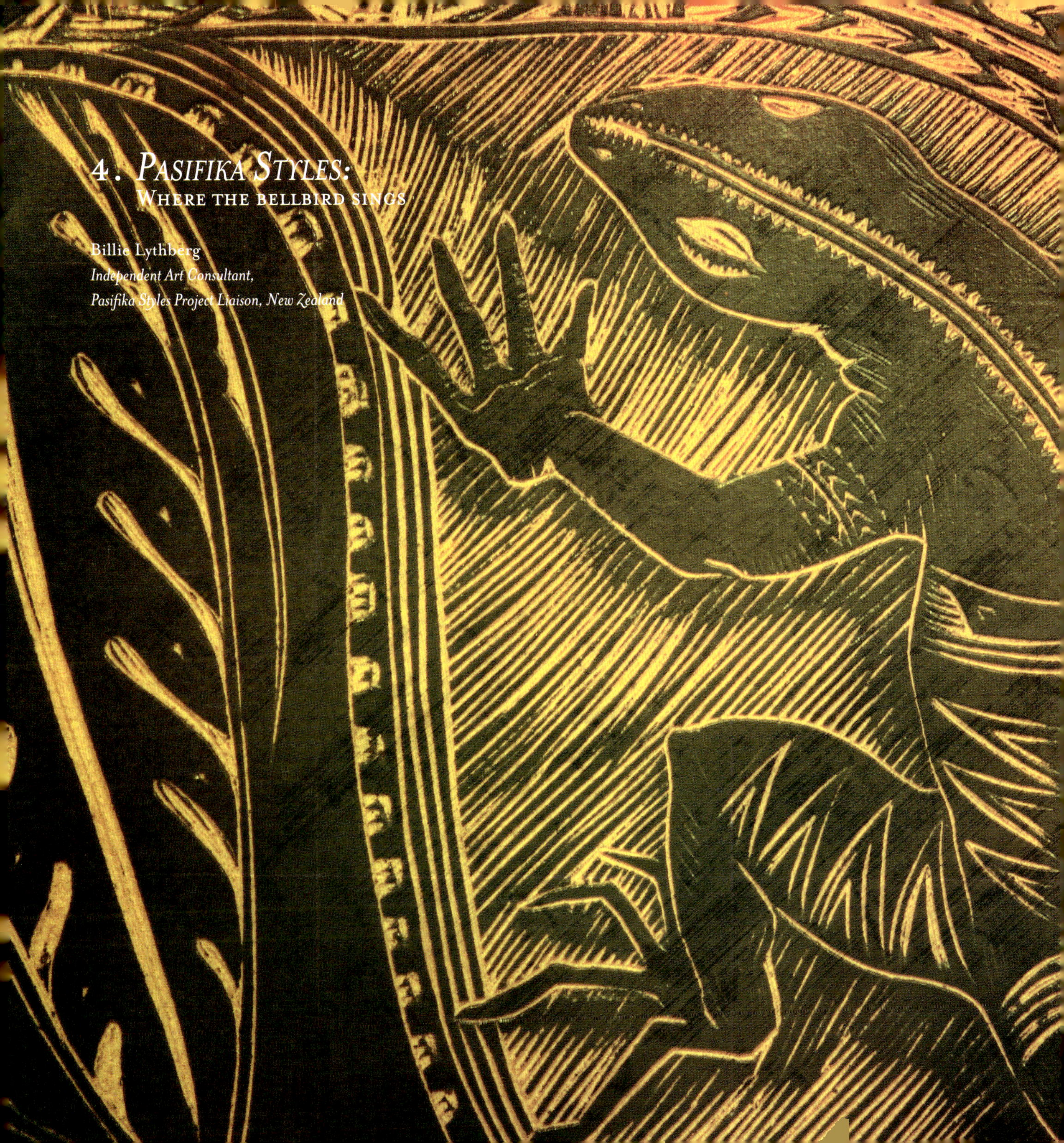

4. Pasifika Styles:
Where the bellbird sings

Billie Lythberg
Independent Art Consultant,
Pasifika Styles Project Liaison, New Zealand

Detail from Michel Tuffery's woodcut *Lau mea ola Laiti* (1988).
Photograph: Kerry Brown.

4. *Pasifika Styles*: Where the bellbird sings

Billie Lythberg
Independent Art Consultant,
Pasifika Styles Project Liaison, New Zealand

A Maori saying that is well-known in Aotearoa-New Zealand[1] explains why people are the most important thing in the world, by comparing the structure of a family to a flax bush:

> If you were to pluck out the centre of the flax bush, where would the bellbird sing?
> If you were to ask me 'What is the most important thing in the world?
> I would reply that, 'It is people, people, people'.[2]

The flax bush is called *te pā harakeke* which means 'the family of flax': the outer leaves, or extended family, shield the inner leaves or parents, which in turn enfold the *rito*, the children at the heart of the bush. If the heart is damaged the bush will die, and there will be nowhere for the bellbird to sing. *Pasifika Styles* reunited the heart of the flax, represented by the artists, with the artefacts they view as their living ancestors. Described by one reviewer as a 'polyphonic collage' (Moutu 2007: 24), the exhibition brought both the people and the song back to the Oceanic collections in Cambridge. In this chapter I will discuss some aspects of the process through which this was achieved, as a team member based in Aotearoa, as well as some precedents and related exhibitions.

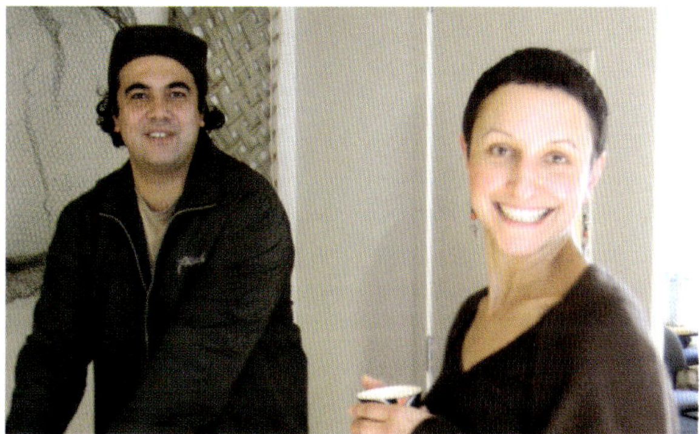

FIG. 22: The author with artist Sheyne Tuffery at the *Pasifika Styles* workshop (*hui or wananga*), Auckland, August 2005. Photograph: Rosanna Raymond.

Pasifika Styles is the first major display of contemporary Pacific art in the United Kingdom, but it is part of a broader continuum of gallery- and museum-based exhibitions of Maori and Pacific art stretching back several decades in Aotearoa and beyond. *Te Maori* (1984), arguably the most influential show to have left the shores of New Zealand, has been extensively discussed in the international literature on museums and cultural representation (Mead 1984; Auckland Art Gallery 1986; see also Clifford 1985; Gathercole 2002; Thomas 1996). The exhibition toured the United States before returning triumphantly home for a national tour called *Te Hokinga Mai* (1986),[3] and included 174 works, largely carvings in wood and stone from private and public collections, some pieces dating back to 1000AD. Though criticised for presenting Maori culture

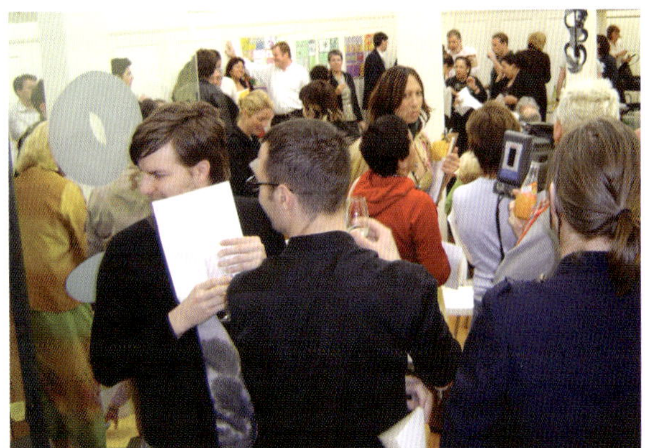

FIG. 23: THE *PASIFIKA STYLES* ARTISTS' AUCTION, OBJECTSPACE GALLERY, AUCKLAND, OCTOBER 2005. PHOTOGRAPH: MIKE WESTON.

as 'not only unambiguously traditional, but also emphatically archaic' the exhibition nevertheless prompted new respect for *taonga* (Maori cultural treasures) in museums and how they were displayed, not least by presenting the works as 'art' rather than 'artefacts' (Thomas 1996a: 295).

Nicholas Thomas has suggested that the importance of *Te Maori* 'arose not only from its content, but also from the extent to which its presentation was authorized by Maori people themselves' (ibid.: 294). The touring exhibition was accompanied by Maori *kaitiaki* (guardians) and 'marked by chants and rituals such as *tapu* lifting [removal of spiritual prohibitions] that emphasized the sacred character of the treasures' (ibid.). When it returned to Aotearoa it was welcomed with a *waiata* (song) composed for the occasion. These acknowledgments of Maori protocol emphasised the relationships between the *taonga* on display and their living descendants, demonstrating that *Te Ao Māori* (the Maori world) is a vibrant, living culture.

By raising the national and international visibility of Maori art, albeit through the exhibition of artefacts from museum collections, *Te Maori* opened the door for appreciation of contemporary works from the wider Pacific region.[4] Though a small group of Pacific artists had gained gallery representation and held individual exhibitions by the late 1980s,[5] the first group exhibition to celebrate the dynamism of Pacific art was *Te Moemoea no Iotefa (The Dream of Joseph)* in 1990, a travelling show developed by the Sarjeant Gallery in Wanganui. As well as staging the first major exhibition of Polynesian Migrant art in Aotearoa, Maori curator Rangihiroa Panoho:

> rejected the reverse exclusivity that often marks ethnic identity politics, and confounded several hierarchical distinctions that generally govern curatorial practice.... Museum artefacts were placed with contemporary art, folk crafts with paintings, archive photographs with contemporary images, and Pacific artists among white appropriators of Pacific style (ibid.: 308).

By exhibiting artefacts together with examples of contemporary art and craft, Panoho's intention was to demonstrate that Pacific migrants to Aotearoa could bring new life to the 'stored culture' in museums (Panoho 1990). He '[gave] voice to the past and the future: the myriad realities of Pacific art were brought together and seen as a whole' (Stevenson 2004: 24). In doing so he brought the relationship between museum-based artefacts and contemporary practices and practitioners to the fore.

Te Moemoea no Iotefa repositioned Pacific art for the public of Aotearoa, and an efflorescence of individual and group shows followed, including 'Pacific' outings held by major regional institutions such as The Dowse Museum, The Govett-Brewster Gallery, and the National Art Gallery. In 1994, for example, Cook Islands artist and curator Jim Vivieaere curated *Bottled Ocean: Contemporary Polynesian Artists*, which toured the country until 1995. Though presented as a group exhibition, *Bottled Ocean* became as much an artwork by Vivieaere, 'a meta-exhibition that made modes of display as well as a body of work its subject matter' (Thomas 1996b: 329). At each new venue he explored different

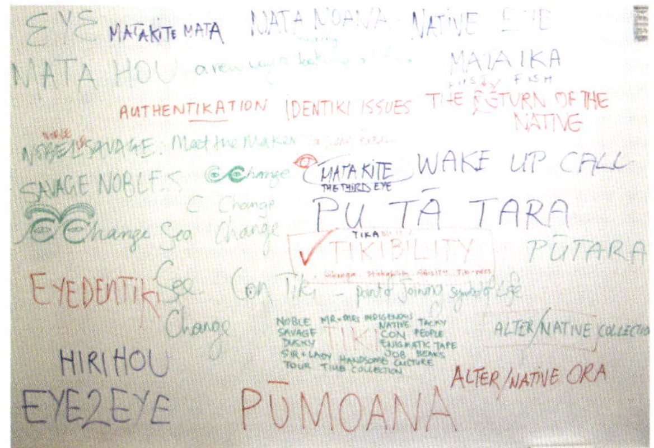

FIG. 24: ARTISTS' SUGGESTIONS FOR THE NAME OF THE EXHIBITION, MADE AT THE AUCKLAND *WANANGA*. PHOTOGRAPH: ROSANNA RAYMOND.

ways of installing the show, utilising a Perspex wall and mirrored floor tiles to push the boundaries of 'display', and reinterpreting individual artists' works.[6] Vivieaere's experimentation arose from his fear that 'having played the "culture card" to establish "Pacific" art, he [might be] trumped by the cliché. He did not want an exhibition of brown artists to be seen as such, or to pigeonhole or label [them]' (Stevenson 2004: 26). Subsequent exhibitions of Pacific art have been founded on organising principles that similarly seek to avoid such 'cultural pigeonholing'.[7]

From the late 1990s a number of exhibitions held overseas have raised the international profile of Pacific artists.[8] One of the most ambitious of these was *Paradise Now?* at the Asia Society Museum in New York in 2004. It showcased the works of artists drawn from the wider Pacific region, including those of European descent, and sought to defy a further cliché so feared and contested by previous curatorial outings; the perception of the Pacific as 'paradise'. Some of the artists were invited to give artists' talks to accompany their works, and the exhibition was also perceived to be supported by the presence of Michael Parekowhai's *Kapahaka* (2003), fifteen cast-fibreglass figures modelled on Parekowhai's brother and clothed as security

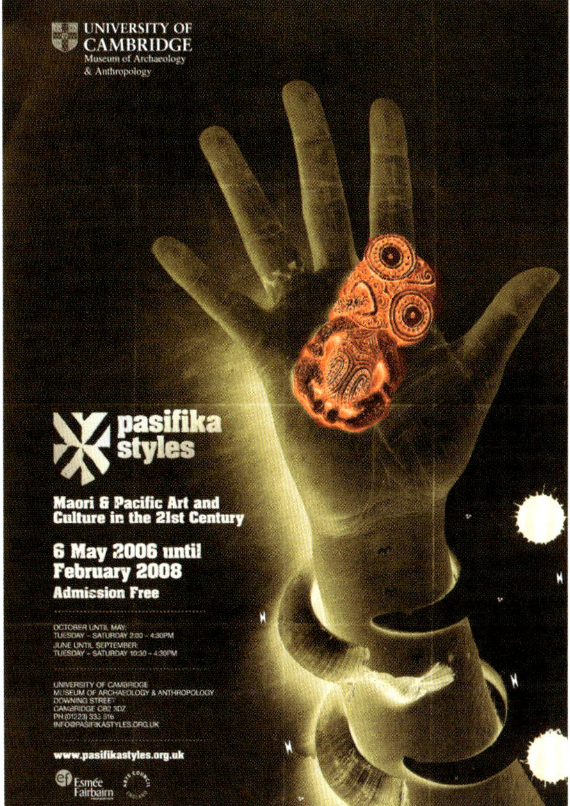

FIG.25: *PASIFIKA STYLES* POSTER, DESIGNED BY DELETE.

guards: 'these figures bring in some of the artist's kin as protection in an unfamiliar world... like having fifteen brothers here to protect the artists' (Myers 2005: 274). However, the show was criticised for:

> [circling] its organizing theme erratically. It alternates between the substantial and the flimsy, the revelatory and the merely didactic, art that argues its case directly and art whose intended (if not actual) effect is supplied primarily by wall labels (Smith 2004).

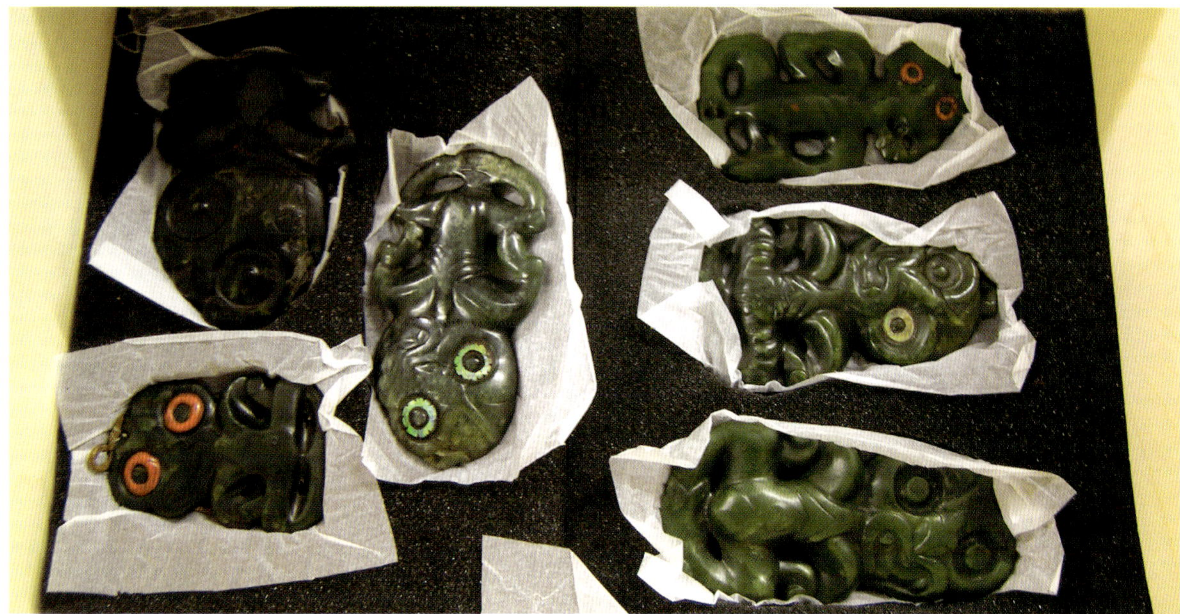

FIG. 26: *Hei-tiki* in their storage box, Museum of Archaeology and Anthropology. Photograph: Carine Durand.

Some of the more nuanced works in the show, noted one reviewer, 'required more knowledge [of the Pacific] than many visitors in New York could be expected to have' (Myers 2004: 274).

Pasifika Styles brings many of the artists included in *Paradise Now?* to the United Kingdom, in an exhibition that seeks to further break down Pacific stereotypes. Unlike previous international shows which have either displayed Pacific artefacts as 'curiosities from an exotic "other"' (Peterson 2006: 66) or sought to unsettle such stereotypes by raising ironic questions, the exhibition creates a platform for immediate dialogue between living artists, artefacts, and the viewing public. The intention here is to sideline curatorial mediation by foregrounding the ability of museum collections to 'instantiate and perpetuate relationships through time' (Henare 2005: 3).

Like *Te Moemoea no Iotefa*, *Pasifika Styles* weaves together 'traditional' and contemporary art produced by Pacific peoples (including Pakeha-New Zealanders of European descent) but adds a further dimension to the way these artworks are viewed by mounting them within a space that functions primarily as a museum. Some of the *Pasifika Styles* artists have had opportunities to show their work in this way before. In 1997, for example, the exhibition *Redress* was mounted at the Auckland War Memorial Museum to coincide with the dismantling of the Museum's Pacific hall. A group of artists led by John Ioane dressed the partially emptied space with site-specific works to mourn the closing of the hall and the ensuing lengthy storage of the Pacific collections.[9] Karen Stevenson discerned that:

> The conflict between ideologies of captured objects and dying cultures and the surging lifeblood of the urban Pacific created an interesting dynamic played out in *Redress*. [Whereas] John Ioane wanted to see the hall

'come alive', to reflect the living vitality of the objects... [Lily Laita] offered the objects and the space its rightful burial (2002: 412).

Among the installations were museum display cases draped by Laita in shroud-like textiles. These challenged the public's preconceived notions of how to behave in a museum: whereas the artist intended visitors to lift the shrouds, people left them alone because one simply does not lift covers off museum cases to see what is beneath them! However, by unsettling the norms of museum display, the exhibition focused new attention on the museum's Oceanic collections: Ioane was asked to interpret one of the 'newly installed artworks' for a museum staff member who walked through the Pacific Halls on her way to work each day. 'It's part of the [museum's] collection', he explained to her. 'It's always been here' (pers. comm., 2007).

Since the opening of *Pasifika Styles* in 2006, the Auckland War Memorial Museum has held a further exhibition of contemporary Pacific art in 2007 to coincide with its major (historically focused) touring show, *Vaka Moana*. This exhibition, *Le Folauga*, brought artists into the museum to speak to the Pacific artefacts in *Vaka Moana*, but housed their artworks away from both the Pacific halls and the Museum's special exhibition space, in two sterile concrete galleries. The ability of the artists' works to converse with the artefacts in *Vaka Moana* was thus limited by their physical separation from them. In Cambridge, pieces made especially for the exhibition respond to the artefacts which are housed there and which in some cases incorporate or are displayed alongside them. The dialogue is both literal and metaphorical: the meetings between artefacts and living people both poignant and empowering. Maureen Lander described how personal and immediate these encounters between people and museum collections could be when she said that 'discovering them is like meeting old friends for the first time – [I feel] a sense of recognition and sadness, and an urge to bring them back into the light and give them new life through referencing them in my art-making process' (*Pasifika Styles* web-log 2007). The centrality of people to the 'things' in the collections at Cambridge was stressed by many of the *Pasifika Styles* artists, who recognised that the task of reinvigorating the collections also extended to the exhibition's visitors. As Michel Tuffery explained, 'it's actually up to the individual to come up with their own way of bringing it alive' (ibid.).

Though the exhibition allows for individual experiences and interpretations, bringing new life to the Oceanic collections at Cambridge was very much a community effort, one which straddled several continents, oceans and time-zones. The rest of this chapter details how this international community was built and held together during the months before the exhibition opened.

Many of the people who would become part of the *Pasifika Styles* project met for the first time at a *wānanga* (working session) held in August 2005, at the University of Auckland (fig. 22). This weekend-long workshop gave the artists opportunities to speak about their work, suggest a title for the exhibition, and drive the curatorial direction of the show. Before the *wānanga*, many had an independent relationship with the show's co-curator and creative director, Rosanna Raymond. Dynamic and charismatic, Raymond is a storyteller and artist with a unique ability to bring people together. Rather than curating a show of artworks *per se*, Raymond approached artists already known to her, albeit on the strength of their work. As the underlying link between all concerned, she promoted comfort and impetus amongst the artists, radiating confidence and excitement alongside fellow curator Amiria Salmond's calm and pragmatic approach.

As the artists described their initial concepts for artworks which would speak to, or about, artefacts held in the museum, it became clear that many of them disagreed with previous interpretations of their work by the academic community, and were anxious to avoid potential misinterpretations of their art in Cambridge. Thus, they perceived a need to *tautoko* (support) not only the artefacts already resident in the museum but also those yet to be created for the exhibition; this support would be dependent on clear lines of communication. As George Nuku explained:

> You should say something clearly to the other world before you present your culture. Be very clear to them about what it is that you are doing and then do it and they will figure it out, because they will feel it. They will feel what you are trying to express in your culture and your world and if you translate that you're almost saying to them that they don't understand - you're not putting any faith or any trust in those people (ibid.).

The artists decided to actively support their work by participating in the visiting artists programme associated with the project, and by presenting a panel discussion at the meeting of the Pacific Arts Association Europe, scheduled to visit *Pasifika Styles* as part of their programme in May 2006.

The *wānanga* bridged gaps between the exhibition's participants, and became a 'shared history' to which the artists and curators could return in future conversations. It has since been spoken of by the artists involved as setting a standard for all future collaborative shows to follow. It was both the ideal and 'traditional' way to convene a project in Aotearoa, and an innovative way for the museum to collaborate with contemporary artists. The *wānanga* closed the geographical distance between the contributors, providing a forum for teamwork and transparent communication, and established warmth amongst the people who would bring that same warmth to the Oceanic collections at Cambridge.[10]

Before the curators returned to the UK, a web-log was initiated by one of the artists, Ani O'Neill, in an effort to help bridge the geographical and ideological distance between the two countries. Group emails were also frequent, and postings on the web-log included photos and video downloads, which maintained a sense of camaraderie and progress among its participants. However, some artists thought the publicly accessible web-log an impractical way to communicate important information, and a few found interfacing with it difficult. Despite this, the web-log played a valuable role for many of the artists as a forum to test ideas and keep in touch (see Paterson this volume); it remains a rich resource of information and personal viewpoints pertaining to the show.

The *Pasifika Styles* artists were charged with breathing new life into the Oceanic collections at MAA, an activity arguably dependent on personal contact with the artefacts held therein. To this end, great emphasis was placed on securing airfares and accommodation so that the artists could spend time in Cambridge before the exhibition began, and explore the museum's extensive holdings. The web-log was used successfully to initiate a fundraising art auction (fig. 23), which was conceived and run by the artists and held in October 2005. The auction raised money for those artists who had not received travel grants from Creative New Zealand (the New Zealand Arts Council) so they might attend the opening of the exhibition in Cambridge. The wider community showed their support for the project by donating a venue for the auction and providing supplies for catering.[11] In a profound demonstration of their commitment to *tautoko* (support) one another and the project as whole, even those artists who had already received travel grants donated artworks to enable their colleagues to join them in Cambridge.

On the evening of the auction a Cook Island drum troupe flanked the gallery doors, calling people into the space and setting the tone for the event. Hosted by artist Shigeyuki Kihara, the auction was a flamboyant and exciting occasion. All of the donated artworks reached reserve, and a significant amount of money was raised, which enabled several artists to travel to Cambridge. The auction underlined the importance of people to the exhibition's success: the artists involved recognised the need to have living, breathing people in Cambridge to sing the exhibition into life.

Although the auction had been initiated by the artists, the task of distributing its funds was delegated by them to the show's curators. All artists who needed funding were invited to apply for funding via email. However, when this important email failed to reach some artists, causing them to miss the submission deadline, the reliance on email as the primary means of communication between the curators and artists was brought into question. Though the deadline for submissions was extended when this became clear, and nobody missed out on applying for funds, those artists who had missed the initial email contact found this incident unsettling.

Email and web-logs are increasingly common means of communication, but their efficacy presumes that all intended recipients have regular access to the internet; some of the artists, especially those living outside major cities, did not. In the absence of the curators, it became apparent that the sense of shared purpose created by the *wānanga* might not hold together if their presence in Aotearoa was reduced to electronic communications and the occasional phone-call. This situation was compounded by the 12-hour time difference between Aotearoa and the United Kingdom, and by the New Zealand summer holidays, which coincided with one of the busiest work periods for the curators. Speaking for the wider group, one artist commented that 'it is hard to keep the focus when you are so far away and we don't see you' (Tracey Tawhiao, pers. comm. 2006).

The artists' communications required structure and the curators required a physical presence in Aotearoa; I fell into this role, becoming both an advocate for those artists who felt they needed one, and a personal representative for the curators. In doing so I was able to maintain regular phone contact with Amiria and Rosanna, and to phone or meet those artists who had difficulties with web-based modes of communication. In this capacity I liaised between the artists and the curators regarding the 'branding' of the exhibition, at one stage chairing a meeting to discuss some artists' concerns. Those who attended the meeting astutely recognised the difference – and relationship – between the exhibition as a lived experience for those who were able to attend it in person, and the exhibition as a representation. Following its closure in the museum, the exhibition lives on in textual and pictorial accounts. The title and promotional images used to brand *Pasifika Styles* are central to these records, and of paramount importance to the way the exhibition is, and will continue to be perceived. Certainly within the arts and academic communities in Aotearoa, only a few individuals had the opportunity to see the exhibition in person. For most, the show exists in cyberspace or on printed pages. This of course does not preclude authoritative discussion of its *kaupapa*, contents, challenges and successes, but it does mean that for most, their experience of *Pasifika Styles* is both constructed and over-determined by its 'branding'.

The title of the show had been discussed at the *wānanga* (fig. 24) and identified as pivotal in defining and communicating the identity of the exhibition. 'Pasifika Styles' was adopted as a working title because of its ability to immediately contextualise the exhibition for potential audiences, sponsors and funding bodies within the United Kingdom. Pasifika also 'speaks to the urban reality of islanders and their attempts to balance notions of identity and loss, migration and place, youth and age, tradition and change' (Stevenson 2004: 31). While 'Pasifika Styles' was approved by the artists as a working title, its use as the formal title of the exhibition and associated events remains contested. As one noted: 'The grass roots found it amusing while high art thought it was frivolous' (Shigeyuki Kihara, pers. comm. 2007).

The exhibition's main promotional image (fig. 25) was similarly problematic for some of the artists. A lengthy emailed communication from Cambridge in February 2006 gave the artists a progress report and showed them a proposed image of Raymond's hand with her distinctive *tatau* (Samoan tattoo), encircled by pig's tusk bracelets and reaching for a *tiki* (ancestral neck pendant) from the museum's collections (MAA Z 6458). Conceptually, it was designed to represent the relationships between Maori (the *tiki*) and the Pacific (the tusks and *tatau*), and between MAA's artefacts and the living artists (Raymond's hand). However, some of the artists felt that the ambiguity of the outstretched hand weakened the metaphorical resonance of the image – was the *tiki* being gifted or taken away? (group email, pers. comm. 2006).

The key concern was that the artists were in danger of being represented as a parody of themselves, a 'style' or 'fusion', terms which 'speak more of fashion than of living art' (Tracey Tawhiao, pers. comm. 2006). In fact, this was specifically something the curators were trying to avoid. The represented reality of *Pasifika Styles* owes much to the styling of the creative director of the show, Rosanna Raymond, one of the group Pacific Sisters, who 'epitomise the vitality and verve of contemporary Pacific art' (Stevenson 2002: 407). Slick, fashionable and slightly edgy, the exhibition's title and promotional imagery lend a street-smart air to the way the show is perceived. Yet the image and title were designed not only to attract a youthful and streetwise audience. Raymond's earlier involvement in a number of academic and outreach projects in UK universities and museums had alerted her to the dearth of knowledge among the general British public about the Pacific, and the difficulties of offering visual cues without reiterating familiar stereotypes. Other potential titles and ideas for promotional images offered by the artists exhibiting at *Pasifika Styles* (fig. 24) were felt by the curators to be too reliant on knowledge about the Pacific for the mainly European audiences that would view the exhibition – they also felt it was important for the title to give an idea of its content. In this, it was necessary to defer to the curators' experience of the United Kingdom; ideas that would work in Aotearoa might have been unintelligible in the UK.

Pasifika Styles literally brought the artists back in touch with artefacts that many view as their living ancestors. The museum's galleries are housed in an historic building filled with objects displayed in beautiful, old-fashioned glass cases. It exists in stark contrast to the white-walled spaces of most contemporary art galleries. Within its stone walls the artists were given extraordinary access to the museum's Oceanic collections. Some spoke of feeling like children in a candy store: Tracey Tawhiao described opening a drawer of *tiki* pendants (fig. 26) and being asked which she would like to include in her installation. 'All of them', she said. 'It's a small cabinet', replied the museum assistant. 'Well you'll need to squash them in then', the artist asserted (pers. comm. 2007).

Maureen Lander has observed that collections housed overseas often contain artefacts without strong provenances, and that in these situations their lack of confirmed documentation can be of benefit to artists wishing to view them (pers. comm. 2007). In Aotearoa, artefacts claimed by *iwi* (tribal groups) are often placed on restricted access. The *tiki* used in the show's main promotional images is one such example of an 'unclaimed' *taonga* (treasure). He was purchased in 1907 by Baron von Hügel, the museum's first curator, from a collector named Webster, but little more is known of his history. By choosing this *tiki* to promote the exhibition, the *Pasifika Styles* design team conveyed the importance of reconnecting artefacts with their living descendants and bringing them into the light.

While bringing the artists to the museum was central to the success of the project, transporting artworks to Cambridge was also of paramount importance. In coordinating the packing and shipping of a large proportion of the works to the UK (with limited funds) I was able to arrange additional sponsorship and was supported by an experienced shipping agent, who knew *exactly* how to get two crates of valuable art, some made from questionable organic materials, to the UK. Once again the wider community supported the artists and curators to ensure the show would be a success.

It is clear that establishing or drawing upon a strong and supportive community is critical to the success of an undertaking as ambitious in scale and scope as *Pasifika Styles*. The *kaupapa* (guiding philosophy) of the project required extraordinary teamwork and communication, and events such as the *wānanga* and the Art Auction in particular demonstrated the artists' commitment to the project and to one another. But communication was not always easy. When the curators were in Aotearoa the project had extraordinary focus and momentum; when they returned to the UK this proved difficult to maintain via email, resulting in some contested decisions.

Through the successes and challenges experienced in the months leading up to the opening of the exhibition, one thing remained constant: the people of *Pasifika Styles* were its most important thing. They drove the *kaupapa* of the show; warmed the artefacts in the Oceanic collection; and brought their song to Cambridge. Many of the artists have already made return trips to Cambridge and other UK museums; for some the exhibition has been a springboard into Artist Residencies and other international opportunities. After the exhibition closes a few works acquired by the museum remain behind to continue this dialogue. Shigeyuki Kihara, whose photographs have been purchased, hopes that one day her descendents will 'come and visit me in Cambridge when I leave the land of the living' (pers. comm. 2007).[12]

Notes

1 Aotearoa is a Maori name for New Zealand, often used conjointly or in replacement of its European name.

2 The Maori version of the proverb is: *Hūtia te rito o te harakeke. Kei hea te kōmako e kō?*
Kī mai nei ki ahau. He aha te mea nui ki tēnei ao?
Maku e ki atu. He tangata, he tangata, he tangata.

3 About 920,000 people saw the exhibition in Aotearoa, and 600,000 in the USA (Te Papa Tongarewa website).

4 See also *Taonga Maori* which toured Australia in 1989-1990 before being shown at the National Musuem in Wellington.

5 These included Fatu Feu`u, John Pule, Jim Vivieaere and Michel Tuffery (Vercoe 2002).

6 Iosefa Leo's sculptures were mounted in and on the exhibition's touring cases; a work by Greg Semu, *Uprising!* was literally cut to size for one installation; a pile of Michel Tuffery's woodblocks were displayed in their bubble wrap in Auckland.

7 For example Giles Peterson curated *Emerging into the Light* (1995); *Pacific Dragons: Art of Protest and promise from 15 nations of the Pacific* (1996); *Te Kare Mowhiti – Romance of the Mask* (1998); *Heart of the Niu* (1998); *Fireworks: Art of the Pacific Age* (1998); *Ring of Fire* (1999); *and Urban Pacific* (2007).

8 These include: *inei/Konei: The Pacific in Photo Art from Aotearoa* (1997) curated by Blair French; *Paringa Ou* (1998) curated by Ian George; *Island Crossings* (2000) and *Longitude* (2007) curated by Giles Peterson; *Paradise Now?* (2004) curated by Melissa Chiu; and *Dateline* (2007) curated by Alexander Tolnay and Rhana Davenport.

9 The Pacific halls did not reopen until March 1999.

10 The notion of keeping *taonga* (treasures) warm is central to many Pacific cultures and was a founding aim of the *Pasifika Styles* project.

11 Thanks to Objectspace Gallery, Delmaine Fine Foods, Waimata Cheese and Kim Crawford Wines for their donations, and Brenda Railey and Shigeyuki Kihara for their leadership and support.

12 Works have also been purchased from Lisa Reihana, John Ioane and Chris Charteris.

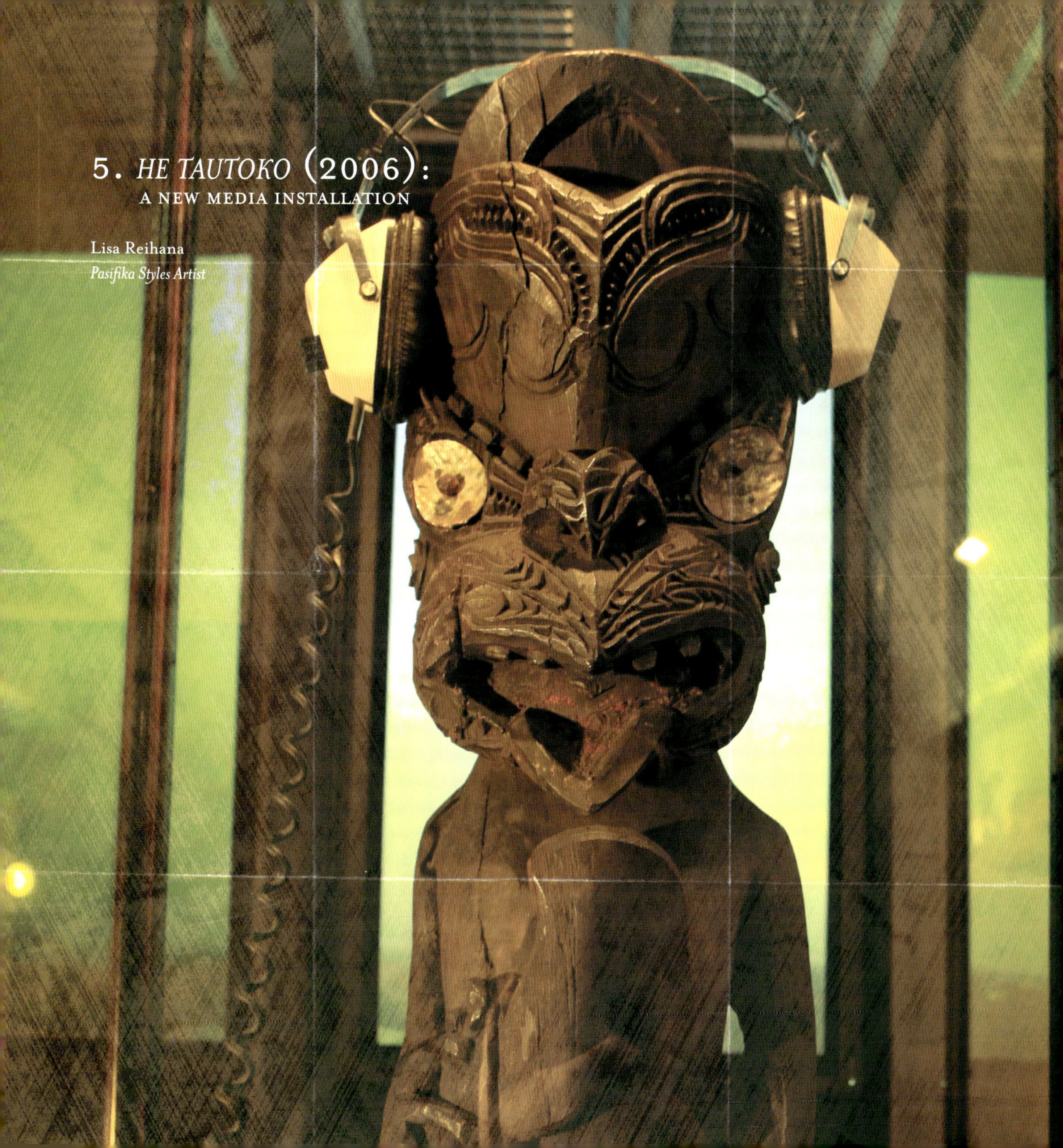

5. *HE TAUTOKO* (2006): A NEW MEDIA INSTALLATION

Lisa Reihana
Pasifika Styles Artist

Detail of Lisa Reihana's installation *He Tautoko* (2006). Photograph: Kerry Brown.

5. *HE TAUTOKO* (2006): A NEW MEDIA INSTALLATION

Lisa Reihana
Pasifika Styles Artist

Artist Lisa Reihana works with a range of materials from video and photography, to sculpture and fashion. She has played a significant role in the artistic development of new media and film in Aotearoa-New Zealand. Her work comments on gender politics, cultural agency and museological interventions, and featured in the Pasifika Styles *exhibition.*

Pasifika Styles is an exciting model that progressive museums can use to re-invigorate their collections. As an artist it presented the perfect opportunity for me to extend my practice, by directly engaging with Maori customary *taonga* (ancestral treasures). My work in the exhibition, *he tautoko* (2006) (fig. 27) is a response to MAA's Oceanic collection. I felt it appropriate to make an *iwi* (tribal) connection, so I sourced a Nga Puhi *tekoteko* (gable figure) carving.

I first visited MAA in November 2005 to view the museum and to record Maori works in the collection onto HDV video. The filmed works include *hei tiki* pendants, weaponry, kauri gum, and *kete* (woven bags) as well as accessioning numbers indelibly written on *pounamu* (greenstone). I used digital filters and editing techniques to create multi-layered images and animated *tukutuku* patterns.[1] The 35 minutes of edited video was then transferred to DVD, which plays back on a plasma screen mounted in portrait format behind the *tekoteko*. The footage of the taonga is interspersed with New Zealand landscapes. The vitrine's glass provided an unexpected bonus – at certain distances the portrait-oriented screen reflects, replicating and creating another horizontal image, an effect not dissimilar to a video wall.

Mounted outside the cabinet is a gold-coloured aluminum casing containing three stereos with Nokia telephone handsets. Three people can concurrently have a unique audio experience while viewing the video-silhouetted *tekoteko* wearing headphones. Each stereo has fifteen minutes of different audio bytes, which play until the handset is 'hung up'.

Different people were approached to gift sounds to *he tautoko*. The soundtracks include songs from the Manukau Institute of Technology Maori choir, and the 'tap tapping' sounds as Maori artist Lyonel Grant carves onto his work the same pattern found on the mouth of the *tekoteko*. During colonial times trading was rife, and the collecting of *taonga* often meant tribal connections and ancestral names were lost. This is also true for the MAA *tekoteko*, who had conflicting provenances written about him on catalogue cards. I used these as a script, recording them in the style of an authoritarian BBC voice:

> Card (1): H.D. Skinner: 'Tekoteko (gable ornament). An excellent example secured by Baron Charles von Hugel, probably at the Bay of Islands. Originally painted with kokowai (native red paint made of iron oxide). At the bottom is the owl's head. H.D.S'.

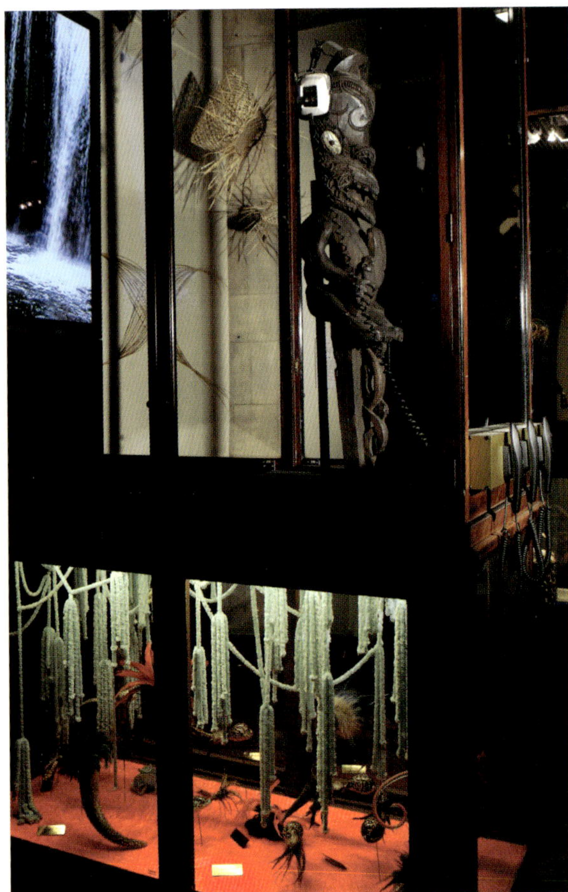

FIG. 27: Two of Reihana's works in the exhibition: *He tautoko* (2006) in the top of the case, and *Fluffy fings* (1998) below. Photograph: Kerry Brown.

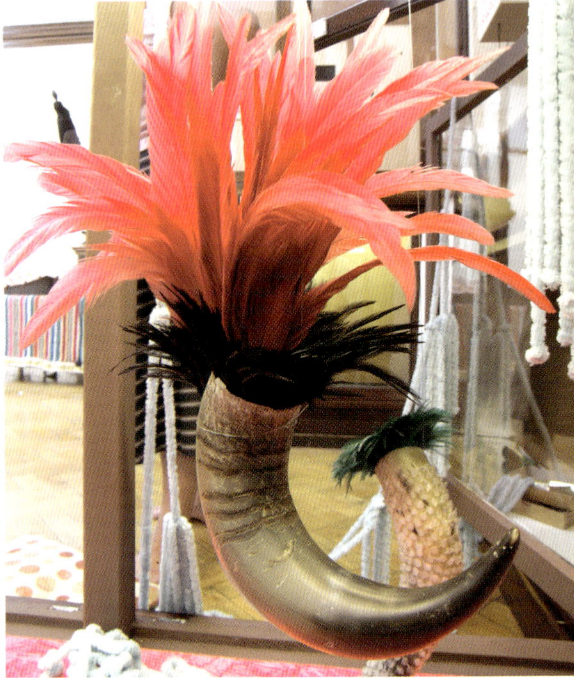

FIG. 28: Detail of Lisa Reihana's installation *Fluffy fings* (2006). Photograph: Kerry Brown.

> Card (2): 'Carved wooden male figure 40 inches long. The hands have five fingers each and the right one grasps a mere. The face is tattooed and the legs as well. They are much attenuated and there are three toes each. Below the figure is a bird-shaped figure'.

> Card (3): 'Gable ornament or tekoteko carved in totara. The style of carving belongs to the central to Bay of Plenty region of the North Island. The figure grasps a club of the wahaika type, and small manaia figures are to be seen at each side of the head near the ears. The cutting is steel-tool work of a vigorous kind...'.

He tautoko translates as 'supporting someone' or 'propping them up'. The *tekoteko* is erected inside a vitrine, contextualised by sounds and images of home. Footage of blue skies signifies that he was once seen on top of a meeting house, silhouetted by New Zealand skies. On the *tekoteko* are 1960s headphones, and when the viewer listens to the Nokia phones, the combination of the two, visually and conceptually, evokes conversing with this ancestor.

Creating a counterpoint to *he tautoko* was *fluffy fings* (1998) installed in the cabinet below. This brightly coloured installation playfully takes on the museological and the aquatic – hand-engraved plaques name the furry and feathery horn works with titles such as '*thingamybobs*' and '*plush tusks*' (fig. 28). The colourful nature of this work appeals to adults and children alike. So that parents could spend more time with *he tautoko*, *fluffy fings* was placed at a child's eye level.

Notes

1 *Tukutuku* are grid-like woven patterns creating panels that line the interior walls of *wharenui* or meeting houses. They are found between *poupou* or carvings and help tell the story of the kin group to which the *wharenui* belongs.

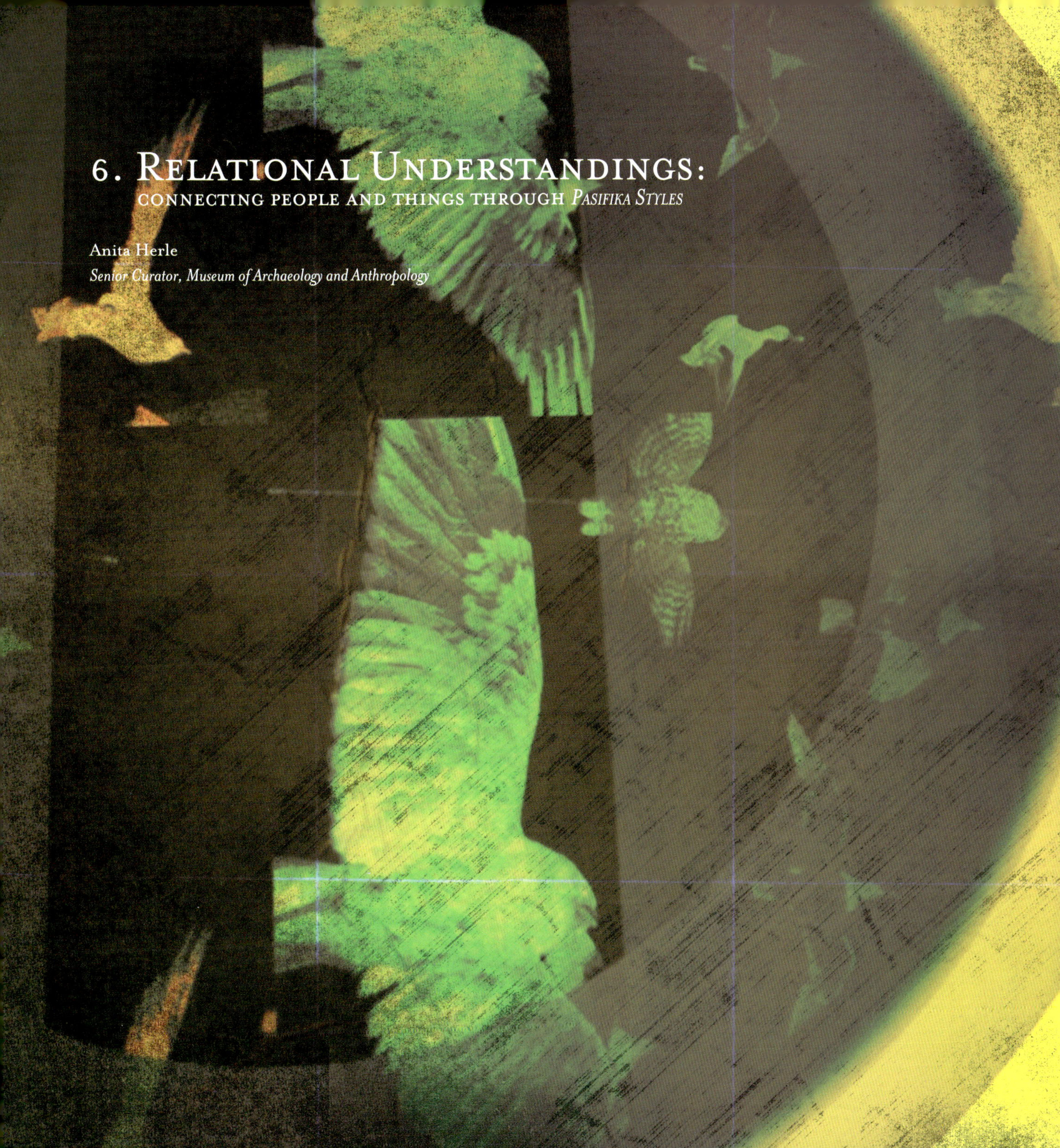

6. Relational Understandings:
connecting people and things through *Pasifika Styles*

Anita Herle
Senior Curator, Museum of Archaeology and Anthropology

Detail from Sheyne Tuffery's *Manu tawhiti rua* (2006). Photograph: Kerry Brown.

6. Relational Understandings:
connecting people and things through *Pasifika Styles*

Anita Herle
Senior Curator, Museum of Archaeology and Anthropology

> Thanks to Cambridge we are able to touch our *taonga* [ancestral treasures], and by touching our *taonga* without white gloves we give life back to the *taonga*. They have had a very long sleep. When we touch them it gives them life and they give us life – it is a reciprocal thing (Che Wilson interview, *Pasifika Styles website*).

The exhibition *Pasifika Styles* is a long-range collective project that addresses in unusually clear and pressing terms many of the debates surrounding cultural property, the performance of culture and the relations between persons and things in the setting of the museum and well beyond. Concerns regarding cultural properties tend to focus on law and ethics, on appropriation and ownership, with media representations typically producing stereotypes that reinforce and polarise the terms of the debate. The common, typically polemical, notion is that rapacious museums are merely a final resting point for captive static objects, with repatriation viewed as simply restorative compensation. A robust challenge to this view was developed in the 'Declaration on the Importance and Value of Universal Museums' signed in 2002 by the directors of nineteen leading museums in Europe and North America (ICOM News 2004:1). The concept of the 'universal museum' asserts that objects are cared for and held in trust for the world, overriding shifting political and ethnic boundaries and enabling the visitor to see 'different parts of the

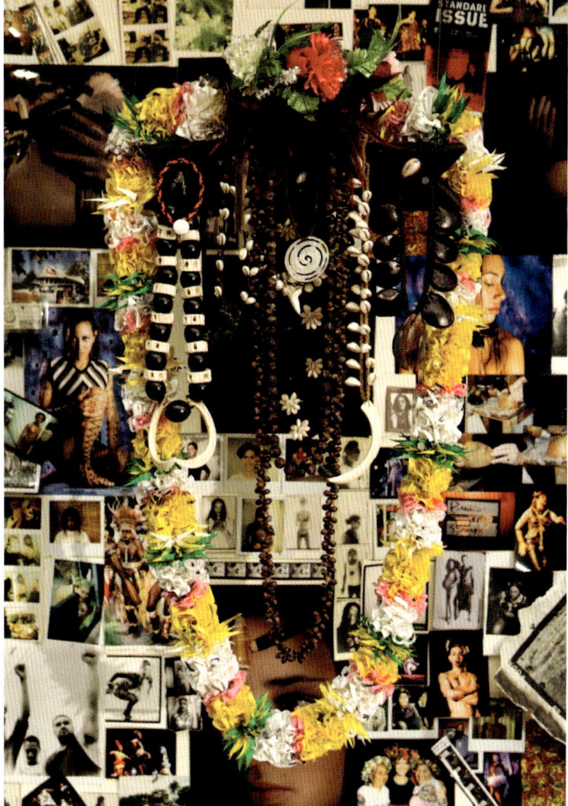

FIG. 29: Draped cross, a detail from Rosanna Raymond's installation. Photograph: Kerry Brown

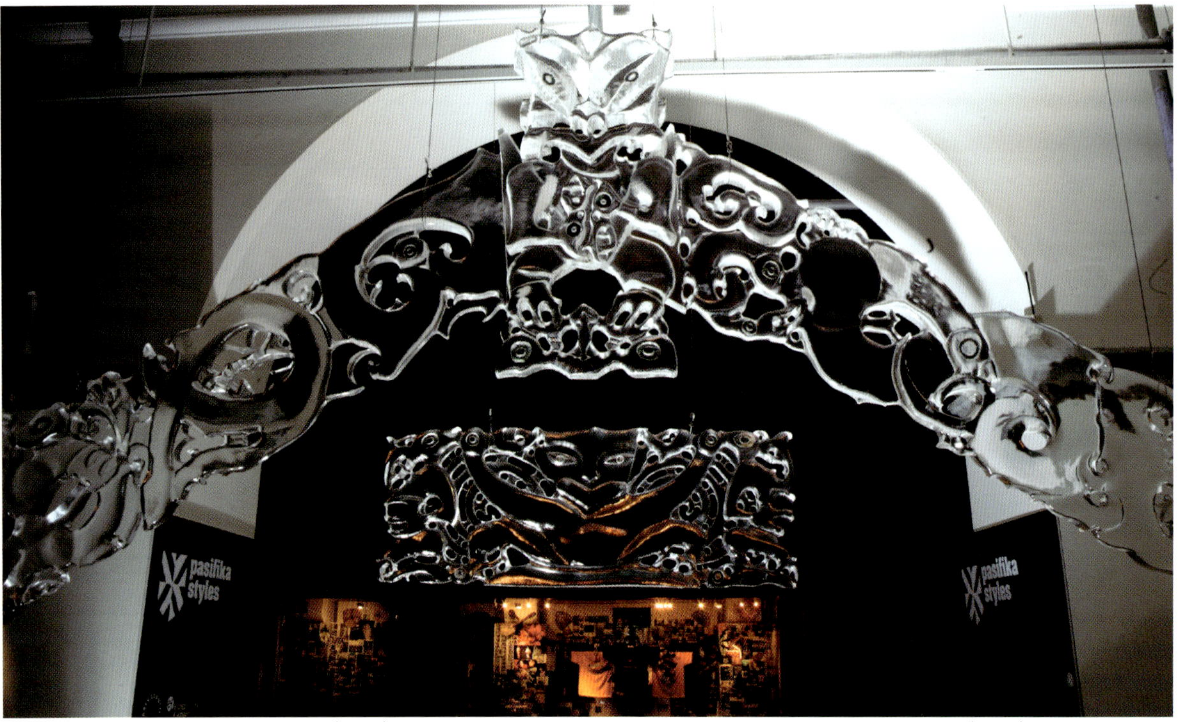

FIG. 30: GEORGE NUKU'S *OUTER SPACE MARAE* (2006), WITH ROSANNA RAYMOND'S INSTALLATION *EYE LAND PART II: WELCOME 2 DA K'LUB* (2006) VISIBLE BEYOND. PHOTOGRAPH: MUSEUM OF ARCHAEOLOGY AND ANTHROPOLOGY

world as indissolubly linked' (ibid.: 7). While many would be in sympathy with the rhetorical position asserted, critics have argued that the declaration is a thinly veiled attempt to bolster immunity to repatriation claims. On both sides of the debate, the hegemonic position of many museums remains unsettling.

The experience of *Pasifika Styles*, and the processes involved in its creation and reception, help shift the focus on utterly fixed objects unambiguously owned by individuals, communities and institutions, to a more relational understanding of the dynamic links between people and things. A central premise of relational models is that entities (both objects and people) emerge from (and thus acquire substance, meaning and value through) the relations in which they are enmeshed. A relational approach to the museum and the objects it contains highlights the productive potential of museum collections and exhibitions to link people and ideas over time and space (Herle 2003). Recent projects, both within the Pacific and between particular Pacific communities and museums in Europe and America, have shifted the emphasis from ownership (in a narrow sense of the term) to considerations of access, use, and interpretation (Peers and Brown 2003; Stanley 2007). In many instances, this shift has re-connected communities with treasured historic objects, re-invigorating their potency and reinforcing the presence of the ancestral past in the present. Furthermore, contemporary art

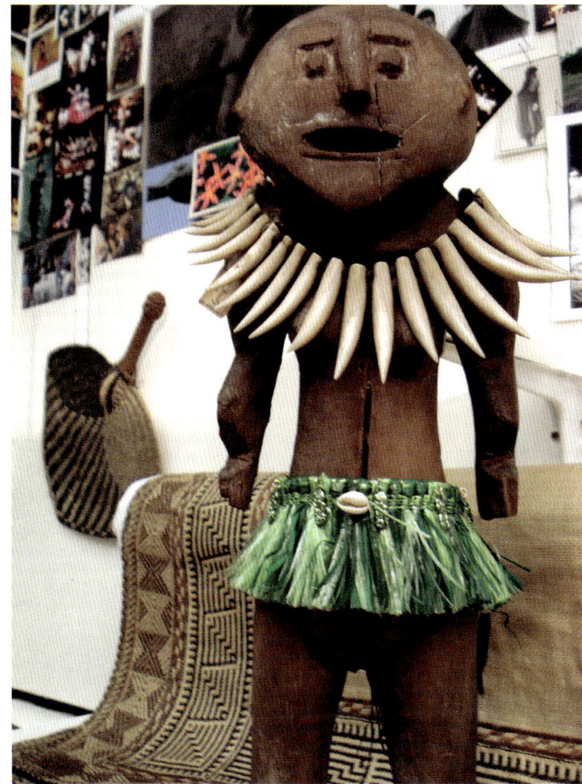

FIG. 31: DETAIL FROM RAYMOND'S INSTALLATION, SHOWING THE FIJIAN "GODDESS" DRESSED BY THE ARTIST. PHOTOGRAPH: ROSANNA RAYMOND.

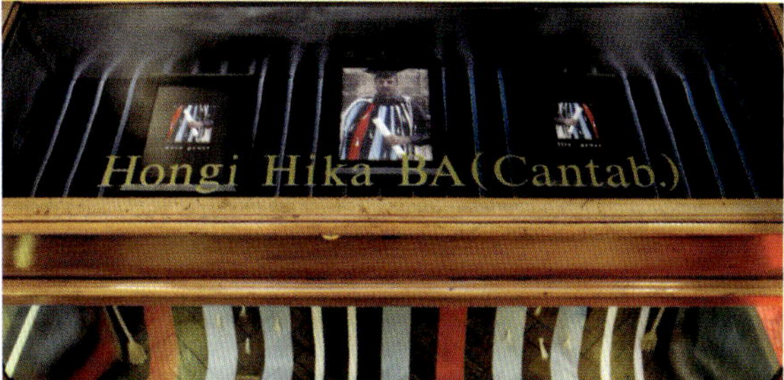

FIG. 32: LISA REIHANA'S INSTALLATION *HONGI HIKA BA (CANTAB.): "AN EMBLEM OF WISDOM...?"* (2006). PHOTOGRAPH: KERRY BROWN.

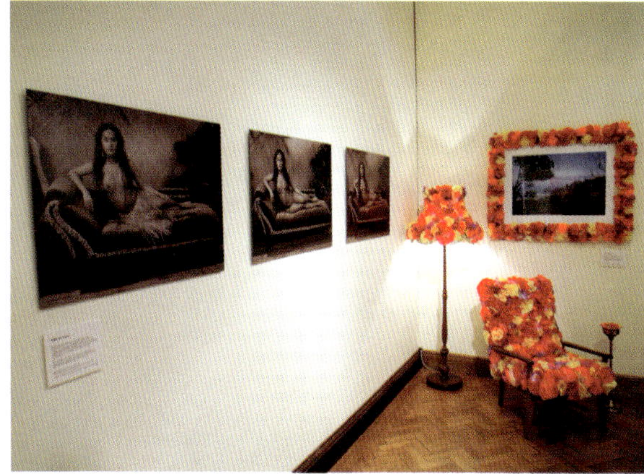

FIG. 33: SHIGEYUKI KIHARA'S TRIPTYCH, *FA'A FAFINE: IN A MANNER OF A WOMAN* (2005). PHOTOGRAPH: MUSEUM OF ARCHAEOLOGY AND ANTHROPOLOGY.

practice, often involving members of diasporic communities, provides an insightful and powerful commentary on ideas about appropriation and reciprocity (Phillips 1998; Thomas 1999).

Rosanna Raymond's leading role as both co-curator and participating artist was crucial to the development of the *Pasifika Styles* project, as was the active involvement of numerous Maori and New Zealand-based Pacific Island artists, many of whom came to Cambridge to participate in its creation, opening and associated outreach activities. *Pasifika Styles* was generated from a less proprietorial form of curatorship, which facilitated members of local and diasporic communities to re-connect with their *taonga* and revitalise the museums collections, both physically and spiritually:

> Working with museums and collections can help bridge the gaps that have opened in the process of housing, collecting and writing about indigenous people over the past 200 years. They could be arenas for cultural exchange, going outside the boundary of the space into everyday life (Rosanna Raymond, label text, *Pasifika Styles* exhibition).

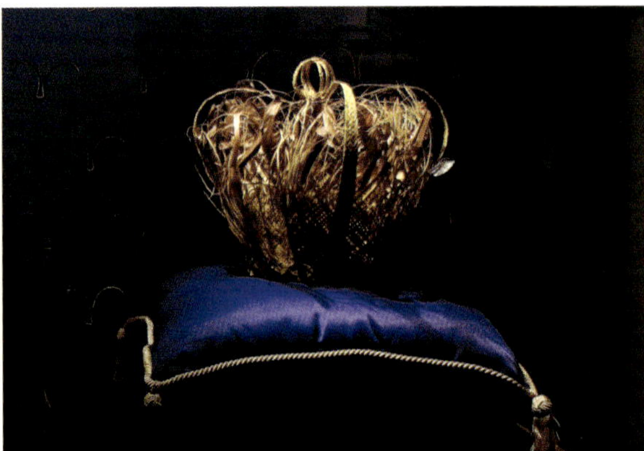

FIG. 34: MAUREEN LANDER'S *CROWN GRAB BAG* (2006). PHOTOGRAPH: KERRY BROWN.

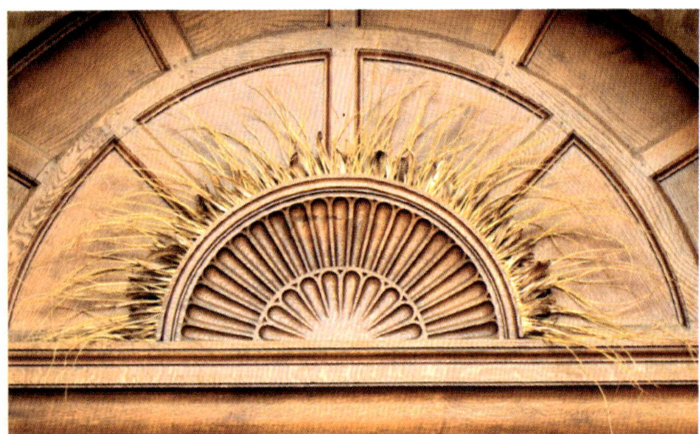

FIG. 35: *TANE RAISES HIS EYEBROWS* (2006) BY MAUREEN LANDER. PHOTOGRAPH: MUSEUM OF ARCHAEOLOGY AND ANTHROPOLOGY.

The poster image for *Pasifika Styles* (see fig. 25) features Raymond's tattooed hand reaching towards a Maori *taonga* , a *hei tiki* neck pendant (MAA Z 6458) collected in 1907 by Baron Anatole von Hügel, the Museum's founding curator. Her arm is decorated with boar's tusk ornaments from Samoa (also in the Museum's collection) and her gesture highlights the living and dynamic aspects of Pacific art. Commenting on the image Raymond stated 'I see him coming into the world of light, re-connecting to the living aspect... and binding Maori with the Pacific' (*Pasifika Styles* web-log).

The exhibition opens with George Nuku's *Outer Space Marae* (2006) (fig. 30), carved from acrylic Perspex and inlaid with paua (*Haliotis*) shell. Its positioning at the entrance of the exhibition highlights the transformation of parts of the gallery into Maori space and the connection between ancestors and their contemporary kin. Adept at moving between cultural worlds, Nuku describes his 'multitudinal self', his ability to take his family and tribe with him: 'When you enact your culture you don't need to translate your culture anymore' (label text, *Pasifika Styles* exhibition).

Visible through the *marae*'s facade, on the opposite side of the gallery, is Rosanna Raymond's large glass-case installation *Eye land Part II: Welkome 2 da K'lub* (2006) (figs. 29 & 31). Raymond's work plays with puns and analogies that tease as well as elicit insightful connections between things. *Da K'lub* is framed with a selection of Polynesian clubs from the museum's collections, arranged along the top of the long case in a manner inspired by the symmetrical arrangements of weapons on the walls of colonial residences and the lay-out of many 'traditional' museum displays. Her *Eye land* is a strong visual evocation of contemporary Polynesian life in New Zealand and beyond. The walls are covered with hundreds of overlapping photographs, posters, magazine covers and ephemera, which document a vibrant and intense period of inter-cultural creativity involving Auckland-based Maori and Pacific Islander artists in dialogue with international youth and fashion culture. As a performing artist and founding member of the art collective Pacific Sisters, Raymond's own art practice has been central to these developments (Raymond 2003). The case also includes many personal items such as photographs, jewellery, ornaments and t-shirts. A Samoan raffia and pandanus skirt from the museum's collection (MAA 1925.151) is displayed alongside a new skirt created by Raymond from plaited yellow plastic and raffia strips decorated with cowrie shells.

Raymond carefully selected specific museum objects to

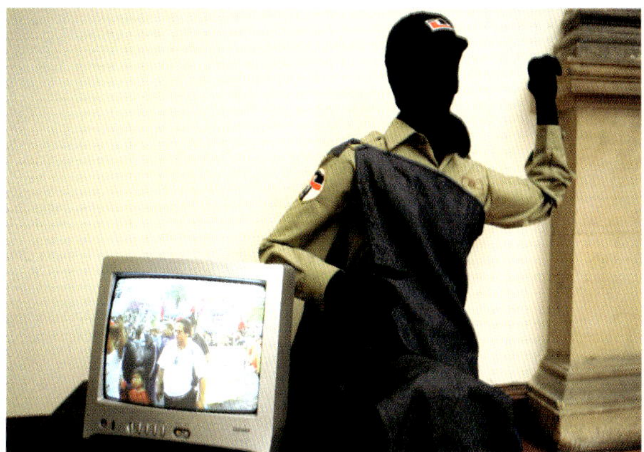

FIG. 36: *Fulltime Revolutionary* (2005) by Kewana Duncan. Photograph: Kerry Brown.

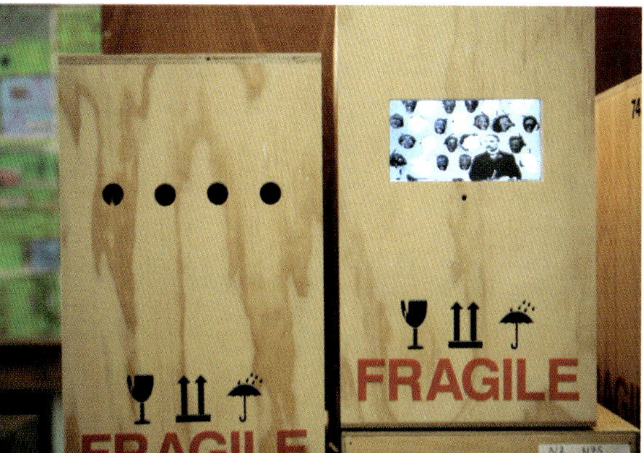

FIG. 37: Wayne Youle's *Hahea* (2006) (left) and *Thanks to the Magic of Religion and Television* (2006). Photograph: Kerry Brown.

include in her artwork, which allude to varied and complex historic relations between Cambridge and the Pacific. A nineteenth-century Samoan mat (MAA 1951.775) is displayed on the case floor with an old hand-written label, which reads:

> King Matafa of Samoa and his Queen sat on this mat to receive Dr Alex Hill [late Master of Downing College in Cambridge] and his wife and son and daughter, at a kava drinking in 1895 when they visited the islands. After the ceremony, King Matafa rose and presented the mat to Dr Hill ... donated by Miss E. Hill 1951.775.

Positioned on the mat, a roughly carved wooden female figure from Fiji, donated by the Museum's founding Curator Baron von Hügel, hints at more ambiguous relations. As a young man, von Hügel worked in Fiji between 1875-1876 recording details of customary life and collecting objects. The catalogue card for the figure (MAA Z 2869) notes that it was 'given to the collector by Ninona, a pretty half caste Kai Loma girl at (Bau) Mbau as her portrait'. While 'portrait' is likely to be a misconstrued reading, the figure appears to have been a memento of a relationship between von Hügel and the girl. Prior to display Raymond was concerned that the figure appeared neglected, so carefully dressed her with a whale-tooth necklace from the collection, a miniature plaited hula skirt she crafted herself and a feather and shell anklet, thus restoring a sense of decorum to the figure and clothing it as it might have been clothed in the past (fig. 31).[1] Researching the Museum's collections, Raymond explained that she feels 'a strong bond to my ancestors when I meet 'artefacts'. It is like a direct line opens up with my cultural heritage, the past becomes present' (*Pasifika Styles* label text).

The living dynamic between the past and present is demonstrated in a powerful and evocative installation by Maori artist Lisa Reihana, a leading figure in the development of multimedia art in Aotearoa-New Zealand (see also Reihana, this volume). *He tautoko* (2006) features a carved wooden *tekoteko* (MAA 1939.70), an ancestral figure originally attached to a house gable. The carving was collected in the 1830s by Baron von Hügel's father near the Bay of Islands, tribal homeland of the artist's father. This region was also the first centre of colonial government and therefore the location from where some

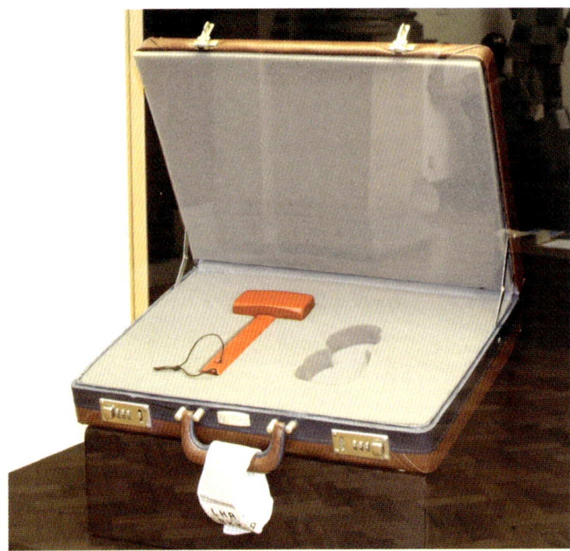

FIG. 38: *THE DO-IT-YOURSELF REPATRIATION KIT* (2006) BY JASON HALL. PHOTOGRAPH: MUSEUM OF ARCHAEOLOGY AND ANTHROPOLOGY.

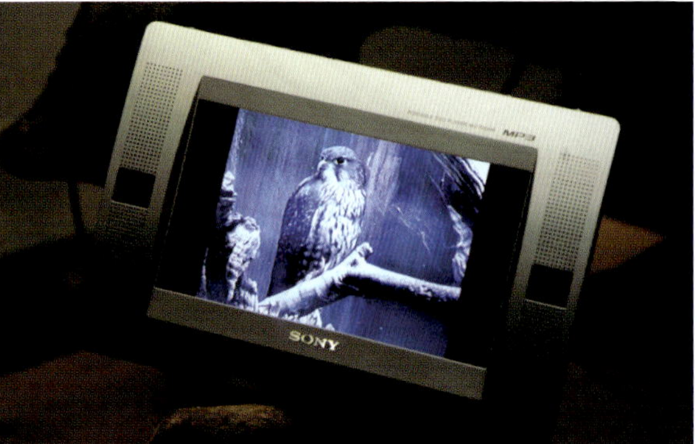

FIG. 39: DETAIL OF ROBERTSON AND MACGREGOR'S WORK. PHOTOGRAPH: KERRY BROWN.

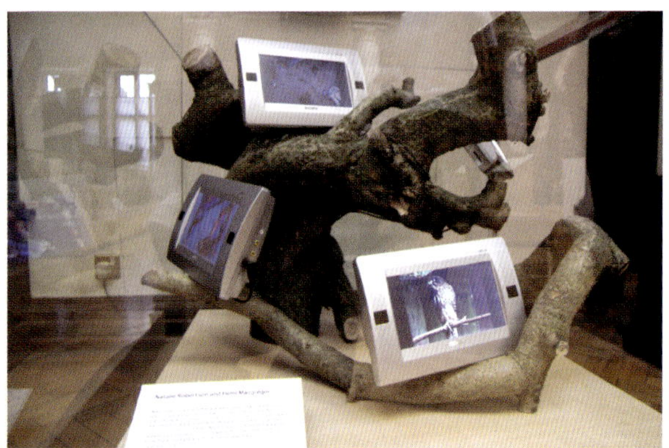

FIG. 40: *TALES OF THE MAORI BORDER* (2006) BY NATALIE ROBERTSON AND HEMI MACGREGOR. PHOTOGRAPH: CARINE DURAND.

of the first Maori objects left Aotearoa. The *tekoteko*, nearly a metre in height, is positioned in the top half of the case so that its iridescent shell eyes look down on the visitor. The figure is wearing large white headphones, plugged into a visitor's listening post, and placed with its back to a video screen displaying digitally manipulated images of Maori collections in the Museum and of the artist's journey between New Zealand and Cambridge. The movements on the screen, the stories and songs (including a rendition of the artist singing 'My Bonnie lies over the ocean') animate the figure, highlighting its continued ancestral presence and ongoing connection to both past and contemporary events. Rather than being didactic, the artist's intention is to activate people into thinking for themselves about the possible meanings created by the re-positioning of objects from the Museum's collections. Commenting on the creation of this installation within the museum, Reihana notes

> It's interesting territory for an artist to work in a museum; they have collections – rich and loaded material. It's not the blank canvas that a gallery usually presents... We call treasured artefacts '*taonga*'. *Pasifika Styles* allows me the opportunity to show people these aren't just objects, they embody the life blood of our living culture (*Pasifika Styles* label text, from an interview with the artist by Sarah Robins).

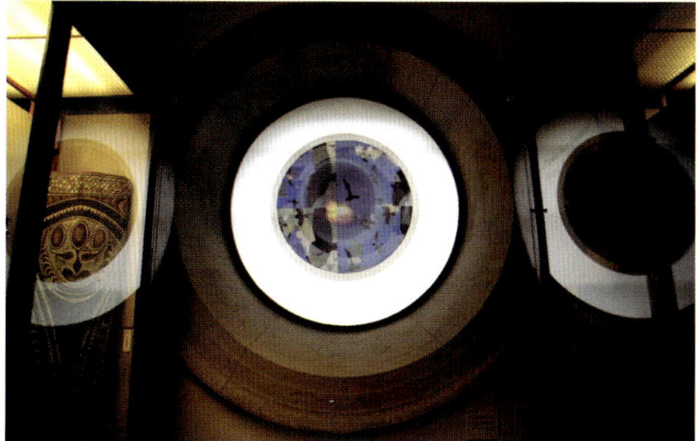

FIG. 41: *MANU TAWHITI TAHI* (2006) BY SHEYNE TUFFERY. PHOTOGRAPH: KERRY BROWN.

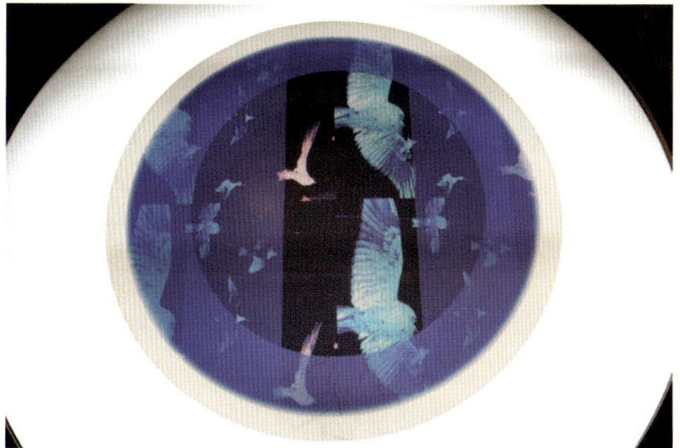

FIG. 42: *MANU TAWHITI RUA* (2006) BY SHEYNE TUFFERY. PHOTOGRAPH: KERRY BROWN.

An adjacent photographic installation (fig. 32) by Reihana, *Hongi Hika BA (Cantab.): 'an emblem of wisdom...?'* (2006) references a critical historic encounter between the University of Cambridge and Hongi Hika (1772?–1828), a Maori chief and war leader of the Ngapuhi *iwi* (tribe). Hongi Hika travelled to England in 1820 on board the whaling ship the *New Zealander*, accompanied by the missionary Thomas Kendall. He spent five months in London and Cambridge, where he worked closely with the linguist Professor Samuel Lee at Queens College. Lee went on to write the first orthography of the Maori language, but Hongi Hika's contribution to this important scholarly work was never formally acknowledged. This is redressed in a series of three photographs, where another *Pasifika Styles* artist, Reuben Paterson, standing in for Hongi Hika, is shown in front of a college wall receiving his long-overdue Cambridge degree. In the photograph Reihana has painted lines over Paterson's face, alluding to Hongi Hika's *moko* (tattooed visage). He wears a Maori cloak composed by Reihana of Cambridge college scarves stitched together and embellished with tassels of goat hair, and holds a rolled degree certificate. The photographs, positioned above the cloak itself, are captioned 'word power' and 'fire power', the latter alluding to the guns Hongi Hika brought back with him from England and used to overrun much of the North Island.

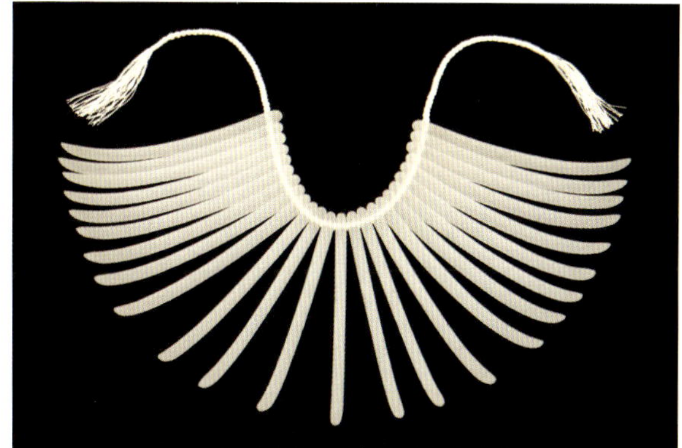

FIG. 43: CHRIS CHARTERIS'S *WASEKASEKA* (2005). PHOTOGRAPH: KERRY BROWN.

Drawing on extensive research on historic Pacific photographs held in museums and archives, artist Shigeyuki Kihara explores the ways in which people and places are collected and classified. Her large and compelling photographic triptych,

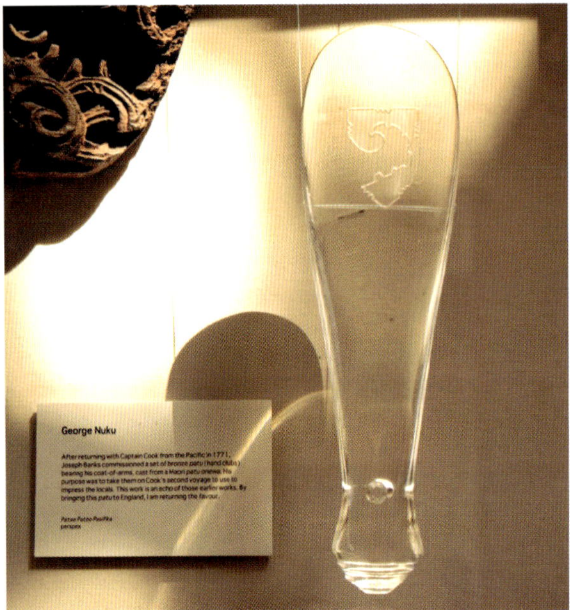

FIG. 44: *Patoo patoo Pasifika* (2006) BY GEORGE NUKU. PHOTOGRAPH: MUSEUM OF ARCHAEOLOGY AND ANTHROPOLOGY.

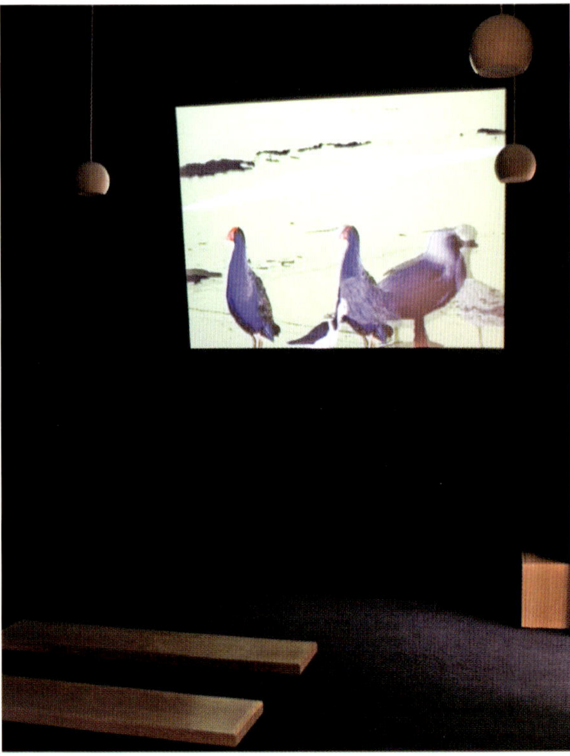

FIG. 45: INSIDE THE EXHIBITION'S AUDIO-VISUAL SUITE. *Manukau: place of wading birds*, A DIGITAL ANIMATION BY SHEYNE TUFFERY, IS PLAYING ON THE SCREEN. PHOTOGRAPH: MUSEUM OF ARCHAEOLOGY AND ANTHROPOLOGY.

Fa`afafine: in a manner of a woman (figs. 19 & 33) challenges stereotypic representations of Polynesian women as sensuous 'dusky maidens' and raises questions regarding the attribution of gender and racial identity. Transgendered and of mixed Japanese and Samoan descent, Kihara positions herself centrally within the series of sepia-toned images which both mimic and critique the techniques of nineteenth and early 20th century studio photography. The artist is posed in a semi-reclined position on a Victorian settee flanked by potted plants with a backdrop covered by a plaited mat. In the first image she is wearing a scant hula skirt, with a floral ear ornament and a strand of beads hanging loosely from her left shoulder. While her posture and expression are identical in all three images, the subsequent photographs are surprisingly revealing. Responding to the voyeuristic and titillating expectations of the genre, in the second image her hula skirt is removed and in the final image a penis protrudes from between her tightly closed legs. While positioning herself as the fictive subject of a typically male, colonial gaze, Kihara looks directly at the viewer, as if to challenge their presumptions. Her re-enactment both highlights and subverts the power of colonial photography to classify and subjugate. The 'reality' of the image is also undermined by the torn edge of the mat background, which reveals a further backdrop and draws attention to the artificiality of the studio setting.

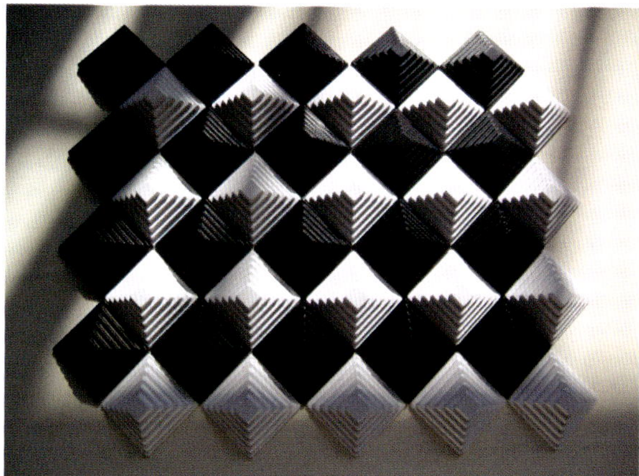

FIG. 46: *Tupu`anga* (ancestor, origin or source) (2005) by Filipe Tohi. Photograph: Carine Durand.

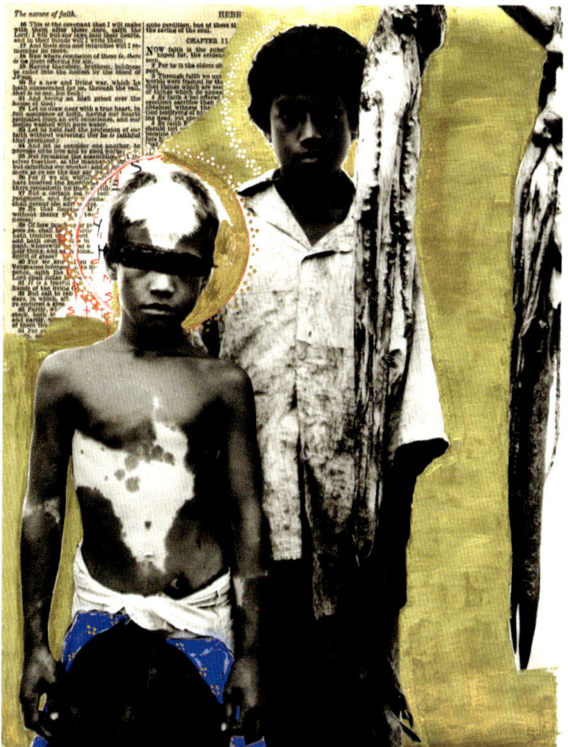

FIG. 47: *Untitled* (2006) by Greg Semu.

> What people see with me is the surface of what's being presented to them, but not necessarily what you would call a reality. I am Polynesian, I am Asian, I appear publicly and live as a woman within my male anatomical body – this is known as *fa`afafine* in Samoa – third gender is the closest western interpretation. The *Fa`afafine* work questions the western classification of races, gender and sexuality. I can never fit into them, but at the same time I ask myself – are they worth fitting into? (Shigeyuki Kihara, *Pasifika Styles* label text).

A series of installations by Maori artist Maureen Lander features her exquisite and at times fanciful weavings, some of which extend beyond the confines of the display cases (figs. 34 & 35). Her artwork has been inspired by over fifteen years of research on feather and fibre objects in museum collections in New Zealand and overseas. She describes the intriguing qualities of objects which have been 'kept in the dark' in museum storerooms: 'Discovering them is like meeting old friends for the first time – a sense of recognition and sadness, and an urge to bring them back into the light and give them new life through referencing them in my art-making process' (*Pasifika Styles* label text). Lander is also interested in the ways objects are interpreted and displayed in museums and how different kinds of meanings are brought up in particular contexts. One of her installations in the gallery, *This is not a kete* (1994/2006) (fig. 17) focuses on a large *kete* (woven bag) which she made specifically for display. Here the *kete* becomes a kind of meta object which invites reflection rather than use (see also Brown, this volume). Lander has created site-specific installations at a number of museums and galleries, including *Mrs Cook's Kete*,

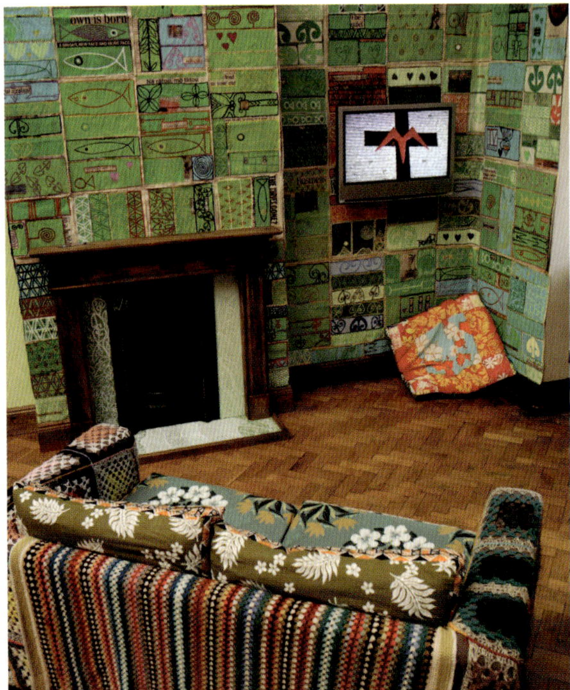

FIG. 48: PART OF *THE LIVING ROOM* (2006) BY ANI O'NEILL AND TRACEY TAWHIAO. PHOTOGRAPH: KERRY BROWN.

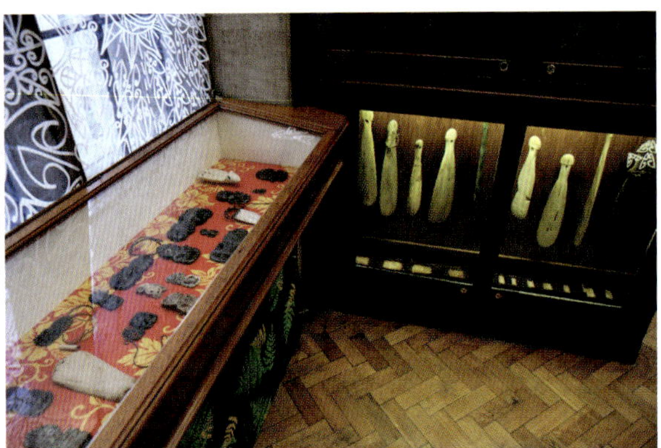

FIG. 49: ARTEFACTS FROM THE MUSEUM'S COLLECTIONS DISPLAYED AS FAMILY HEIRLOOMS IN *THE LIVING ROOM*. PHOTOGRAPH: KERRY BROWN.

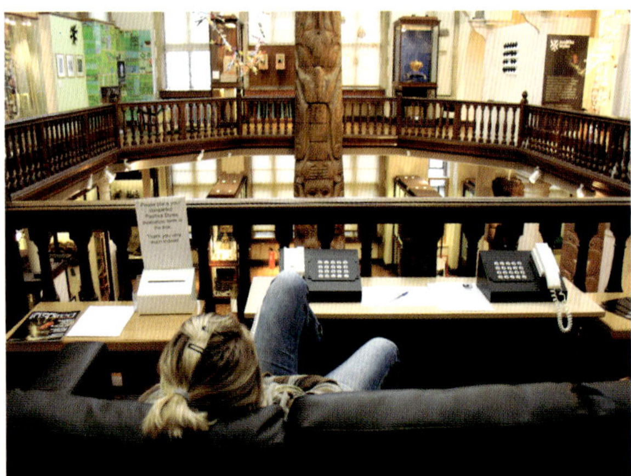

FIG. 50: THE SOUND STATION, WHERE VISITORS TO THE EXHIBITION LISTEN TO INTERVIEWS WITH THE ARTISTS BY SARAH ROBINS. PHOTOGRAPH: AMIRIA SALMOND.

originally developed at the Pitt Rivers Museum in Oxford and adapted for *Pasifika Styles*.[2] Developing customary weaving skills for new contexts and creatively incorporating new material and techniques, Lander's artworks directly challenge the distinction between traditional and contemporary. 'One of the main things that I have learnt from Museums is that weavers were always innovating in response to new materials, developing new technologies. So I have come to believe that that is what is traditional – to be innovative – and in that way there is a continuum' (Maureen Lander interview, *Pasifika Styles* website).

Another continuum between past and present evident in the exhibition is the strong link between land and indigenous identity and the creative use of artwork to assert political entitlements to customary resources. Lander's main installation *Crown Grab Bag* (2006) (fig. 34) features a magnificent fibrous crown perched on a royal purple silk pillow embellished with golden tassels. The work references the New Zealand Foreshore and Seabed Act of 2004, which empowered the New Zealand government, 'the Crown', to override tribal rights to pursue customary claims to the foreshore and seabed through

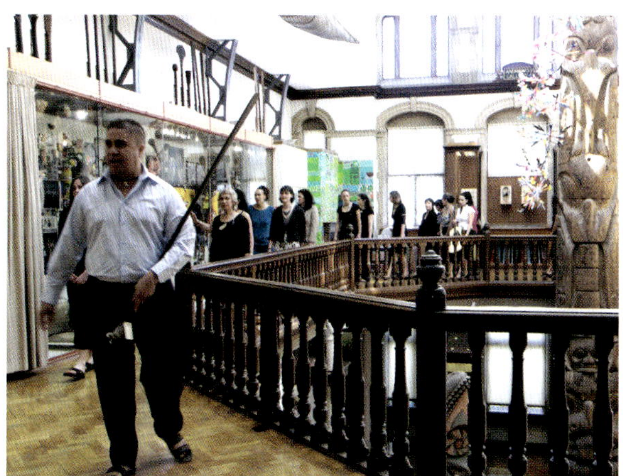

FIG. 51: CHE WILSON LEADING THE BLESSING OF THE EXHIBITION, 5 MAY 2006. PHOTOGRAPH: CARINE DURAND.

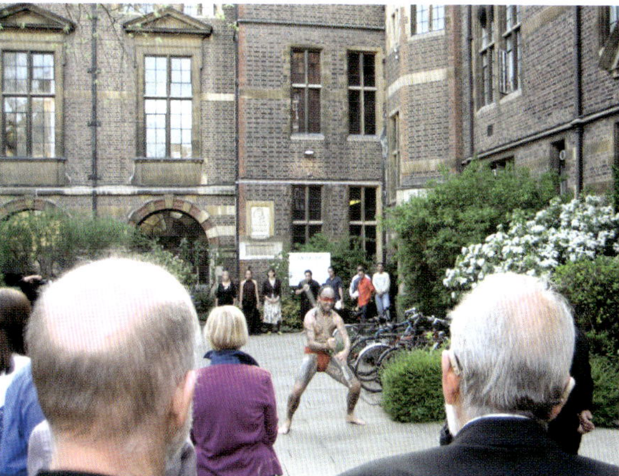

FIG. 52: GEORGE NUKU'S *WERO* AT THE OPENING OF THE EXHIBITION. PHOTOGRAPH: JOSH BELL.

the courts. Lander's crown is delicately woven from a variety of fibres, including plant materials that grow along the foreshore – the creation of the crown itself is thus a subtle but defiant act of re-appropriation. Shells and fishing hooks from the museum's collection are placed on the base of the case. Strands of *pingao* fibre, stitched into the fabric lining at the back of the case, form inverted U-shapes representing the raised eyebrows of Tane (god of the forest). According to Maori legend, following a dispute between Tane and Tangaroa (god of the sea) Tane's eyebrows were flung on to the sand dunes, which mark the liminal space between the forest and the sea. Here Lander connects contemporary political conflicts to legendary battles. This part of the installation is reflected on the other side of the gallery in a large-scale version arranged over the archway leading through to the Museum's stores. In this work, *Tane Raises his Eyebrows* (2006) (fig. 35) Tane expresses his surprise and disapproval at the Crown's decision to expropriate resources which are collectively owned and used by Maori people and which connect them back to their ancestors. This theme is also picked up in Kewana Duncan's costume piece *Fulltime Revolutionary* (fig. 36)

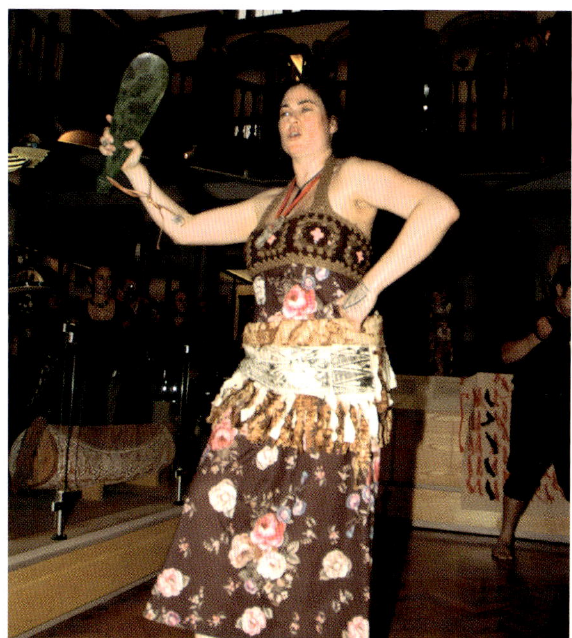

FIG. 53: CURATOR AND ARTIST ROSANNA RAYMOND PERFORMING AT THE EXHIBITION OPENING WITH A GREENSTONE *MERE* FROM THE MUSEUM'S COLLECTIONS. PHOTOGRAPH: SHERRY ROBERTS

which includes a video presentation of the massive *hikoi* or protest march against the confiscation of the seabed and foreshore of Aotearoa.

Fuelled by the entangled colonial histories embodied within museum collections and contemporary artworks, the exhibition space is a powerful forum for contemporary political debates. While *Pasifika Styles* provides the opportunity for artists to re-connect with and breath new life into their *taonga*, which have been carefully preserved by the museum over many decades, the exhibition also offers a forum to express frustrations and raise questions about museum practices of collection and containment. Wayne Youle's installation (fig. 37) is composed of numerous modular storage boxes, stacked together in a locked display case. Some were crafted by Youle himself, based on those formerly used to store preserved Maori heads in the Museum prior to their repatriation; others are actual Museum boxes containing Maori artefacts. The labels on the boxes both follow and extend the Museum's classification system, from functional categories and object types such as 'weapons' and 'adze heads' to 'someone else's stuff' or 'visitor (special)'. One of Youle's boxes displays a nineteenth-century photograph of British military officer Horatio Robley in front of his substantial collection of *toi moko* or tattooed Maori heads (Robley 1896). It alludes to the fascination of Western collectors for these highly exoticised human objects, which prompted a grisly trade in the nineteenth and early twentieth century and epitomized the macabre extremes of collecting. Belatedly, many museums have cooperated with Maori requests for their repatriation and these ancestors are quietly and steadily making their way back home. The notion that artefacts or *taonga* are still alive is suggested by the breathing holes drilled into some of the storage boxes and via the headphones attached to others. The sounds of breathing or scratching, as if something or someone inside was attempting to escape, are a powerful evocation of the pain of alienation and separation.

> Museums are that kind of hush-hush, clean, untouchable, tapu kind of space. You wanna touch everything but you can't. It's a thing I'd like to explore, like what's behind all those boxes (Youle, *Pasifika Styles* label text).

The right of museums to hold material from other cultures is most forcefully challenged by Jason Hall's *The do-it-yourself repatriation kit* (2006) (fig. 38). An open leather briefcase, with baggage tag from London's Heathrow airport attached to the handle, contains a club hammer. The interior foam lining, with a recessed compartment in the characteristic shape of a *tiki* ornament, makes the intended purpose of the hammer obvious. Ironically the installation, which seems to advocate the forceful liberation of *taonga*, is itself positioned within a museum display case. While the suggestion of smash and grab may be interpreted as overtly threatening, its positioning within the Museum is perhaps best understood as a demand for recognition and engagement.

While several of the artists' installations incorporate historic pieces from the Museum's collections, contemporary artworks have also been used as interjections in the main anthropology gallery, bringing a renewed vitality to the predominantly historical displays. Next to the Maori case is a video installation, *Tales of the Maori Border* (2006) (fig. 39 & 40) by Natalie Robertson and Hemi Macgregor, which refers to Maui, a shapeshifter and important figure in Polynesian legends. Opaque window inserts with avian designs composed by Sheyne Tuffery (fig. 41 & 42) accentuate the spiritual importance of birds in the Pacific, where feathers are also an important symbol of wealth and status. Chris Charteris' alluring greenstone pendants and necklaces made of Perspex 'whale's teeth' stand out against the symmetrical arrangement of Fijian ivory and shell ornaments based on nineteenth-century display aesthetics (see fig. 64). Charteris pays great attention to materials and form, activating the energy inherent within his creations:

> Before I start making, I think about what sort of energy I wish to portray. In making these works I have contemplated what would be appropriate for a chief or a person with big *mana* to wear. What would have enough power, status and impact (*Pasifika Styles* label text).

George Nuku's placement of a specially carved Perspex *patu* (hand-club) in the Maori display case in the permanent gallery is an eloquent evocation of the productive potential and ambiguities involved in the movement of objects and ideas between the Pacific and the UK. Nuku's *Patoo Patoo Pasifika* (2006), gifted to the Museum and inscribed with a version of the *Pasifika Styles* logo (fig. 44), refers to much earlier exchanges through which Cambridge acquired eighteenth-century Maori *taonga* collected during the voyages of Captain Cook. The label for Nuku's *patu* reads:

> After returning with Captain Cook from the Pacific in 1771, the naturalist Joseph Banks commissioned a set of bronze *patu* (hand clubs) bearing his coat-of-arms, cast from a Maori *patu onewa*. His purpose was to take them on Cook's second voyage to use to impress the locals. This work is an echo of those earlier works. By bringing this *patu* to England, I am returning the favour (*Pasifika Styles* label text).

The distinctive spaces and environments created within the *Pasifika Styles* gallery also reveal the different regimes of the senses at play (Edwards et al, 2006: 1-31). In Europe there is a long history of privileging visual perception, reinforced by colonial practices that attempted to impose Western hierarchies of the senses as well as Euro-American museums and galleries which cultivated particular ways of seeing now seen as paradigmatic. A critical aspect of the 'politics of liberation' in museums involves challenging the sensory relations between people and objects. The artists' engagement with ancestral *taonga* is not limited to visual appreciation and the presentation of the artworks similarly invites a range of sensory engagements. Sounds from the art videos, shown in a cinematic viewing area (fig. 45) subtly permeate the gallery. Two of the artists' installations include head-phones on listening posts, as described above, and interviews with individual artists, recorded by Sarah Robins, are accessible on audio hand-sets at a purpose-built audio station looking out over the gallery (fig. 50). Filipe Tohi's tactile and interactive *Tupu`anga (ancestor, origin or source)* (2005) (fig. 46) is composed of a series of black and white rectilinear shapes, which the visitor is encouraged to fit together to make a variety of forms. His work is based upon the ancient Pacific Island art form of *lalava* (lashing) that was used for joining and binding materials together. He describes *lalava* patterns as a 'mnemonic device for representing a life philosophy. *Lalava* patterns advocated balance in daily living and were metaphorical and physical ties to cultural knowledge' (*Pasifika Styles* label text).

Ani O'Neill and Tracey Tawhiao's *Living Room* (2006) (fig. 48) creates a sensuous and cosy ambience, with dappled light filtered through Tawhiao's curvilinear designs painted over the window. Her textured wallpaper, made from pieces of newspaper, is over-painted with lustrous colours to obscure many of the stories and to highlight particular phrases such as 'lend us your ear', 'we're looking for people to take us to our future' and 'a foothold in paradise' – in what she describes as an attempt to 'find the news beyond the newspapers' which so often contain ill-informed and negative portrayals of Maori and Pacific peoples. Photographs by Greg Semu, exploring the impact of Christianity on his Samoan people, hang next to the mantelpiece (fig. 47). Visitors to the exhibition are encouraged to sit on the customised sofa, covered by O'Neill with a patchwork of brightly coloured floral-patterned fabric, and to feel the tactility of the crocheted throw. They can watch 'television' via a video screen playing a documentary commissioned for the project from New Zealand-Samoan academic and broadcaster Lisa Taouma, featuring interviews with many of the artists. Here they are able to speak all-but-directly to the viewers about their work, framed within the political and social context of their lives and ambitions. Two Edwardian display cases in the *Living Room* (fig. 49), arranged to resemble household cabinets, contain a variety of personal *taonga* – greenstone *hei tiki*, pieces of barkcloth, tattooing implements and hand clubs, all from the museum's collections. These objects are not labelled as artefacts but are rather displayed as personal and family heirlooms within this domestic settling. Their meanings are embodied in the personal and social relations of their production and use. This popular area of the exhibition is very different from the static room-sets found in other museums; visitors often 'hang out' in this comfortable and familial interactive space.

During their visits to Cambridge, the *Pasifika Styles* artists engaged with the museum and its collections on many levels. Che Wilson composed a *waiata* (traditional song) for *Pasifika Styles* (reproduced at the beginning of this volume) – which was sung on and off throughout the installation and was performed at the opening by members of Ngati Ranana, the London Maori Club, together with many of the artists. With care and respect, *taonga* were handled, caressed, smelled and used in ceremonies and performances. While acknowledging the role of museums in preserving these artefacts, Nuku expressed his frustration at their separation from daily life:

> I feel sorry that the *taonga* aren't breathing like they would out in the garden or wherever, getting damaged and getting sweaty Maori hands fondling them and snot and tears all over them and being kissed and stuff (*Pasifika Styles* label text).

The museum agreed to the request that specific items from the collections be used in the opening ceremonies, confident that the cultural descendants of their makers would ensure their well-being. Che Wilson, a distinguished Maori orator, together with his relative Gerrard Albert, developed the *tikanga* or protocol surrounding the opening of the exhibition. Che officiated on the day (fig. 51) carrying a *taiaha* staff (MAA Z 6381 – see also Wilson this volume) and wearing a *korowai* (cloak) made by Raymond, which they nicknamed a *sugawai*, referring to its innovative style that blended aspects of hula skirt and cloak.[3] He led the formal blessing that took place before the exhibition opening, involving the artists and museum staff, which was intended to lift the spirit of the *taonga* and unite together the participants in the exhibition's creation (see also Elliott this volume). Prior to the spectacular opening event, guests were required to wait outside the museum while Wilson explained what was to follow. Suddenly artist George Nuku emerged for the *wero* or ceremonial challenge, intended to test the intentions of incoming visitors. Displaying his full body *moko* (tattoo), he charged towards the visitors, wielding his Perspex *taiaha* (club), chanting loudly with hisses and a protruding tongue (fig. 52). His vigorous and agile movements were a forceful demonstration of the power and strength of the Maori people. Guests were then invited to come inside, where they were welcomed by members of Ngati Ranana and Beats of Polynesia, a Cook Islands group, with singing, drums and chants. Throughout the evening, bullroarers were swung in the gallery, traditional instruments were played and Raymond performed with a greenstone *mere* (hand club) from the Museum's collection (fig. 53) (see also Elliott, Wilson and Veys, this volume).

The power of the opening and the strength of the exhibition overall was made possible by the collective efforts of artists and curators, facilitated by museum staff relinquishing strict authority over the collections and methods of presentation. In this way *Pasifika Styles* demonstrates the importance and potential of acknowledging different kinds of expertise and interests in the objects they hold in trust. Here, the Museum itself shifts from being a hegemonic institution, aligned to the pedagogical and self-serving interests of state (Bennett 1995; Hooper-Greenhill 1989), to a restorative agent, which provides a forum for debate and creative dialogue. *Pasifika Styles* demonstrates the potency of developing the collaborative capacity of *kaitiaki* or guardians, both of the objects and of crucial relationships between people and their *taonga*.

Notes

1 Early accounts record that Polynesian figures of this kind were often clothed, wrapped or otherwise adorned with feathers and fibre when in use, the coverings being integral to the object's spiritual potency.

2 The woven artefacts produced by Lander for this installation are now in MAA's permanent collection.

3 The creation of the *sugawai* is a salient example of how inter-personal relationships and artistic innovation come together in the creation of valued cultural objects.

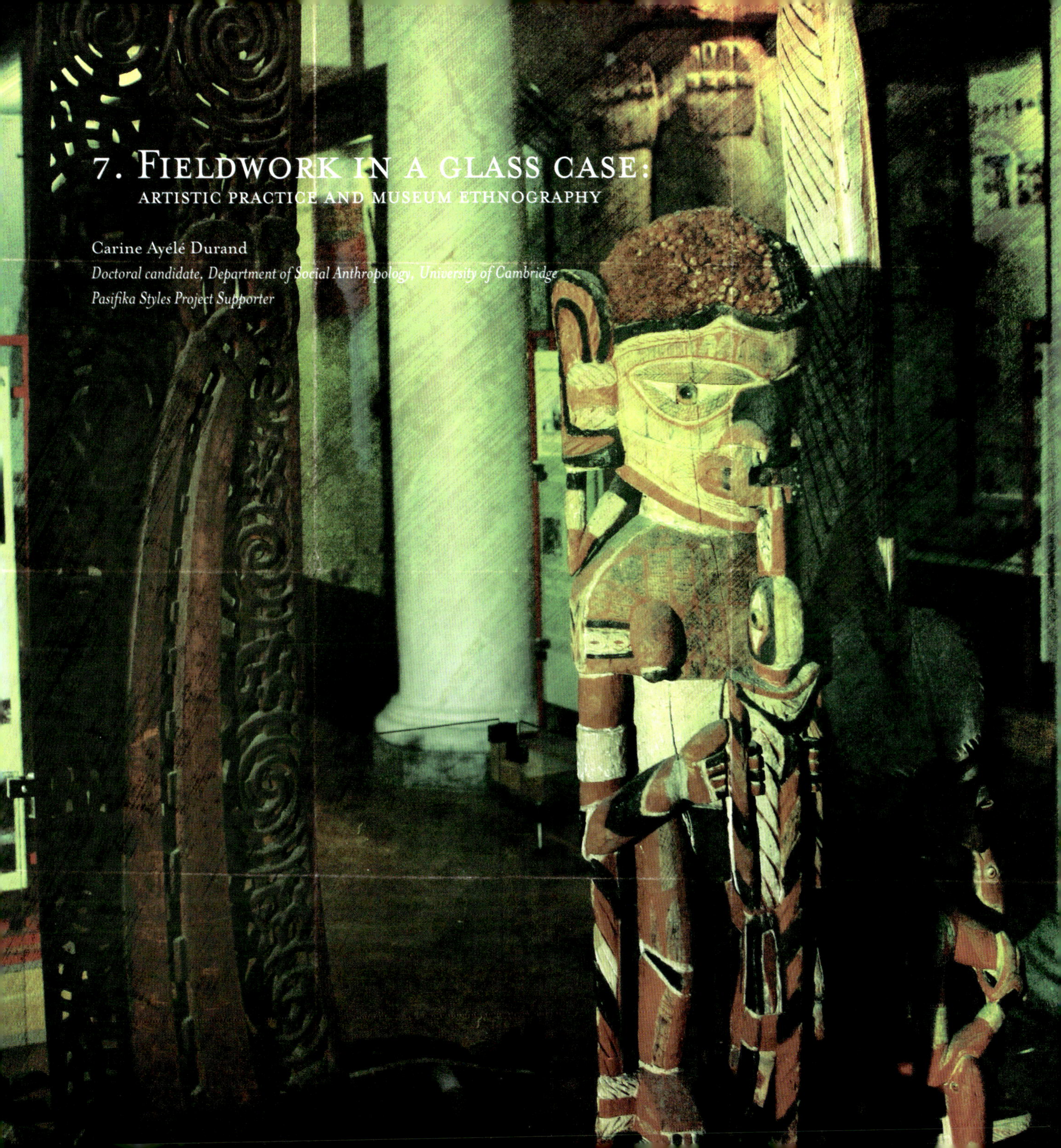

7. Fieldwork in a glass case: artistic practice and museum ethnography

Carine Ayélé Durand
Doctoral candidate, Department of Social Anthropology, University of Cambridge
Pasifika Styles Project Supporter

Historic Pacific artefacts on display in the Anthropology gallery, Museum of Archaeology and Anthropology. Photograph: Kerry Brown.

7. Fieldwork in a glass case:
artistic practice and museum ethnography

Carine Ayélé Durand
Doctoral candidate, Department of Social Anthropology, University of Cambridge
Pasifika Styles Project Supporter

Since the late 1980s, several initiatives involving artists/artisans and indigenous groups have been launched which challenge the view that museums are merely archival spaces 'devoted to the collection and preservation of material objects' (Stocking 1985). In response to the persistent notion that objects in museums are removed from the contexts of life activity in which they are produced and used and thus appear socially inert

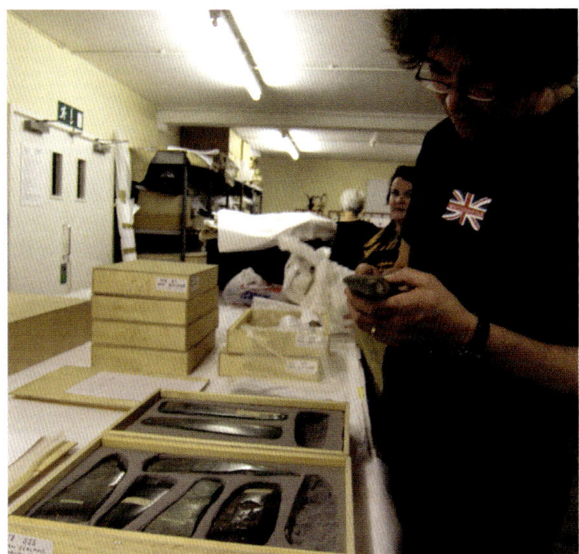

fig. 54: Artist Chris Charteris studying artefacts from the museum's collections, April 2006. Photograph: Carine Durand.

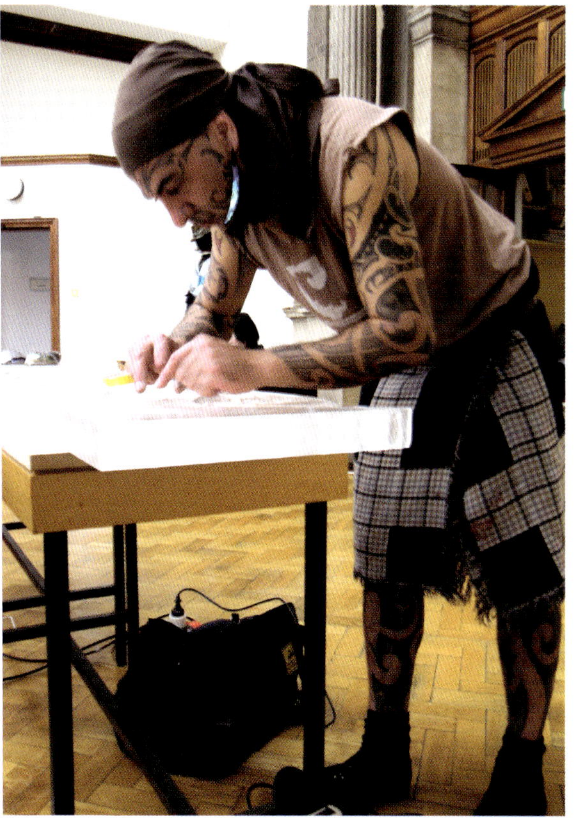

fig. 55: George Nuku carving, April 2006. Photograph: Carine Durand.

(e.g. Boas in Jacknis 1985: 104; Ingold 2000: 346; Appadurai 1986: 4), the intention of such collaborative projects is to demonstrate that museums might rather be seen as dynamic forums in which people and objects are assembled to reflect upon contemporary concerns (Latour 2005; Stocking 1985). These include the controversial concept of indigeneity and the participation of indigenous groups in international debates regarding access to and the ownership of their cultural heritage. In employing an ethnographic approach to museums and people's engagements with objects, I aim to describe the processes through which artists / artisans and museum professionals collaborate in terms of social relations, using examples derived from my own fieldwork. From November 2005 to May 2006, I observed and participated in the *Pasifika Styles* project, assisting the artists in the mounting of their installations and in their studies of the Museum's Oceanic collections (fig. 54 to 56). During this research, I was interested in how the artists sought to restore the process of creation 'hidden behind' the finished objects (Ingold 2000) through the deployment of creativity and specific artistic skills. Regarding the historic objects as an important source of inspiration, they also sought to demonstrate how such artefacts continue to be valued in contemporary society.

As the project unfolded, it became clear that the artists' knowledge and skilled practice offered insights into both 'material' and 'cultural' aspects of the objects that were highly valued within the museum environment. This made me reconsider how 'mainstream'[1] museums and academics relate to people who have a cultural connection to their collections, as well as how those people might go about asserting a greater degree of control over research into their own culture and material heritage. In the process, my own research methodologies were reconfigured in ways that have a broader relevance to current debates and methodological initiatives in museums studies and social anthropology.

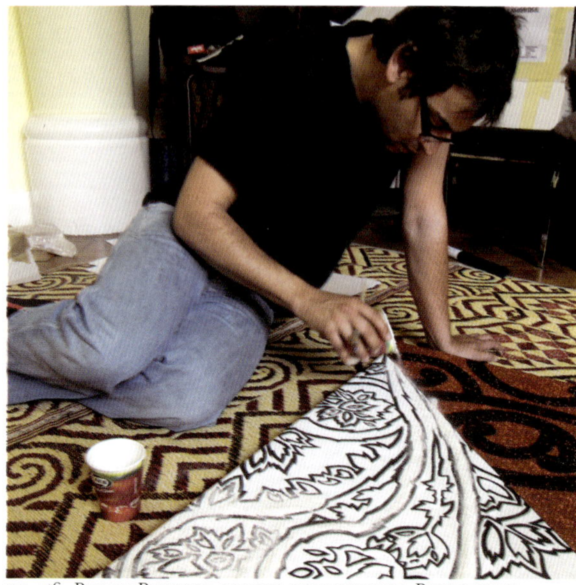

FIG. 56: REUBEN PATERSON AT WORK IN THE MUSEUM. PHOTOGRAPH: CARINE DURAND.

ARTISTIC PRACTICE AS A FORM OF ETHNOGRAPHIC FIELDWORK

Over the past two decades, in an attempt to challenge disciplinary preoccupations with language and writing, some anthropologists have begun to develop research methods and techniques focused on skilled practice and the production of artefacts (Gunn 2005; Henare 2003; Ingold 2000). The intention is to pay more attention to artefacts and their singular properties, to combine research and practice, and to dispose of the idea that a 'division of labour' should exist in Anthropology between 'those who study "systems" of society and culture and those who work on material culture and museums' (Henare 2003: 54; see also Strathern 1990). Over the last decade, such methodological approaches have led to increasing collaboration between anthropologists in the 'field' or in the museum on one hand, and artists / artisans on the other (e.g.

Gunn 2005; Herle 2003; Leach 2004, 2007). The objective of such initiatives is often to demonstrate that artistic creativity and the development of skilled practice help to generate new forms of knowledge and understanding.[2] Scholars have also begun to consider novel relationships between artistic practice and anthropological methods (Coles 2000; Foster 1995; Schneider 1996). Some argue that artistic practice is as 'legitimate' a form of ethnographic expression as the already academically sanctioned written and visual discourses in anthropology (Schneider 1996: 183, 185).

Participating in the *Pasifika Styles* exhibition, I became involved in the interactions and discussions surrounding the selection and display of a wide variety of objects, including artefacts drawn from the museum's historic collections as well as artworks commissioned for the exhibition and brought from the Pacific or created by the artists in the museum. It appeared that the Maori and Pacific Island artists involved in the project were conducting their own 'fieldwork' both within and outside the museum and that, through their artistic installations, they were offering alternative ways of selecting, arranging and presenting the 'data' they collected. In December 2005, for example, I assisted Lisa Reihana in the production of her video installation based on contemporary and historic Maori artefacts held at MAA (fig. 57). After selecting artefacts that she could relate to her Maori background from the stores and from the Maudslay Gallery, containing the main anthropology displays, Reihana shot footage of each piece for forty to forty-five minutes. After helping her to move the artefacts from the museum workroom to an office we had transformed into a photographic studio, I documented her research methodology and artistic approaches to the collections through the medium of photography. Using a wide range of filming techniques, including extreme close-up and long shots, Reihana demonstrated innovative ways of engaging with objects. Her aim was to generate new connections and relationships between the museum artefacts, her own background and the new artwork. In addition, through filming the details of the carving or weaving techniques of

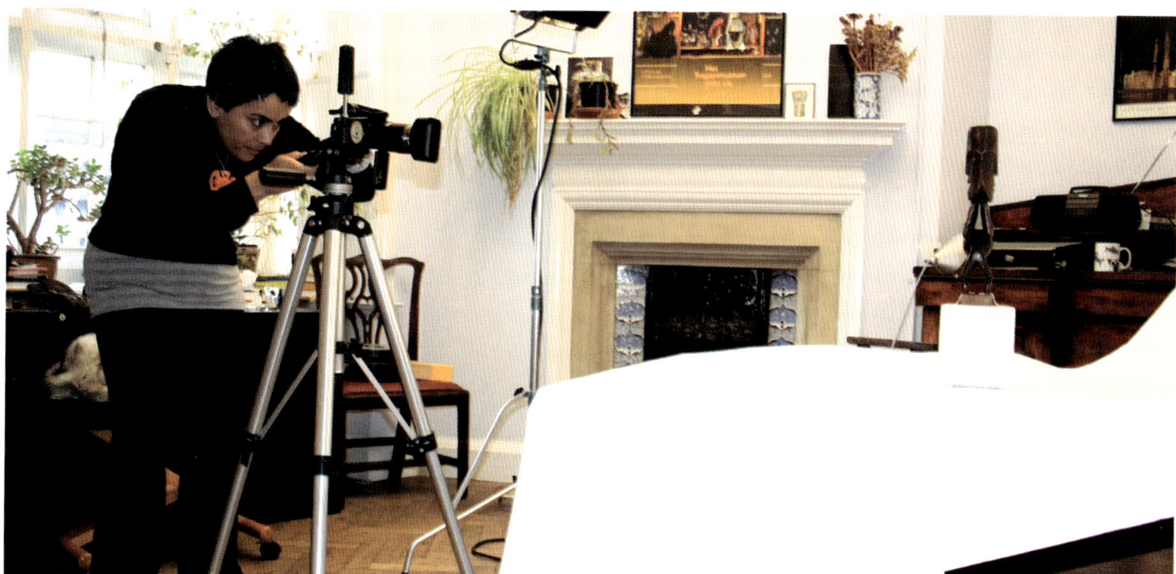

FIG. 57: ARTIST LISA REIHANA FILMING ARTEFACTS FROM THE MUSEUM'S COLLECTIONS, DECEMBER 2005. PHOTOGRAPH: CARINE DURAND.

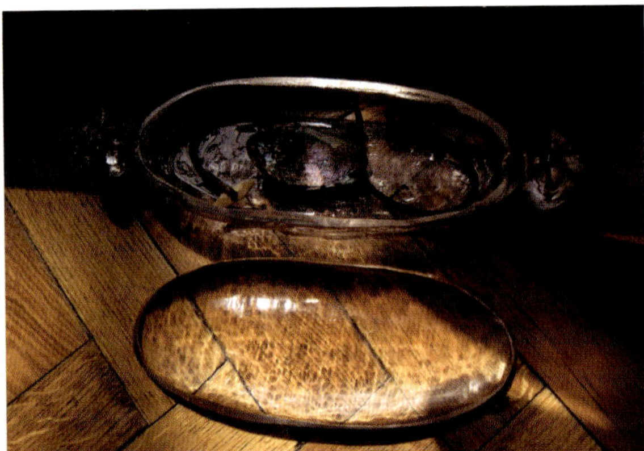

FIG. 58: CARVED PERSPEX *WAKAHUIA* BY GEORGE NUKU. PHOTOGRAPH: CARINE DURAND.

each object, she sought to offer to the public different ways of looking at museum collections.

Other ways of conducting 'fieldwork' in the museum were demonstrated by artist George Nuku (figs. 55 & 58). In May 2006, in preparation for the exhibition opening, Nuku used museum workshop facilities to create additional elements in Perspex for the *Outer Space Marae* he had brought from New Zealand. Assisting him, I could see how the public engaged with his installation. Nuku encouraged the visitors to touch it and then discussed why he had chosen to work with contemporary materials. Nuku and Reihana both observed and participated in the *Pasifika Styles* process several months prior to the exhibition opening. They selected, arranged and presented the information they wanted to share with the public, drawing on their experience within their own communities as well as on their active engagement with people and objects at MAA. They both spent a considerable amount of time in the museum while working on their artworks. It enabled them to observe a wide range of museum activities including access to the storage, conservation methods, and the introduction of technological devices. Regarding the mounting of their installations as a collaborative process, Nuku and Reihana were willing to share their concerns with museum professionals and visitors. Developing novel research methodologies as well as creative ways of engaging with the objects, they thus transformed the gallery into a dynamic learning space where people could better reflect upon their own assumptions about creativity, traditions, and innovation.

'*Eye land*': Rosanna Raymond's installation

Perhaps the best example of this kind of museum-based fieldwork, however, was found in the work of Rosanna Raymond, whom I assisted in the preparation of her major installation *Eye land Part II: Welcome 2 da K'lub* (fig. 59). While working alongside Raymond, I focused on learning skills in practice as a research method to be used when conducting ethnographic fieldwork in the context of museums. My own methodology was thus strongly influenced and informed by those of the artist. At the beginning of my research, I focused on deploying conventional techniques of ethnographic participant-observation. My first intention was to conduct formal interviews with Raymond, in order to analyse her engagement with historic collections and contemporary artworks both within and outside the museum environment. She suggested that we could instead talk about these issues while working together on her display case. As it turned out, this suggestion completely changed my approach to the field and my relationship with the artist. From February to May 2006, she allowed me both to observe and participate in her research within the museum, which combined formal documentation of historic objects (by bringing her own knowledge to bear on individual artefacts as well as consulting the museum archives and database) and the creation of new artworks. In New Zealand, Raymond had been an active member of The Pacific Sisters – a multicultural group of Maori and Pacific Island designers, makers and performers – and had learnt 'traditional skills and oral tradition' from the 'Sisters' and her community elders (Raymond 2003: 201). In the United Kingdom, this knowledge and practice allowed her to offer to museum professionals better understand-

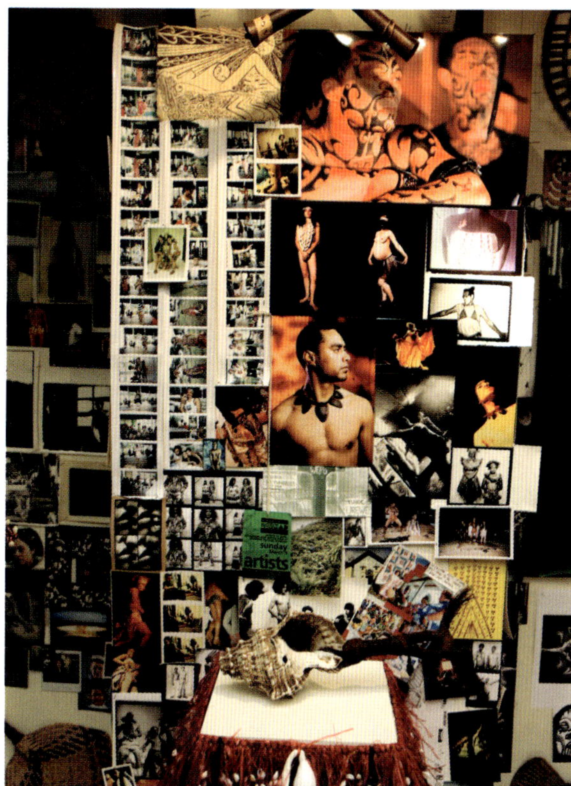

FIG. 59: DETAIL FROM RAYMOND'S INSTALLATION, SHOWING THE INCORPORATION OF HISTORIC MUSEUM ARTEFACTS ALONGSIDE POSTERS, PHOTOGRAPHS AND NEWLY CRAFTED WORKS. PHOTOGRAPH: KERRY BROWN.

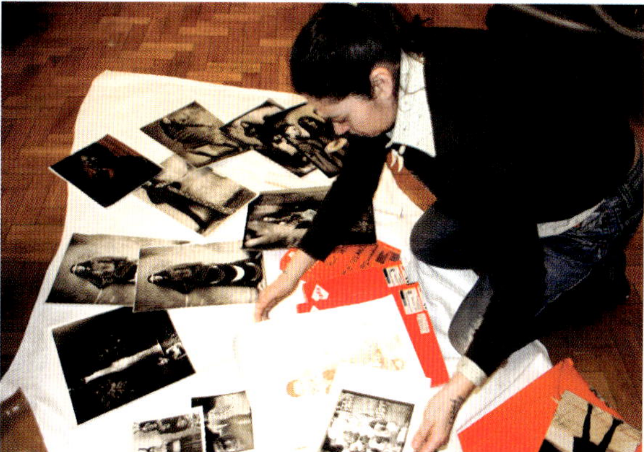

FIG. 60: ROSANNA RAYMOND SELECTING IMAGES FOR HER INSTALLATION. PHOTOGRAPH: CARINE DURAND.

ings of the ways in which the objects in their care are put together - not only materially but also in a broader cultural sense. *Eye land Part II: Welcome 2 da K'lub* (2006) can be defined as Raymond's 'vision' of Aotearoa New Zealand and as an instantiation of her own particular visual and object-oriented brand of fieldwork. Travelling to New Zealand in 2005 on a research trip in preparation for the exhibition, she purchased artworks and contemporary artefacts and conducted interviews with the artists participating in the *Pasifika Styles* project. Documenting these encounters through the medium of photography, she decided to integrate these images and objects into her installation. In so doing, Raymond aimed to demonstrate that her artwork was also a way of selecting, arranging and presenting 'ethnographic' data collected in 'the field' (fig. 60). The installation of her display case thus became a context within which I learned new methods of ethnography and developed skilled practice, being taught for example the matting technique of attaching shells on to a raffia and plastic skirt (fig. 61). Through learning these techniques, it became evident that the act of making is integrally connected to those of storytelling and of building social relationships. While participating together in the making of artworks and artefacts, we talked about a wide variety of themes including the acquisition and transmission of knowledge, inter-generational issues among Maori and Pacific Islanders in Aotearoa New Zealand, and political and economic indigenous concerns. Through creative practice and artistic skills, Raymond's work generates 'new' connections between different generations and communities, historic collections and contemporary artworks, past and present, artists and museum professionals. *Eye land* became a 'field site' as well as a 'field diary' within which Rosanna and I could work through broad issues including indigenous peoples' efforts to gain greater control over

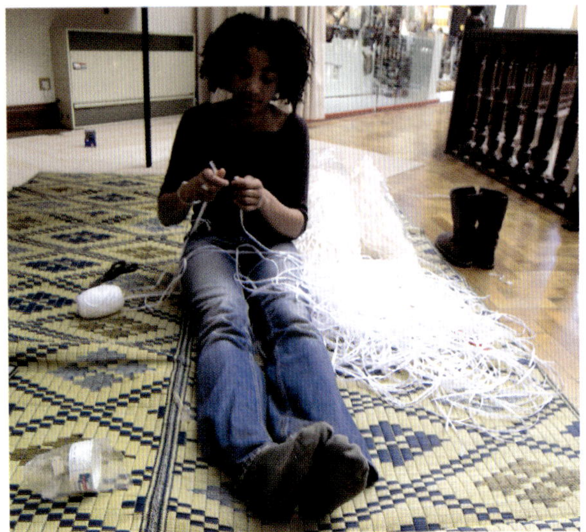

FIG. 61: THE AUTHOR HAND-KNOTTING A RAFFIA HULA SKIRT. PHOTOGRAPH: ANI O'NEILL.

their cultural heritage in museums.

In likening artistic practice in museums to a form of ethnography, my intention is to reflect on alternative ways of selecting, arranging and presenting ethnographic 'data'. The point is not to suggest that anthropologists ought to transform themselves into artists or vice-versa. Rather, in discussing how anthropologists and artists engaged through objects in this particular project, I intend to emphasise shared concerns and to suggest new possibilities for creative exchange between anthropology and art. My own contribution to Raymond's display case enabled me to further reflect on the exchange of knowledge and methodological practice between artists, anthropologists and museum professionals.[3] The artists used their creative skills to assemble elements collected during their own 'fieldwork' in the museum environment within their installations. Anthropologists willing to experiment with alternative ways of presenting ethnographic data might gain considerable insights from such artistic approaches.

Acknowledgments

This paper was initially written for the Conference *Migratory Practices: contradictory and complementary exchanges between anthropology, art, craft and design*, Manchester, 5th - 6th September 2006. I am grateful to Amiria Salmond and Rosanna Raymond who kindly commented upon various drafts of the piece. Many thanks are also due to the artists pictured in this paper: Chris Charteris, George Nuku, Reuben Paterson, Rosanna Raymond, and Lisa Reihana and to the curators of MAA, Amiria Salmond and Anita Herle. I thank Thera Mjaaland who provided very useful suggestions for the presentation of the pictures. My gratitude goes also to AHRC and Trinity College, Cambridge for financial support.

Notes

1 I use the concept of 'mainstream museums' here to refer to major European institutions (e.g. The British Museum, University of Cambridge Museum of Archaeology and Anthropology) that hold ethnographic collections assembled mainly between the early 18th and late 19th centuries. 'Mainstream museums' is opposed here to indigenous or local museums recently built by communities who aim to regain a greater control over their cultural heritage.

2 Leach has recently called the value of such initiatives into question (2007: 167-188).

3 My observations of the *Pasifika Styles* exhibition differ hence from Leach's evaluation of the New Technology Arts Fellowships' project (NTAF) (Leach 2007: 167-188). I have suggested here that artists and museum anthropologists engaged in the *Pasifika Styles* project developed a useful exchange of knowledge and methodological practice.

8. Fusion/Confusion

Reuben Paterson

Ngāti Rangīitihi, Tūhourangi, Ngāi Tuhoe[1]

Pasifika Styles Artist

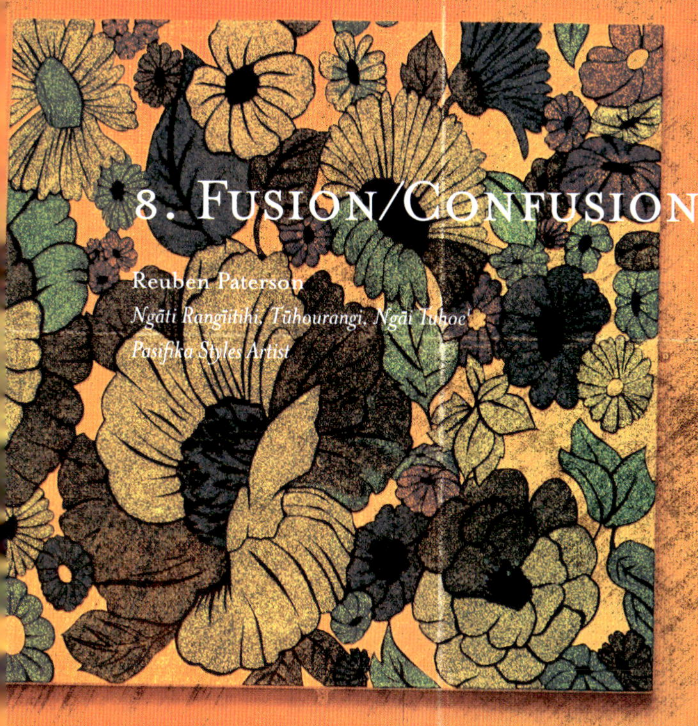

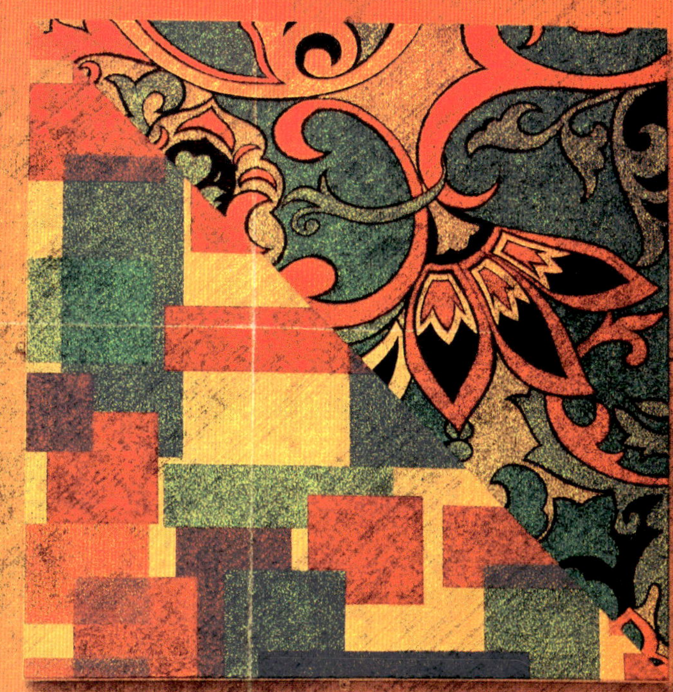

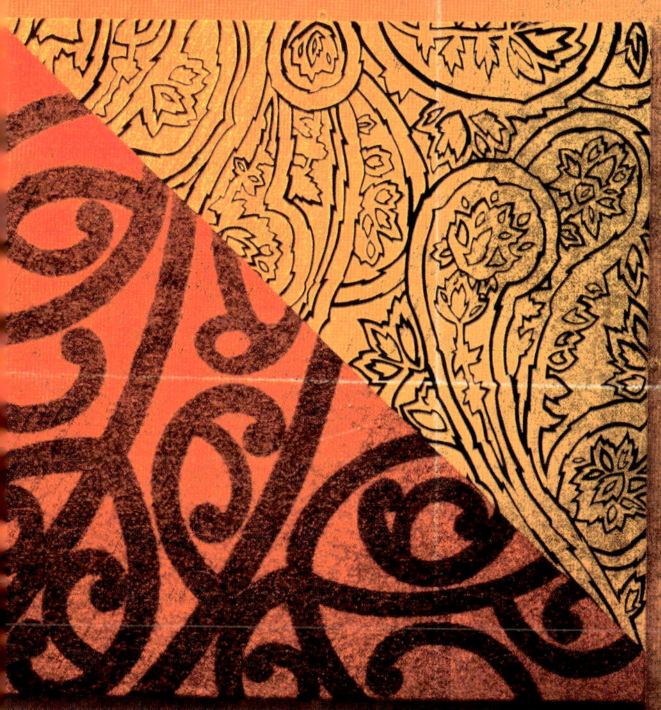

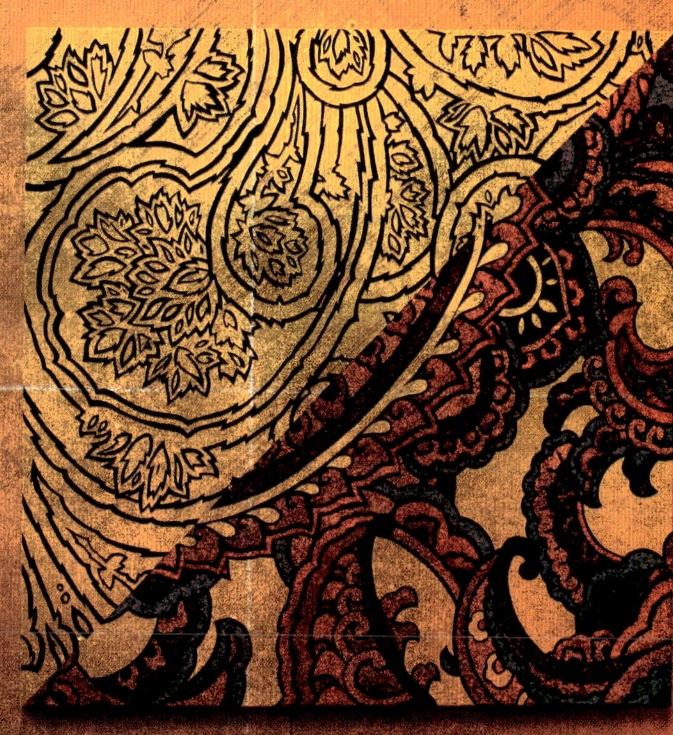

Detail of Reuben Paterson's works on display in the *Pasifika Styles* exhibition. Photograph: Kerry Brown.

8. Fusion/Confusion

Reuben Paterson
Ngāti Rangītihi, Tūhourangi, Ngāi Tuhoe[1]
Pasifika Styles Artist

Having moved as an artist to the island of Ikaria in the Aegean Sea thirteen months before the opening of the *Pasifika Styles* exhibition, I was looking forward to a reunion with friends and colleagues in Cambridge during a month-long residency at the Museum as part of the Visiting Artists programme. Being away from New Zealand during the unfurling of the exhibition's *kaupapa* meant that I was out of the Auckland *hui* or *wānanga* loop (see Lythberg, this volume). Though I wasn't able to join the artists and curators for that weekend, I was soon able to catch curatorial developments on the *Pasifika Styles* weblog, which provided a unified way to respond to and post on events leading up to the opening. With such vast seas between England and New Zealand (let alone the Aegean) the curators should be acknowledged for their investment in making sure the voices of the artists were respected and in enabling us to travel, creating a dynamic presence for our Pacific cultures. Representing ourselves is our own responsibility; only we can ensure the honesty and truth of the cultural image a museum or gallery will present of us. This is where such a project, with artists actually being involved in the project's development and travelling to the museum, breaks new ground.

Within the curatorial and artistic journeys of *Pasifika Styles* there is also a connection to the historical migrations of Maori from South East Asia and the travels of Captain James Cook during his three Pacific voyages. In Cambridge now sit collections of our *taonga* or treasures which Cook and his crew acquired, and these are one of the main inspirations behind the exhibition. Philippe Vergne's observation that in the current condition of globalization 'what we are witnessing... seems to be a new stage in world development, not unlike the Enlightenment' seems pertinent here. His imperative to 'identify the genealogy of the global subject... so that the others do not remain other' (2003: 19) resonates with Maori concepts of *whakapapa*, the way in which we define our identity through genealogies of people and place.

Whakapapa now has a global resonance thanks to Maori traditions of global engagement. It is a historic fact that we have shared, exchanged and inspired a wealth of cultural ideas with the world, first via colonization and most recently through the internationalization of our art and culture. We thrive in a climate of challenges, which demonstrate our resilience and have shaped the meaning of Maori visual culture in the twenty-first century. This is relevant particularly within New Zealand, where city migrations, ethnic mixes, and our evolution toward an organised or recognisable national culture sees more Maori and Pacific Island cultural imagery co-opted as signifiers for our country. Yet I question the ability of New Zealand to acknowledge its own authentic cultures at a deeper level. The union and trade across cultures bring us many homogenized wonders, but not a singular national identity that represents

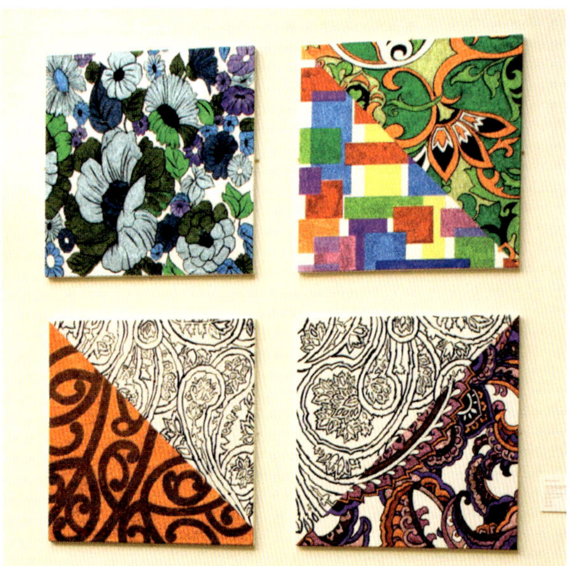

FIG. 62: THE AUTHOR'S WORKS ON DISPLAY. CLOCKWISE FROM TOP-LEFT: *EVERYWHERE YOU GO, ALWAYS TAKE THE WEATHER WITH YOU* (2004-05), *SLAUGHTER SOMETHING INNOCENT* (2006), *LEAVING* (2006), *ME AT HOME* (2006). PHOTOGRAPH: KERRY BROWN.

the truth and character of our first people.

Looking back home from Greece I could also acknowledge (alongside Greek patriotism) the influence on our world and humanity of Grecian antiquity; this effect became the work I made for *Pasifika Styles*. It was more about being Maori and inspired by the contexts of my own global travel than a response to the particular collection of *taonga* within the museum, but the amplitude of being Maori is in our *taonga* even when they reside away from us. Through globalization I assimilated the practice of separation, as do our treasures in your museums. Greek-inspired philosophies of Empiricism, Epicureanism and pragmatism helped me to record my observations of culture and transfer it into new work. These philosophical frames help me to produce artwork that challenges explanations of Maori philosophy in Western and European terms in that 'Maori identity and Maori "knowing" are at its very core' (Mason 2005: 105).

Living in Greece and travelling through Europe I witnessed how culture and the movement of people have created new spaces of cultural confusion and seduction in galleries around the world. In the absence of clear cultural ownership or understanding, art on one hand is unburdened and free to speak its own language. This sense of an open communicative space has been described by Lucy Lippard when she wrote that 'there are vestiges in every place that are not altogether culturally determined, or that interact with cultural assumptions to form a kind of hybrid location' (1997: 278). But on the other hand such 'hybridity' silences echoes of the deep connections we have to where we come from. Fusion creates a new confusion.

While reading 'Time and Place' by Peter Eleey in the art magazine *Frieze* (2005: 115) I felt eager to refute, like a pro-globalist, that 'art, like produce, loses its flavor when shipped half way round the world; that its local identity is a perishable commodity whose most intense effects are found closest to its source'. But are we, as participants in the viewing process, comfortable with locality functioning in an artist's practice? While in Ikaria I worked with the gourd, an object that has a practical function in both Greek and Maori cultures. What does an Ikarian gourd from Greece (as an object familiar to many cultures) become when decorated by a New Zealand Maori? Instead of losing flavour, might the gourd not be enhanced by the coming together of cultures?

In the four 'Anti-Globalization' works of mine exhibited in the *Pasifika Styles* exhibition (fig. 62) pattern, detail and colour are analogous to the affordability and wide availability of ornamentation that became contested with the advent of mass production and machine-made decoration. At the same time they draw on Maori artistic traditions emerging from a very different visual and cultural universe. In traditional *whakairo* or carving, as in *kōwhaiwhai* (the painted rafter designs inside the *wharenui* or meeting house) the creation of pattern is integral to the image even when it is highly elaborated. 'During the time that one of these carving forms is being enacted the carving plays a non-verbal supporting role – an accompanist as it were to the melody now being offered. So just as the figure emerges from the body of the timber, so does the *kōrero* (speech) from the body of the carving' (Bevan-Ford: 1994: 13). All four paintings share a common cultural and material language as products of a globalized lifestyle: the materials were sourced from America and issued through Germany and the UK; they have been exhibited in Spain, New Zealand, and England; and they were created in Athens, Greece, Auckland, New Zealand, Pescara, Italy and a final work in Cambridge, England.

Having now returned home and been part of an important show I feel I can ask whether museums should consider if, in this age of international travel, you truly need these objects in the same way we do. These *taonga* have a history, and it's necessary to consider why and how they got to be where they are now, and what they can do for you. Do they simply support patriotism or propaganda in your continuing history? Are Maori what you experience through these *taonga*, or does cultural relativism stand in the way of what Aotearoa has to offer in the now? I would argue that anthropological museums need to be refashioned with the help of artists and museum staff in order to prove that our cultures did not die and to highlight their living and vibrant existence. When educated in this way we not only share an understanding of each other's cultures but can see the differences between us as well as the similarities. Inside and outside of globalization, we must find joy in the beauty and simplicity of who we are and where we each come from. *Mauriora*!

Notes

1 These are the artist's Maori tribal affiliations.

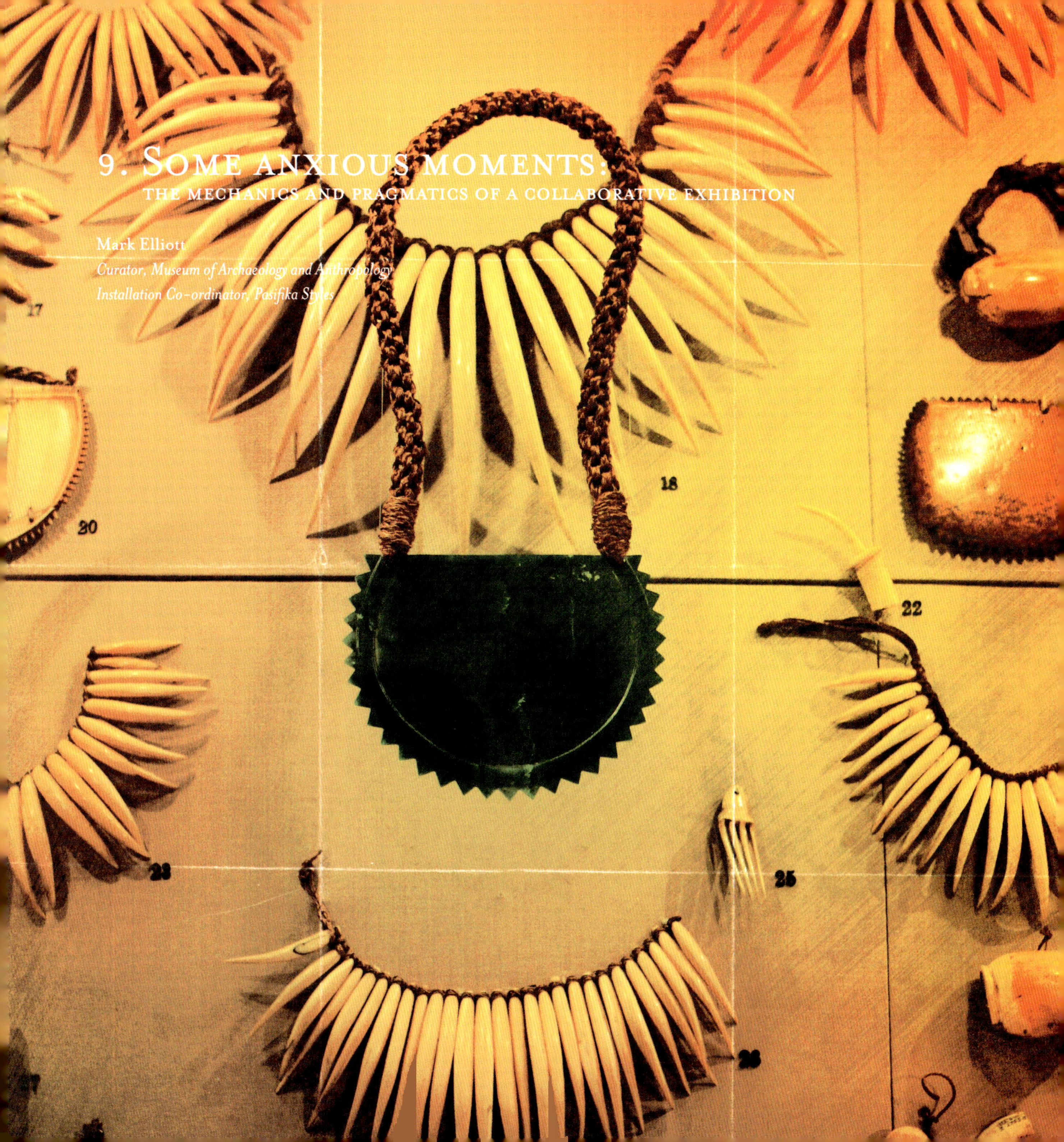

9. Some anxious moments:

The mechanics and pragmatics of a collaborative exhibition

Mark Elliott
Curator, Museum of Archaeology and Anthropology
Installation Co-ordinator, Pasifika Styles

Chris Charteris's *Kouma* (2005) displayed among historic Fijian artefacts in the museum. Photograph: Kerry Brown.

9. Some anxious moments:
The mechanics and pragmatics of a collaborative exhibition

Mark Elliott
Curator, Museum of Archaeology and Anthropology
Installation Co-ordinator, Pasifika Styles

Early in the afternoon of Friday 5 May 2006 I stood in the hot, sun-drenched top gallery of the Museum of Archaeology and Anthropology, alongside fellow staff and the artists and performers of *Pasifika Styles*. I looked at the displays around me – the gleaming Perspex of George Nuku's *Outer Space Marae* hanging, at last, at the entrance to the exhibition; Ani O'Neill's *etu `iti*, two smiling rows of little stars swathed high above the main anthropology gallery; Reuben Paterson's glitter paintings twinkling in the afternoon sun. Below us, the Museum's historical collections from Oceania and around the

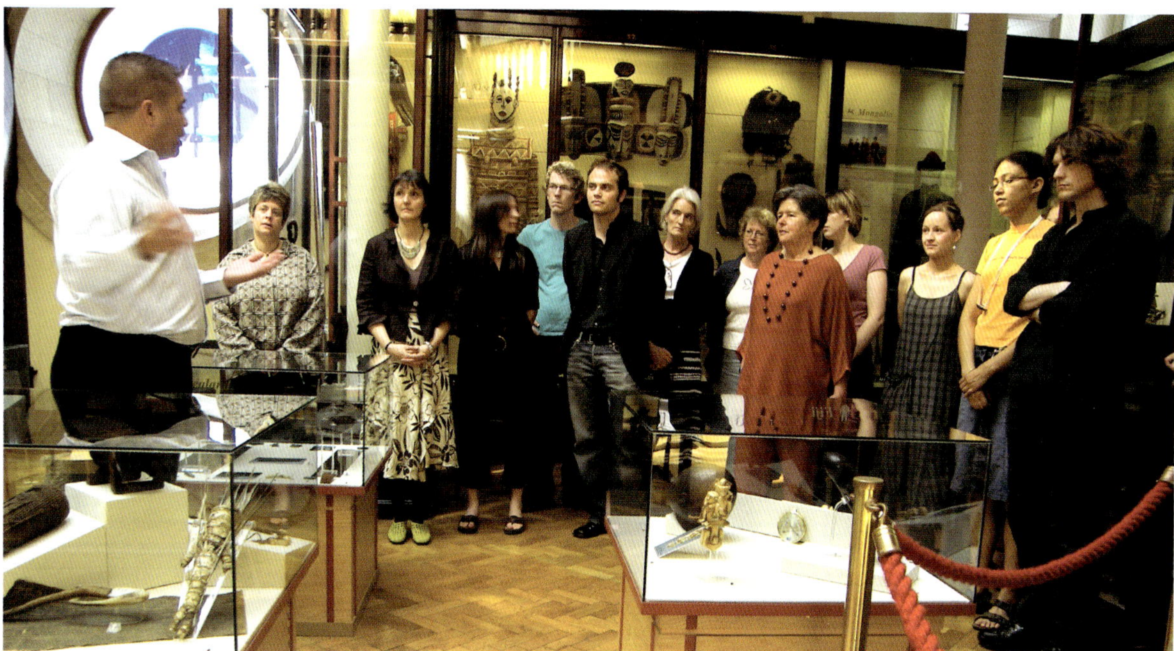

FIG. 63: Che Wilson addressing Museum staff during the *whakarite*, or blessing, 5 May 2006. Photograph: Carine Durand.

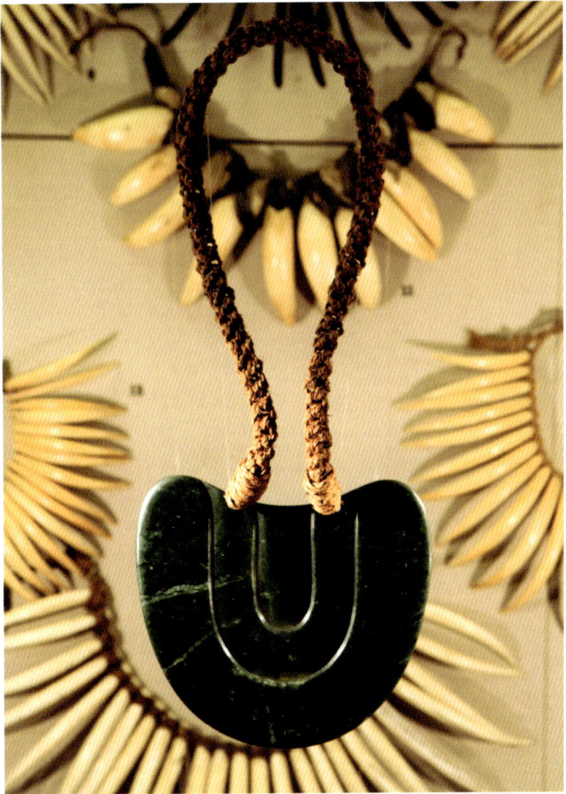

FIG. 64: 'THE NEW GUYS WITH THE OLD GUYS'. CHRIS CHARTERIS'S *SAVAGEWARE* (2005) SHARES A CASE WITH FIJIAN WHALE IVORIES COLLECTED BY ANATOLE VON HÜGEL AROUND 1885. PHOTOGRAPH: KERRY BROWN.

world echoed the work of a new generation of Pacific artists.

While not the Museum's first project with originating communities, the exhibition that had taken shape over the previous weeks was unlike anything any of us had done before. Visual and performing artists had descended on our little institution and, politely but implacably, taken over. Weeks of frenetic activity in the gallery, following years of hard work by the co-curators and the exhibition team inside and outside the Museum, were culminating in an equally frenetic opening night. The last coat of paint was drying in the *Living Room*, the last artwork had been installed, and the last label was about to be put in place. We were very nearly there.

Before the exhibition could open, however, Pacific protocol demanded a formal blessing. This was a chance to stop and take in what had been achieved and to contemplate what in many ways was the point of the project; the reuniting of people and their ancestral artefacts or *taonga*. As we stood in the gallery, a change was coming over many of us, resulting not only from heightened emotion and lack of sleep. We had already been led through the permanent anthropology gallery by Che Wilson, holding a *taiaha* from his own *iwi* or tribal group now held in the Museum's collections (MAA Z 6381) up into the space of *Pasifika Styles*. Now we were participating in a *whakarite* – the blessing of the culmination of all our labours.

For me, and others similarly unfamiliar with the cultures and protocols of Polynesia, the *whakarite* was a profoundly moving experience. It was explained that it was an essential ceremony to lift the *tapu* from these galleries and the assembled *taonga*, which had been lying here for generations. This would make the space safe for us and for the visitors we would soon welcome at the public opening. Participation in the ceremony generated a powerful sense of inclusiveness; through it, we – Pacific Islanders, Maori, Pakeha,[1] Europeans, North Americans – became *tangata whenua* ('People of the Land' or simply 'locals' in Maori), so that later we would be able to welcome our guests. In a sense the artists were made museum people and we were all made Pasifika people. We were all being included, but crucially on terms set down by the Pasifikans themselves.

This is an account of how the exhibition came together, and the processes through which I and other members of the *Pasifika Styles* team became involved in relationships formed and embellished through the mediation of museum artefacts, people, places, and experiences like the *whakarite*. In academic debates about museums and people variously described as

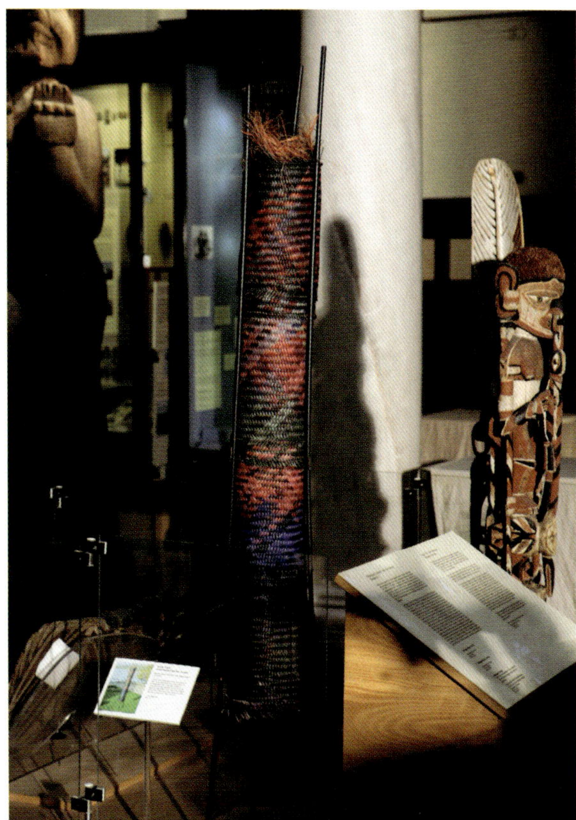

FIG. 65: *Pacific Totem* (2002) BY DONNA CAMPBELL, ON LONG-TERM DISPLAY IN THE MAIN ANTHROPOLOGY GALLERY. PHOTOGRAPH: KERRY BROWN.

'source communities' or 'communities of origin', much is made of the need for mutual respect and consultation (e.g. Ames 2003; Clifford 1997; Lavine 1992; Rosoff 2003). Collaboration, it is said, involves both listening to the point of view of the other and, equally importantly, expressing one's own, because the reality (often assumed and therefore rarely explored) is that both parties bring something valuable to the relationship. Perhaps the most important element is that both parties *care*. Empathy is a tricky subject to discuss in an academic context, despite its centrality to museum practice, ethnography, or indeed any 'cross-cultural' interaction. Yet it was empathy, and a personal commitment to the project on the part of all of its key participants, that enabled this unique collaborative experiment in museum display to happen.

The Museum of Archaeology and Anthropology (MAA) is one of the oldest museums of its kind in the UK, with one of the largest and most remarkable collections of Oceanic artefacts. Since its foundation in 1884 it has played a central role in the development of both sociocultural anthropology and archaeology, and its collections and activities reflect this strong academic tradition. More recently, MAA has led the field in initiating active collaborations with individuals and groups from communities with an interest in its collections. Much of this work has developed in the context of academic research projects led by curators together with scholars, experts and practitioners from groups such as the Zuni in New Mexico, communities in Nunavut in northeastern Canada, and Torres Strait Islanders (e.g. Herle 2003).[2] Not all museum staff involved in *Pasifika Styles*, however, were as experienced in working so closely with people of diverse cultural backgrounds. With some thirty-four artists engaging remotely or in person with the collections, the scale and complexity of the exhibition were such that it drew on more of the Museum's resources than previous projects. All this, and the occasional clash of working styles and expectations which resulted, made this one of MAA's most ambitious exhibitions.

Most of the exhibition team had mounted shows at MAA and other institutions, but the diversity of jobs involved in a large international project like *Pasifika Styles* meant that all the Museum's staff, including the curators, were faced with an unprecedented variety of challenges. Beyond dealing with the difficulties of getting all the works to the Museum and installed, developing marketing strategies, drafting press releases, compiling mailing lists and negotiating sponsorship deals were only

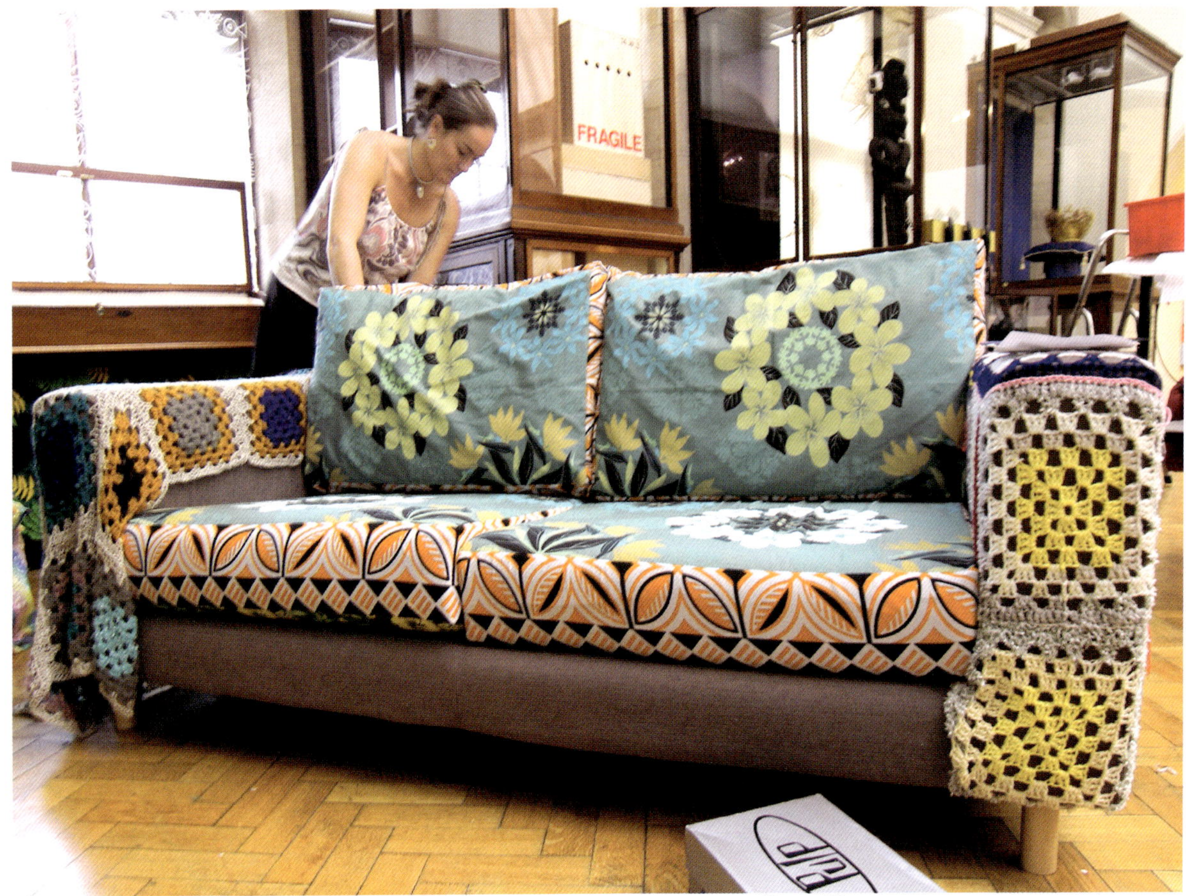

FIG. 66: ANI O'NEILL CUSTOMISING A COUCH FOR *THE LIVING ROOM* INSTALLATION, A JOINT WORK WITH TRACEY TAWHIAO.

some of the tasks the young and slim-line exhibition team had to deliver, often without the benefit of in-house experience. In addition they would have to deal with an influx of creative and assertive visitors, all keen to get the show on the road and to participate in and direct the installation of their work. The arrival in Cambridge of the *Pasifika Styles* artists was thus anticipated in some quarters with a degree of trepidation.

The Visiting Artists programme involved some twenty New Zealand-based artists, some of whom were working on site-specific installations that needed to be completed in the days leading up to the opening (fig. 66). Many of their artworks were in media or formats of which Museum staff had little or no experience. Some artists were producing video works, which required varying degrees of technical input; others were constructing and installing audio-visual units that demanded specialised attention. Communication was an important issue; it was not always clear in advance of an artist's arrival what precisely they were bringing with them and the kind of help they would need. The logistics of transporting and installing the works were equally demanding. Planning and coordination had to be done across time zones via telephone and email, providing many opportunities for misunderstanding. The majority of the works arrived from New Zealand by ship in late April, but there was great uncertainty surrounding one of the largest and most striking pieces. Until the very last moment we were not sure if George Nuku and his massive meeting house façade would ever make it to Cambridge. If and when it did, accommodating the piece within the historic museum building would be challenging. Where precisely would it go? Who would install it, and how?

Tensions surfaced and were heightened as the opening date drew near, fuelled by practical anxieties though sometimes expressed in other terms. For some it was mystifying that this Museum, with such a prominent academic tradition, was investing so many of its limited resources in an exhibition of contemporary art, albeit from a region where we have particular strengths in terms of research and collections. Such controversies are perhaps not unusual.[3] Coming at a time of considerable internal change and expansion within the institution, however, these misgivings added to and were intensified by pre-existing uncertainties.[4]

Art/Ethnography. Again.

Looking back, many of the concerns expressed within the Museum were rooted in categories through which we define our work and that of others. What place does 'art' have in a museum of archaeology and anthropology? The tension between 'art' and 'artefact' is an old one, perhaps as old as the discipline of anthropology itself.[5] The marginal position that museums have occupied in relation to anthropology compounds anxieties around the use of the term 'art' in anthropological literature. What became clear during the preparation of *Pasifika Styles* was that these loaded categories were not only a source of controversy within the museum. They were equally salient to the way in which we as an institution were perceived by others.

In interviews undertaken by the curators in preparation for the exhibition, some artists had expressed ambivalence, even antagonism, toward museums as institutions which fix in time their cultures and the people – their ancestors and by implication themselves – who produced the artefacts on display:

> Glass cabinets just make it law of the land: you people are less than us. But ... I'm glad museums exist because... maybe it's made us sharper and quicker. Yeah. Warriors need good enemies to be great warriors. What's the use of having a weak enemy when... you become complacent? (John Ioane, from an interview with Rosanna Raymond, 2005).

The conception of curators Rosanna Raymond and Amiria Salmond was to create a space in which contemporary works could engage with the historic collections in the Museum. This effect is powerfully achieved in the gallery by the interpolation of recent works with older pieces: the 'new guys' alongside the 'old guys' as one artist described it (figs. 64 & 65). While this lends a great deal to the impact of the exhibition, it was not an uncontroversial decision. If some in the museum had reservations about an 'art show' in the galleries, this anxiety was more than matched by concerns on the part of some contributing artists that, by showing their work in a museum, they would be seen not as 'contemporary artists' but as 'Pacific' or 'indigenous' artists, or simply as ethnographic exemplars. Though anticipated, these concerns nonetheless brought complications for the curatorial team, most notably in the composition of exhibition text.

The distinctive exhibitionary strategy of classical ethnographic display involves contextualising artefacts with information on the culture or group from which they were obtained. This paradigm, in which the identity of individual makers is elided in favour of technological or sociological detail, is at odds both with art gallery practice in which the artist's individuality is seen as key to the interpretation of the work, and with the ideal, popular among artists, of letting the work speak for itself. There was discussion about whether *Pasifika Styles* should include labels explaining what *taonga* are, or *tapu*, or *toi moko*, or even giving a background to the Treaty of Waitangi or the Maori Foreshore controversy. In the end, to avoid didacticism and to enable as wide a range of potential visitor interpretations as possible, most of the labels drew on interviews with the artists conducted by the curators and by Sarah Robins, foregrounding themes such as authenticity, identity and perceptions of museums. These were supplemented by audio tracks of many of the interviews themselves, available via two sound stations at one end of the gallery as well as through the website, and by Lisa Taouma's documentary *Represent* (2006) screening regularly in the *Living Room*, featuring excerpts of similar interviews set into a broader account of the rise of contemporary Pacific art and identity.

A local audience might feel the need for more explication of the return to New Zealand of *toi moko* (preserved Maori heads), for example, to better understand Wayne Youle's powerful works, or of the repatriation issue more generally so that they 'get' Jason Hall's playful and provocative *The do-it-yourself repatriation kit* (2006).[6] But perhaps this comes down once again to the tensions inherent in exhibiting contemporary art in a museum of archaeology and anthropology. The issue is central to our curatorial practice: are we guided by what the audience wants, or what the owners/makers of the works want? Well, you can't always get what you want. Perhaps sometimes you shouldn't. In this and other ways *Pasifika Styles* prompted us to rethink the nature of ethnographic exhibition.

By the time we had reached the end of the *whakarite*, however, many of these questions had been resolved, or set aside for the time being. Working together on installing the exhibition had brought about a sense of common purpose that transcended many of the anxieties felt on both sides. Here we were aided by the *taonga* themselves, at once the objects of debate and the agents that brought us together. When a Maori war trumpet (MAA Z 6614) was played by musician Jerome Kavanagh, for example, in the run-up to the opening, all present felt the power of that moment. The deep resonant note that echoed around the gallery prompted first silence, a few tears, then a series of responses in song. Throughout the installation, *taonga* repeatedly acted to bring people from different cultural and professional backgrounds together. These instances demonstrated that all of us shared the same respect and love for these amazing things (to express it in European terms). The point is made eloquently by artist Che Wilson, speaking from New Zealand (see also Wilson, this volume):

> I didn't like institutions, I just saw them as a bunch of thieving bastards, you know, who collect all these *taonga* and they don't let them live. And then I went to England and [found] a completely different approach... OK, the odd person we met was... stuffy: 'leave me alone with my objects!' But in a funny way what I saw in England is that the people looking after our *taonga* – they had an *aroha* [love] for our *taonga* which we over here don't. Over here what I saw was just *mana*, you know: "I am the curator of this. This is my patch"... But the personal relationships that I was able to build [in England allowed me to see] people who actually care about the *taonga*. OK, they call them 'objects' but that's just their job, you know, and you can't get precious about them calling them a thing because... those are just cultural differences (from an interview with Rosanna Raymond and Amiria Salmond, 2005).

Wilson's words sum up better than any of my own what I and perhaps many of us at the Museum took away from our work on *Pasifika Styles*. Although punctuated by very real tensions and disagreements, the process of mounting the exhibition ultimately brought more mutual recognition and understanding than discord. To a great extent this was the result of all of us, ultimately, just getting on with it. We had all invested a great deal in the project and it was important that it be a success. 'Success' meant more, and different things, to some than to others. But as Wilson asserts, it's not always helpful to get bogged down in terminology. As museum professionals we are predisposed to behaving in a certain way towards the 'objects' in our care, the people who identify with them, and the 'information' that surrounds them. What is clear from the example of *Pasifika Styles*, and highlighted by other contributions to this volume, is that such predispositions have to be held up for reflection and subject to negotiation for all parties to the exchange to gain the most from collaboration. This, after all, best serves the *taonga* and those who care for them.

Notes

1 New Zealanders of European descent.

2 Much of this work is current and therefore not yet published. Earlier collaborations at MAA include the collection, documentation and display of Tamu shamanistic material by Nepalese Shaman Yarjung Kromchhain Tamu (Herle 1994).

3 Since the 1990s, many ethnographic museums have begun to review their contemporary role in relation both to local and international communities, in response to the demands of communities themselves as well as those of funding bodies, and in the context of various theoretical developments (see e.g. Peers and Brown (eds.) 2003; Simpson 2001).

4 *Pasifika Styles* coincided with a major administrative reorganisation of the Faculty of Archaeology and Anthropology, of which the Museum is part. It also came as the Museum's long-serving Director David Phillipson retired and was replaced by Nicholas Thomas.

5 See Faris (1988) and Price (1991) on the tension between art and 'artefact' in museum display and scholarship in the 1980s. Stocking (1985), provides a longer view of similar professional and scholarly debates.

6 Conversations with visitors in the gallery, as well as written feedback in the form of visitor surveys and comment cards, suggest that this is the experience of some visitors. At least one reviewer shared this view (see Weeks 2006: 51).

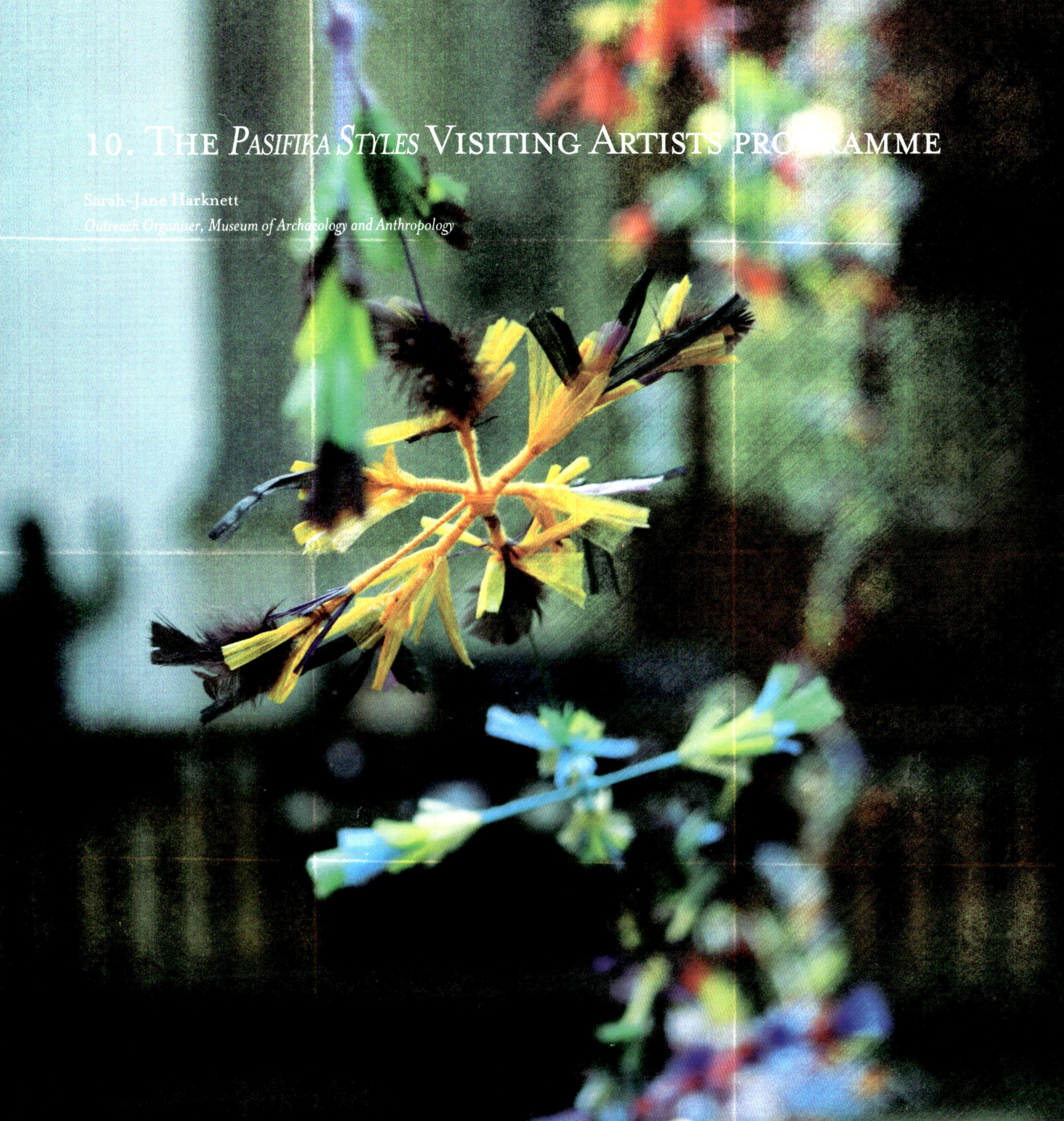

10. The *Pasifika Styles* Visiting Artists programme

Sarah-Jane Harknett
Outreach Organiser, Museum of Archaeology and Anthropology

Detail of Ani O'Neill's `*etu iti* (2006). Photograph: Kerry Brown.

10. The *Pasifika Styles* Visiting Artists programme

Sarah-Jane Harknett
Outreach Organiser, Museum of Archaeology and Anthropology

According to curator Rosanna Raymond, the Visiting Artists programme was

> '...a crucial part of *Pasifika Styles*. We wanted to provide a platform that also catered for the living heart of art practices in Aotearoa today, as well as reaching out to audiences unfamiliar with the culture. The artists brought with them the dynamic needed to enliven the collections, creating new narratives and establishing new relationships with the legacy of collecting and housing *taonga* over the last two centuries' (pers. comm., 2007).

The curators of the exhibition were eager to make use of the unique skills that the visiting artists would bring, engaging with a broad audience through a series of workshops and community outreach opportunities. The resulting schedule, supported by funding from Arts Council England and the Esmée Fairbairn Foundation, included events before the exhibition opened, during its early stages, and a year after the opening.

The pre-exhibition programme

In August 2005, the pre-exhibition programme designed to engage with Cambridge communities began with a pilot workshop in the museum. This day-long, drop-in workshop for children led by Rosanna Raymond and the Manaia Maori Performing Arts Company included drawing, writing, poetry, movement and performance, and allowed the children to hear, share and perform stories infused with Maori song and dance.

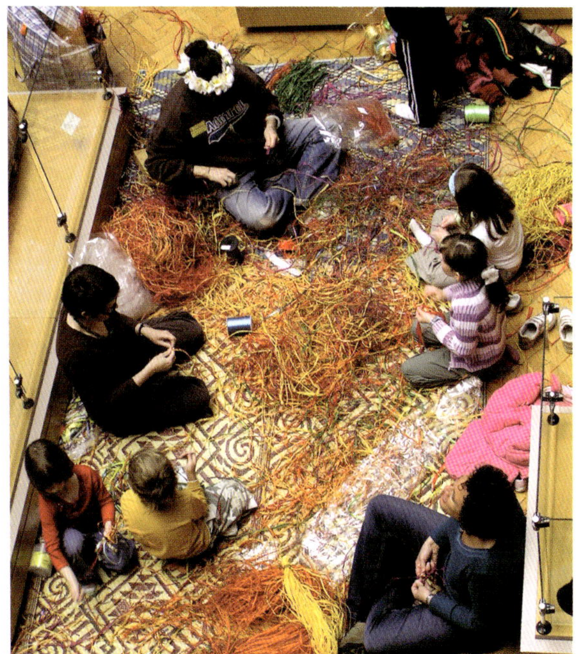

FIG. 67: *Titi iti* (small hula skirt-making) workshop, part of the *Pasifika Styles* Festival programme, May 2007. Photograph: Jocelyne Dudding.

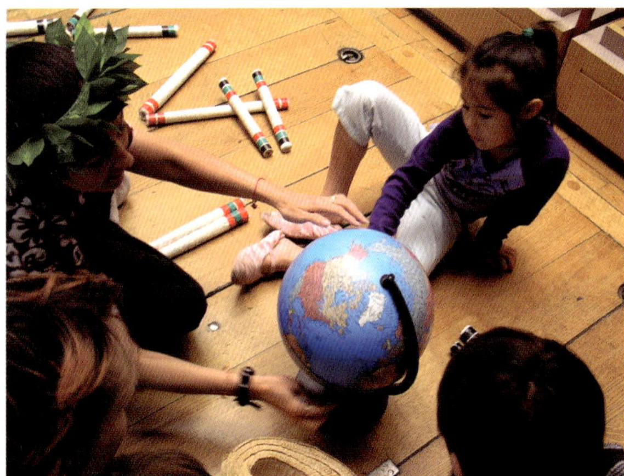

FIG. 68: POINTING OUT THE PACIFIC ON THE GLOBE. PHOTOGRAPH: JOCELYNE DUDDING.

The workshop quickly revealed that these young people had little prior knowledge and understanding about the Pacific. Most were unsure about New Zealand's geographical location, and this was their first exposure to Maori culture, history and language. The exercise provided a baseline for the general audience for the rest of the workshop programme. Although the workshop was widely publicised, it failed to attract large audiences, partly because of the timing (a warm, sunny weekday in the school summer holidays), but also perhaps because of lack of knowledge about (and possibly interest in) the Pacific.

In November 2005, the pilot workshop was followed by three Maori storytelling events by Rangimoana Taylor; the first a performance with Rosanna Raymond at the Museum, then a sign language interpreted performance in Norwich, and a story-telling workshop in Cambridge. These were advertised widely through local press and events websites and promoted extensively through storytelling groups and deaf communities. Even so, attendance was disappointing, although feedback from participants was extremely positive:

> Engaging, enlightening, informative and thoroughly enjoyable. Thank You.

> I am half Maori but have been brought up in Great Britain. I found this performance a wonderful way to learn about Maori legends and stories. Having been to a performance in 2003 [I] was excited about seeing Rangimoana again and hearing the stories again.

> Stunning. What can I say? So much more than mere entertainment! I was so moved, so enthralled. I learnt a lot and could listen forever. Thank you, thank you, thank you. Best fiver ever spent.

In April 2006, during the run-up to the opening of the *Pasifika Styles* exhibition, a series of workshops were held in which the Manaia Maori Performing Arts Company worked with marginalised young people aged 16-19 from the Cambridge City Council's Entry Into Employment Scheme (E2E). The workshops focused on *mau taiaha* (a traditional form of Maori martial arts) as a method of engagement, but also introduced the participants to other aspects of Maori arts and culture, including *poi* (flax balls on long strings, swung in traditional dances) and stick games (where batons are thrown in rhythmic patterns between pairs of people in time to a song). The intention was to train the participants to a level in *mau taiaha* where they could provide a short performance piece at the end of the workshops for family and friends. Although this final performance did not occur because of the high turnover of participants, feedback demonstrates that the students were enthusiastic about the workshops.

During this same period two of the exhibiting artists, Ani O'Neill and Reuben Paterson, led practical sessions on Maori and Pacific Island arts in local schools and ran a workshop day at the Museum. O'Neill's installation at the exhibition was to be called *'etu iti'* – 'Little Stars'. In her three sessions she taught the children techniques such as binding, threading, plaiting, weaving, and stitching, to make star-shaped sculptures from a variety of found, recycled and natural materials. Participants contributed towards the creation of Ani's dramatic installation in the *Pasifika Styles* exhibition, where their 'stars' were suspended across the gallery space. Reuben Paterson's concurrent sessions started with an introduction to the people of the Pacific, their culture and traditions, before showing the beautiful patterns to be found in *kōwhaiwhai* (painted rafter panels), which appear as painted scroll designs, abstract and curvilinear in form. Reuben explained the background and meanings of some of the patterns and the traditional colours as well as introducing his own artworks, which draw on that artistic tradition. Participants then used *kōwhaiwhai*-shaped sponges and glitter to create their own artwork.

Community Engagement after the Opening

In May 2006 the *Pasifika Styles* exhibition opened to the public, with 15 of the New Zealand-based artists present in Cambridge as part of the project's Visiting Artists programme. Later that month Maureen Lander, one of the exhibiting artists, led two workshops at the University Botanic Garden, both of which sold out well in advance. In 'Fun With Flax', she taught participants how to create a range of small objects from flax leaves, using a variety of braiding and plaitwork techniques. Her second workshop, which lasted for two days, was entitled 'Sandals and Bags'. Maureen also gave a talk one evening in the museum to an interested audience of local weavers.

During late June and early July of 2006 Kahutoi Te Kanawa and Bethany Edmunds, both Maori weavers from New Zealand, led three days of workshops at White House Arts in Cambridge. These covered the harvesting of New Zealand flax (*Phormium tenax*, actually a type of lily), extracting its fibre, traditional dye techniques using heated stones from a small fire pit, and the techniques of Maori decorative *tāniko* finger weaving. The workshops were aimed at members of the Cambridgeshire Guild of Spinners, Weavers and Dyers, as well as of the United Kingdom Institute of Conservators, though other participants heard about them through the *Pasifika Styles* grapevine. Feedback again indicated that they greatly appreciated the opportunity to experience techniques and processes of weaving from a different culture:

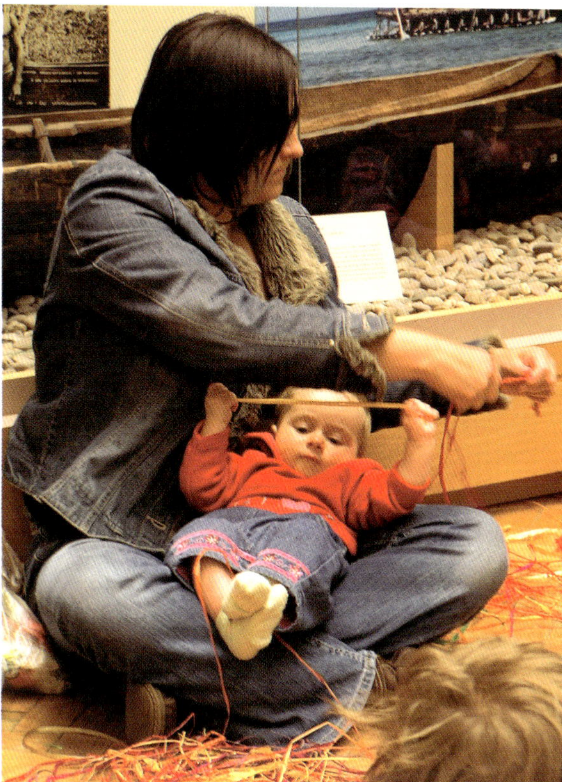

Fig. 69: People of all ages were welcome to participate in the *Titi iti* workshop. Photograph: Jocelyne Dudding.

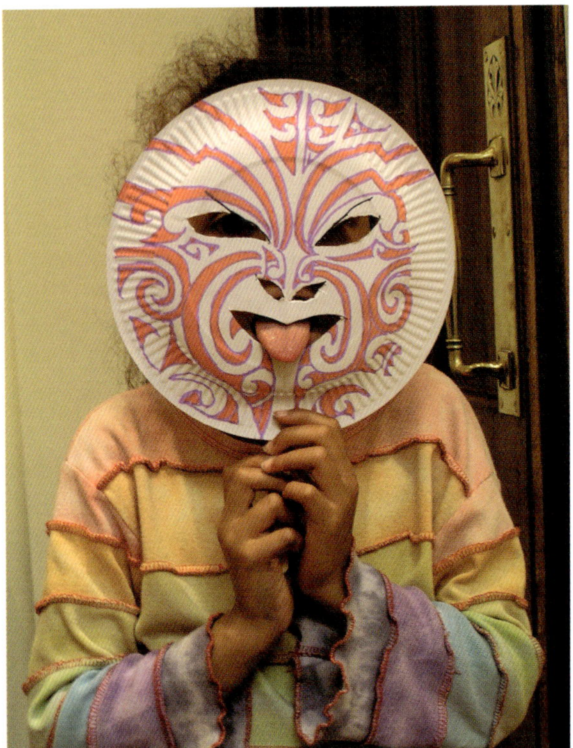

FIG. 70: A PARTICIPANT IN GEORGE NUKU'S MAKING FACES WORKSHOP, OCTOBER 2006. PHOTOGRAPH: JOCELYNE DUDDING.

I feel very privileged to have learned so much about the Maoris, their culture and their dyeing and weaving methods from such a renowned teacher as Kahu... I jumped at the chance to attend this workshop and I enjoyed every minute. The technique for spinning the fibre was fascinating as was the dyeing process – so different from our own and made magical by the accompanying legends.

Kahu and Bethany taught us as much about Maoris and their history as about weaving with NZ flax. They brought the whole workshop alive with their legends and explanations. They inspired me to spend hours on Google finding out more as Maori weaving is not often included in general books on weaving. I particularly liked the fact that Kahu and Bethany did absolutely everything as authentically as possible. Some people would have been content to make do with UK dyeing facilities - ie a stainless steel pan on an electric cooker - but they dug a pit for the fire, used the right type of stones, brought their dyebath with them and used a beautiful calabash pot. It was all this attention to their heritage that made it so perfect... it was a chance in a lifetime as far as I was concerned.

In May 2007, a year after the exhibition opened, a family activity day was held in the Museum to coincide with the *Pasifika Styles* Performing Arts Festival. At this event, members of the group Beats of Polynesia taught games from the Pacific, hula dancing and helped participants to make a hula skirt (fig. 67 to 69). There was also a storytelling session and the opportunity to contribute to a giant Pacific 'barkcloth'. A general lack of prior knowledge about the Pacific was again evident, but the audience's responses were once more enthusiastic. Further activities are planned for the period leading up to the closing of the exhibition in February 2008.

CONCLUSION

As Outreach Organiser at the Museum, I found the Visiting Artists programme of *Pasifika Styles* the most stimulating part of the project. The opportunity to meet and learn from such an interesting and diverse group of people was a real privilege.

This is not to say that it was without its challenges. Trying to get sufficient documentation in place for artists from New Zealand to visit UK schools was a time-consuming (albeit highly necessary) process.[1] Working across time zones and almost solely via email provided its own communication problems, and some of the artists were travelling or away from their documents when initial contacts were made. Certain requests from artists involved in running workshops were not always easy to fulfil; multiple rolls of brightly coloured raffia, for example, are not a common thing to find in the UK, many people do not want their flax bushes 'trimmed' and some venues would rather not have a large fire pit dug in their grounds! It was sometimes complicated to explain to those who ran particular venues what the artist would like to do or use, when so many of their cultural references are completely unknown in the UK. Some artists were perhaps expecting to present very similar sessions in UK schools to those that they lead at home, and occasionally these expectations needed modification. I work with some excellent primary schools in Cambridgeshire, but given our climate and Health and Safety regulations, was not sure that they would be happy using an angle grinder at an outdoor workshop!

The expectations that the artists had about Cambridge before they arrived were sometimes difficult to meet in the midst of the most intense period of activity. Being a relatively small institution, with few staff, and office space at a premium, we could provide only one room for our visitors to use on site. As a lot of display equipment was also stored in this room, it quickly became a multi-use space with staff, artists and volunteers competing to complete tasks on every available surface (including the floor), although it had originally been intended as an out of the way space for people to relax. The artists, however, were extremely accepting of our shortcomings, and were prepared to be flexible when circumstances dictated. The final programme is one that I look back at now with pride.

I would not have been able to complete the tasks allocated to me without the assistance of a team of dedicated volunteers, who gave up hours of their time to help with the exhibition and project. I was amazed at the commitment of some of our students, who were happy to take on routine tasks with the same good humour as they always demonstrate when helping with events. Unusually, I found myself with no task to do on the exhibition opening night, as our extremely capable team had it all in hand.

As I have little previous experience of Pacific cultures, the opening was a very interesting, moving and refreshing experience. It felt a luxury to take time out of exhibition preparations and all the last minute trouble-shooting and organising to be a part of the ceremonies, but I was so glad to have been able to take part. I didn't feel like a casual observer at all; Che and others involved in proceedings made Museum staff feel as much a part of the team as the artists, recognising our different contributions and drawing us together. Openings are often more like endings for people who are closely involved in the exhibition process - the end of our contribution before the public views it, the end of (most of) the hard work, a respite before the evaluation process kicks in again. The ceremonial aspect of the opening reminded me that this was the first sight of the exhibition for our visitors, their first opportunity to engage with the art. It felt like a true celebration, a recognition of achievement, a symbol of how far we had all come to make the exhibition a reality.

Notes

1 The artists had to apply for police clearance from their country of origin in order to run workshops - not easy for artists not based at the time in their home country.

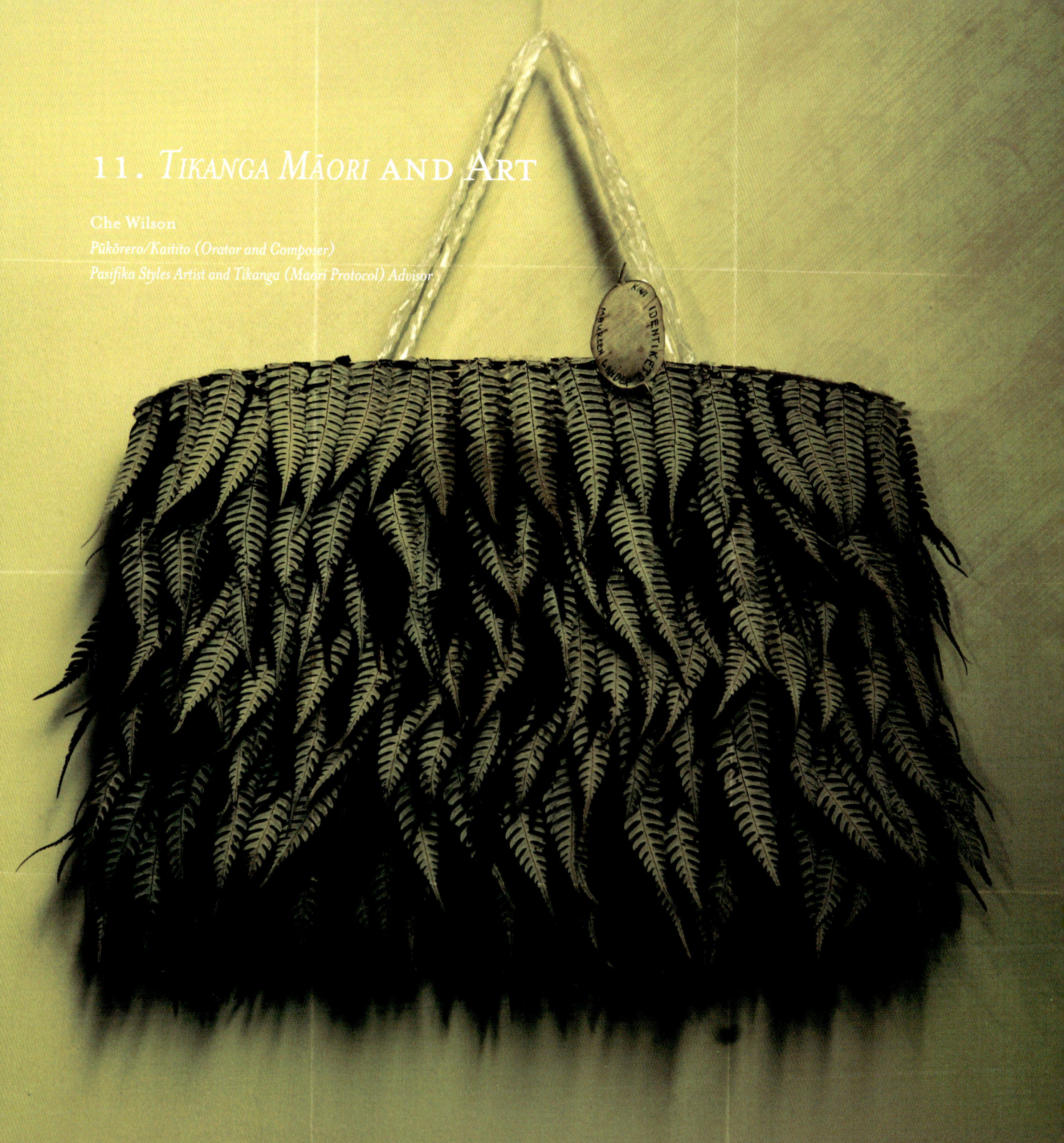

11. *Tikanga Māori* and Art

Che Wilson

Pūkōrero/Kaitito (Orator and Composer)

Pasifika Styles Artist and Tikanga (Māori Protocol) Advisor

Kiwi Identikete (2006) by Maureen Lander. Photograph: Kerry Brown.

11. *Tikanga Māori* and Art

Che Wilson
Pūkōrero/Kaitito (Orator and Composer)
Pasifika Styles Artist and Tikanga (Maori Protocol) Advisor

My first connection to *Pasifika Styles* started in 2003 when I first met Rosanna Raymond at Ngati Ranana, the London Maori Club. Our connection evolved over time into a relationship of support and learning, during which time the *Pasifika Styles* project was conceived. I agreed to *tautoko* (support) this *kaupapa* by providing advice and practical help with *tikanga* (Maori protocols) and attended the curators' presentation at New Zealand House to representatives of UK-based Maori and Pacific Island communities, potential funders and the NZ High Commissioner. This event showed me that I wanted to get involved both as *tikanga* advisor and artist.

At the end of 2004, I left the UK to return home and continued to support the development of the project through email and phone calls. As our *tuāhine* (sisters) developed and

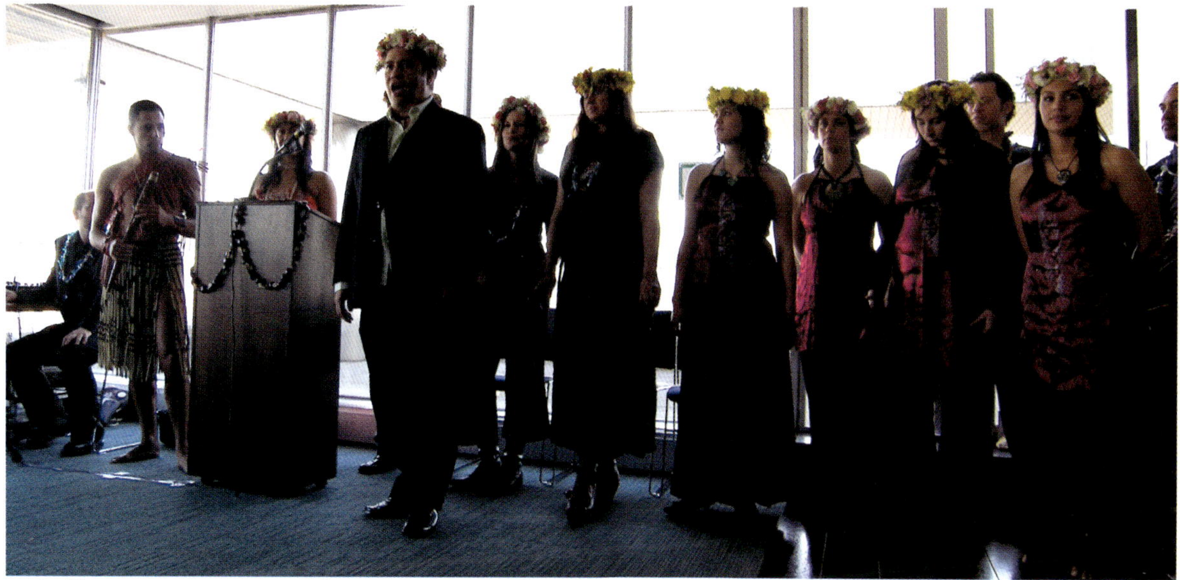

FIG. 71: The author officiating at the London launch of the *Pasifika Styles* project, 28 April 2006. Photograph: Carine Durand.

shaped *Pasifika Styles*, they returned home to Aotearoa to fulfil the age-old *tikanga* of bringing this *kaupapa*, *kanohi ki te kanohi* (face-to-face). After months of preparation involving *wānanga* (workshops), *kai* (sharing food), emails, phone calls and blogging, I crossed the Great Ocean of Kiwa to arrive back in the UK with my *tuakana* (senior relative) Gerrard Albert to bless the *Pasifika Styles* exhibition and ensure the spiritual well-being of all involved.

Preparing for the blessing and opening was a mix of working with Ngati Ranana, the Pasifika community in the UK, dealing with the artists and negotiating with the sometimes wary *tikanga* of the museum. This was a great time for Gerrard and me to hone our skills in dealing with people with a range of backgrounds and thoughts about *tikanga Māori* and *tikanga Pasifika*. It also allowed us to better understand how to navigate the waters of foreign processes including health and safety!

There was also the dynamic of having to prove myself to the artists. For some I was *just* a *tikanga* person, plus I was the new artist on the block. After helping with making a few lolly *lei* (necklaces) and floral *pare* (head garlands) the London media launch was a success and when I performed a poem of mine, *E noho nei au i tawhiti pāmamao*, I was allowed into the clique! This was an interesting time; it was as if, as a group of artists, we were a stand of kahikatea trees. Below ground we shared a root system, but above we appeared as different and sometimes completely individual trees. At times the kahikatea stand was overpowered in a wood of grand old oaks. In other respects some of the trees had grafts from a range of trees from all around the world. On some occasions, some of the kahikatea trees didn't even realise that below the grass was a simple root system that supported the whole stand. We had to continually remind ourselves that the taproot of the kahikatea derives from our shared ancestry back to Tahiti-nui, Kahiki-roa and Tawhiti-pāmamao.

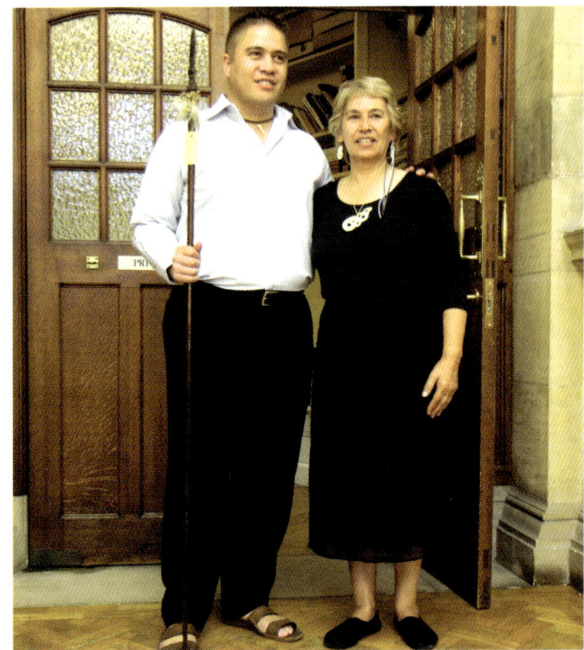

FIG. 72: THE AUTHOR WITH NGATI RANANA *KUIA* ESTHER JESSOP AT THE BLESSING OF THE EXHIBITION. PHOTOGRAPH: CARINE DURAND.

The week after the press launch was the big day in Cambridge (fig. 71), a private blessing followed by the public opening of the exhibition. We had all agreed to maintain the *mana* of the blessing by keeping it private. As a ceremony to *whakawātea* (spiritually clear) the artists and staff involved and to *whakarite* (spiritually prepare) the *taonga* for a two-year journey of *pūkana* from the *taonga* in the exhibition at the visitors, we didn't want the blessing to be presented as a performance for the benefit of anthropologists, it was more about ensuring the spiritual safety of all involved. The presence of cameras, intruding into *tikanga* space, meant that some *karakia* were not said verbally, but were rather performed in line with *whare wānanga* teachings to protect the integrity of these sacred words. The blessing was sealed as Ngati Ranana *kuia* Esther Jessop (fig. 72) sent her *karanga* to the *taonga*, calling on them to reveal themselves to the world of light.

After a *kai* (sharing of food) to complete the blessing we then had the public opening that evening. This was a time where the Old Oak gave a helping hand to the Kahikatea; Rosanna Raymond, Jerome Kavanagh and I were able to use *taonga* from the museum's collection in a public ceremony celebrating the coming together of people and *taonga*. Rosanna wielded a beautiful *mere pounamu* that sang an amazing song; Jerome gave life to a *pūkāea* and I brandished the *taiaha* of an ancestor from my own tribe Kiriona Rupuha. Kēmureti, *e mihi kau ana* – the spirit has been set free. This spirit has broken down barriers and I have since used a *mere pounamu* in public from the British Museum collection, which has opened the doors of museums at home.

Pasifika Styles, a gift to the tranquil waters of the River Cam, a gift from the Great Ocean of Kiwa, emerging as a fusion of past, present and future life. This exhibition has been guided by the ancestors, by Sina the Goddess of the Moon and can be likened to a *rāpaki*, a woven skirt or kilt. The fibre has been beaten for softness, each thread was twisted together for strength, and in its final state it swirls and flows, catching the light. It has been marked in the stars that this *rāpaki* will dance on many more stages around the world in a range of forms for eternity. Te Moananui-ā-Kiwa – toitū e!

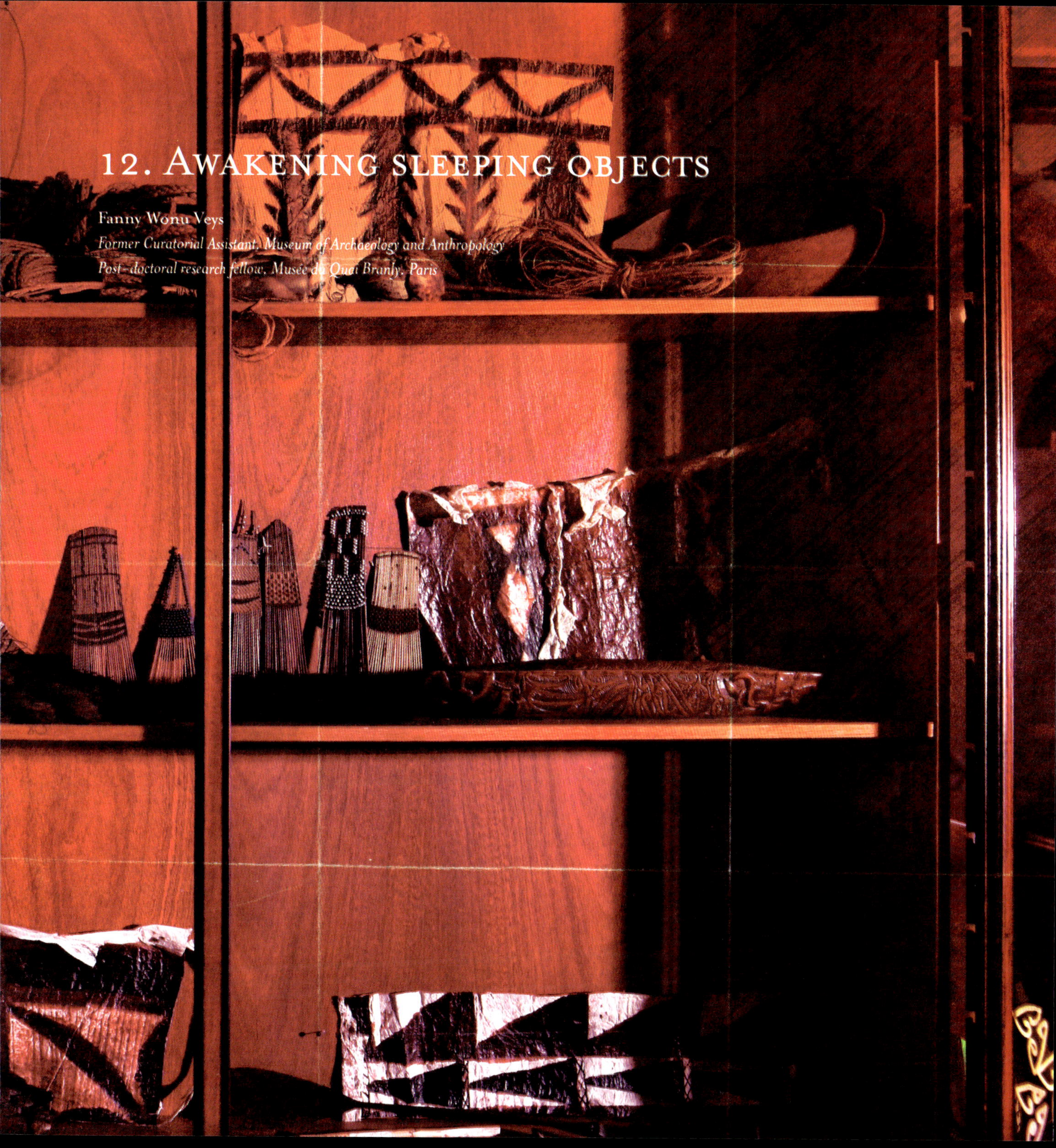

12. Awakening sleeping objects

Fanny Wonu Veys
Former Curatorial Assistant, Museum of Archaeology and Anthropology
Post-doctoral research fellow, Musée du Quai Branly, Paris

Bark cloth, combs, *wakahuia* and other items from the museum's collections on display in *The Living Room* (2006) Ani O'Neill and Tracey Tawhiao's installation.

12. Awakening sleeping objects

Fanny Wonu Veys
Former Curatorial Assistant, Museum of Archaeology and Anthropology
Post-doctoral research fellow, Musée du Quai Branly, Paris

In February 2006, I took up the role of curatorial assistant for Anthropology at the Museum of Archaeology and Anthropology, an appointment which coincided with the lead-in to the opening of the *Pasifika Styles* exhibition. I had already participated in the weekly meetings of the project team, where the curators developed and explained the different facets of *Pasifika Styles*. Now, however, I was to coordinate the artists' research visits as well as the gala opening night, both major responsibilities. Whilst the former task fell within the normal remit of my role as curatorial assistant, event management was not in the job description! This account of the artists' visits, culminating in the opening night, shows what was revealed through the engagements that took place between historical anthropological objects and contemporary artists who originate, or whose ancestors originated, from those places where the objects were collected. It is written both from the viewpoint of a museum professional concerned with ensuring the accessibility of collections with minimal impact on the objects and from a more personal interest in the contemporary importance of historical Polynesian artefacts.

Although the timing of the artists' trips to Cambridge was not specified by the curators (who indeed hoped they might spread themselves over the two-year duration of the project) most artists understandably wished to come for the exhibition opening and the conference that followed shortly after. The coincidence of so many visitors at one time, particularly during the installation of a major show, meant that good forward planning was essential. In coordinating the artists' research visits, I began by sending out an email well in advance of their arrival in the UK, inviting them to examine material from the museum's collections by appointment and to specify their area

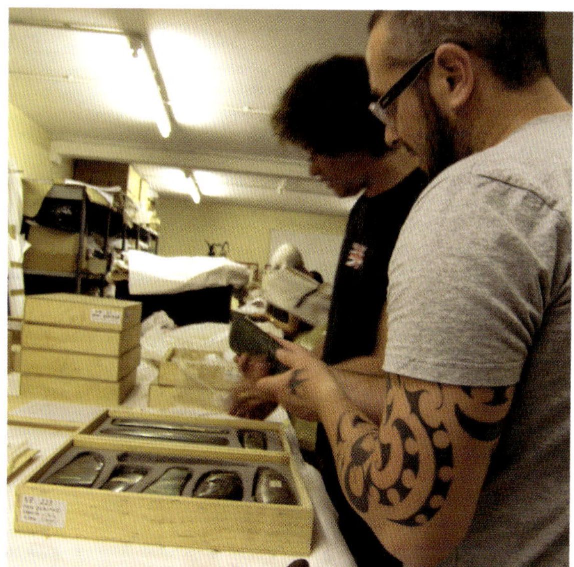

FIG. 73: Artists Wayne Youle and Chris Charteris handling *toki* (adze heads) from the museum's collections, April 2006. Photograph: Carine Durand.

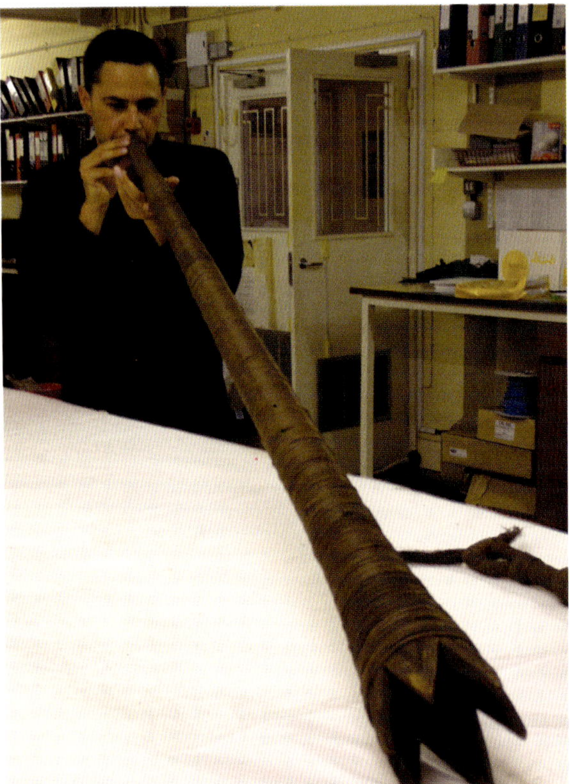

FIG. 74: Musician Jerome Kavanagh tests the sound of a *pukaea* from the collections in the museum workroom. Photograph: Carine Durand.

of interest. Twelve of the artists who visited at this time took up the opportunity, viewing, smelling, caressing, and sometimes singing to objects from Aotearoa-New Zealand, Samoa, Tonga, Fiji and the Cook Islands.[1] Some, such as Che Wilson and Chris Charteris had been awarded special research grants by the museum, as they knew very precisely what they wanted to see and had offered to share their expert knowledge.[2] Others had a more general interest in particular regions or archipelagos; materials such as bone, greenstone and feathers; or techniques including lashing, binding and weaving (fig. 73).

Most of the Polynesian material at the Museum is located in the same building as the galleries, and not in the external stores. Those objects not on display are kept in boxes, drawers or on shelves, and are therefore physically rather than visually accessible. The disadvantage of boxes and drawers is that one cannot pick out objects at a glance, but must rather rely on the computerised database to locate specific things. Some artists conducted this research remotely, using the online version of the database, others waited until they arrived at the Museum. Once we had narrowed the search down to particular items of interest, we would go into the storage area, pick up the box(es) and start to look together at the objects. It was this process that sparked my interest because of the similar ways in which the various artists from different backgrounds, working in a variety of mediums, experienced the objects. I am using the word 'experiencing' here to stress the fact that encountering the museum's collections was more than a merely visual meeting. Of course visually striking artefacts attracted interest and admiration for their intricate surface carving, ingenious lashing patterns, complex weaving techniques or exquisite shape. Equally important though were auditory, tactile, and olfactory aspects, and upon opening a box, objects were often greeted with dance, songs and personal address: Che Wilson welcomed the artefacts with a Maori greeting; Ani O'Neill analysed the intricate binding of feather objects; Lisa Reihana engaged in conversations with a carved male figure; and Tracey Tawhiao caressed *hei tiki*. On other occasions, Bethany Edmunds enjoyed the smell of Maori cloaks; Wayne Youle, Chris Charteris and Hemi Macgregor talked enthusiastically about the weight of particular stone and whale's tooth neck ornaments; Rosanna Raymond danced as objects were removed from their dark boxes; and Maureen Lander found aesthetic pleasure in the way the light was caught in the shell back of fish hooks. Natalie Robertson and Jason Hall examined the techniques used to make personal adornment pieces; and Filipe Tohi explained

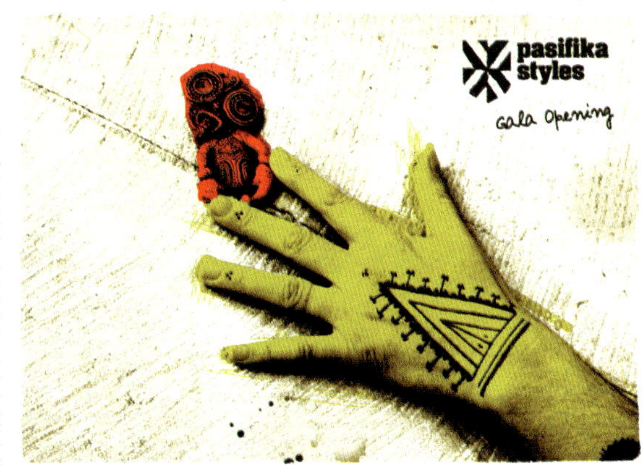

FIG. 75: INVITATION TO THE OPENING OF THE *PASIFIKA STYLES* EXHIBITION, DESIGNED BY DELETE. PHOTOGRAPH: CARINE DURAND.

the mathematical principles lying behind lashing after seeing examples of blades bound to the adzes' hafts. Artefacts were touched, lifted, shaken and smelled. If their condition and materials allowed it, gloves were taken off to enhance the sensory experience. The examining of objects was thus a multisensory 'performance' involving bodily actions such as dance, walking around with the objects, and speech. For the artists, this performativity established an intimacy with the objects' former owners, and also, in a way, with the museum as a safeguarding institution.

During the opening on 5 May 2006, where I was coordinating aspects from catering to *tapu*-lifting and performances, the interaction between artists and museum objects was clear not only to the museum staff but also to the public attending the opening (fig. 75). A carved *taiaha* (fighting staff), from Che Wilson's region of Whanganui, New Zealand, was held by him while he was leading the formal ceremonial opening of the exhibition. During that night's performances one of the museum's *patu pounamu* (greenstone hand clubs), secured by a cord through its handle, was used as a musical gong. A gripping moment during the opening was the playing of a *pūkāea*, a long wooden trumpet from the collections. The Museum holds two such instruments: one was collected on Captain James Cook's first voyage of exploration (1768-1771); the other was acquired in the nineteenth century. The wood of the Cook piece proved too porous to be played, making the other trumpet the only option. Not only was this object handled, touched and lifted, new life was literally blown into it. After it had been silently sleeping for over a century, Jerome Kavanagh, a musician specialising in *taonga pūoro* (Maori musical instruments) gently brought it to life (fig. 74). Relationships between past and present, artists and their ancestors, museum staff, the artists and the public were rekindled and forged as these artefacts were awoken once more.

NOTES

1 These were Ani O'Neill, Che Wilson, Lisa Reihana, Rosanna Raymond, Wayne Youle, Chris Charteris, Filipe Tohi, Hemi Macgregor, Maureen Lander, Natalie Robertson, Jason Hall, Niki Hastings-McFall and Tracey Tawhiao. Bethany Matai Edmunds and Kahutoi Te Kanawa visited the collections during a later visit to Cambridge.

2 Che Wilson's visit, during which he was accompanied by his senior relative Gerrard Albert, formed part of a tribally-funded research project into collections from their area. Chris Charteris's research focused on body adornment pieces which have long been a major influence on his artwork. Both applied for and were awarded grants from the Museum's Crowther Beynon Fund.

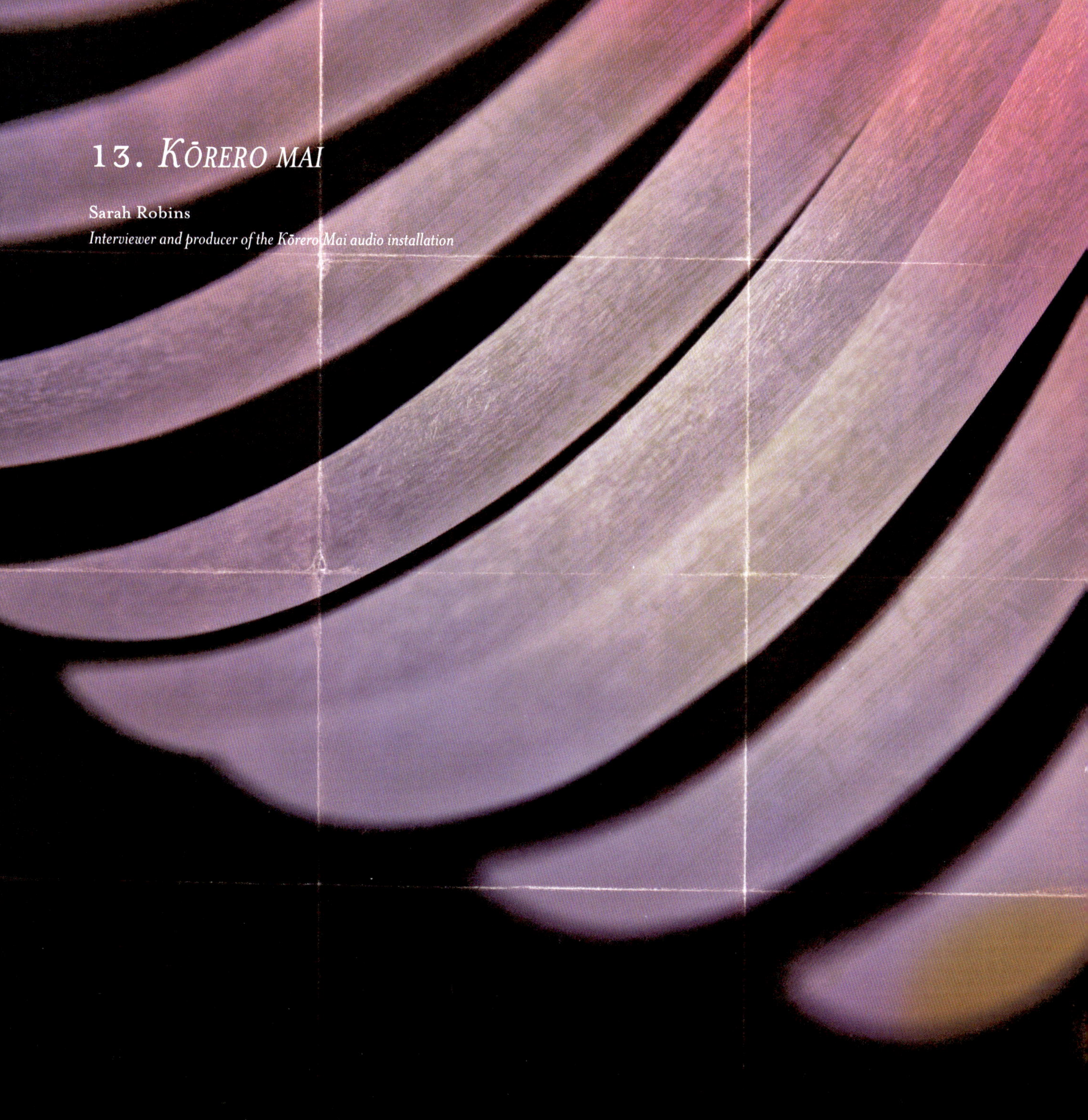

13. *Kōrero Mai*

Sarah Robins
Interviewer and producer of the Kōrero Mai audio installation

Title page Detail of Chris Charteris's *Wasekaseka* (2005).
Photograph: Kerry Brown.

13. *Kōrero mai*[1]

Sarah Robins

Interviewer and producer of the Kōrero Mai audio installation

By and large, audio guides at art museums and galleries tend to be didactic, academic tools designed to give exhibition visitors a greater understanding of a show by placing each artwork in a wider context – historical, political, economic, social etc. – and offering an explanation of the imagery, symbolism and techniques used. While this leads to a greater appreciation of the exhibition, these guides, along with wall texts, usually offer just one perspective – that of the authoritative 'expert' or institution. They are often dry in nature, dense with information and assume a high degree of background knowledge or education. And perhaps most significantly, they can limit our own independent thinking about the work on display. The spoken and written word are so commanding that they demand priority over the act of looking, such that we no longer 'see' the work in front of us and allow our own thoughts to form. In contrast, the *Kōrero mai* audio project was conceived to allow the maker of each artwork a voice in the *Pasifika Styles* exhibition and an opportunity to provide a context or complement of their own choosing to the work.

I had known Rosanna Raymond for several years prior to *Pasifika Styles*. I wrote two or three articles about her work and she, in turn, asked me to write an essay for an exhibition catalogue she produced showcasing her artwork and poetry. For two or three years we tossed around ideas of working on a larger project together – perhaps a Pacific Sisters production would work well in New York? (I was living there at the time)... but the 'Sistas' were now scattered across the globe, complicating the process of putting a show together, raising the costs involved and other projects competed for everyone's time and energy. We let that idea go but Rosanna and I kept in touch, occasionally bouncing ideas around and catching up in person where possible. I was studying radio production when I heard that she and Amiria had launched into preparations for *Pasifika Styles*, and had become reacquainted with an age-old love of listening to people share their stories. It seemed to me that an international – albeit predominantly British - audience such as an institution within the University of Cambridge might attract, would benefit from some contextualisation for the themes that the show would likely address, and what better way than through the voices of the artists themselves? The curatorial team responded positively and quickly to my proposition for an 'alternative audio guide' and in a few short months, Rosanna and Amiria had secured funding to cover the production costs, we'd hammered out a brief and a timeline and I started contacting artists to arrange times to meet and interview them.

I envisaged a range of voices and sounds that would offer greater access to the work and the place and time from which it had sprung. Not only would we hear the contributing artists talking about the creation of their work, the issues that influence them, provoke them, entice them and drive them to create, but we would also gain a greater sense of who they are: accent, the nuances of speech, a sense of attitude and the like. That in their thinking aloud, we, as listeners and viewers, would come to rediscover that thinking is *allowed* ... independent thinking, rather than frustrating attempts to digest great wads of art jargon.

As it was our intention to have as many of the audio tracks as possible available on listening stations at the time of the exhibition opening, the interviews were conducted several months in advance (dates are noted on the transcripts). They are necessarily, therefore, a snapshot in time of each artist's thinking about *Pasifika Styles*, and in some cases, the final artwork differed quite substantially from the work-in-progress at the time the interview was conducted. Although I knew of many of the artists by reputation, I personally knew only a few in advance of the interviews and some of the artists were reticent, understandably suspicious of being recorded. Others were expansive, effusive, funny, nervous, political – again, a snapshot of a moment in time, often amidst everyday life in their studios, homes, or offices. All were sincere and passionate about what they do and why they do it. I didn't ask a standard set of questions of each artist, other than that they introduce themselves in a way they considered appropriate, but ideas and themes were common to many and recurred time and again. Sometimes I reminded the artists that the audience seeing this show may have very limited knowledge of the climate in New Zealand and the Pacific – past or present – which caused them to reassess their words, but in the main, these are their thoughts. My job was primarily to take my voice out of the conversation and edit the interview as honestly as possible. Hopefully a sense of this generation of artists comes across in the audio tracks.

Ever ambitious, *Kōrero mai* was in many ways a work-in-progress itself, even up to the point of production. In its original conception, it was to be a podcast, with additional material added as the exhibition and accompanying festival progressed,

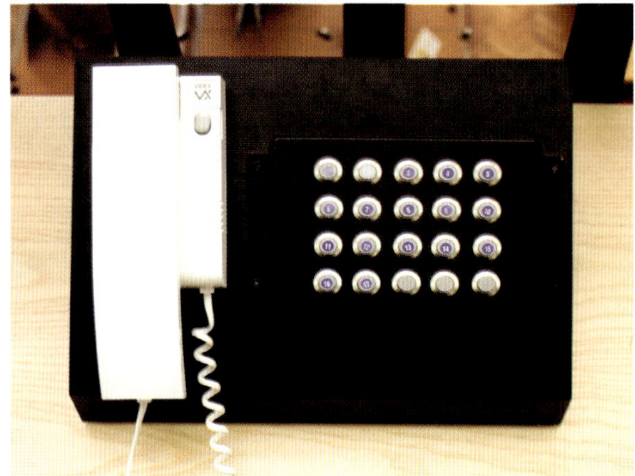

FIG. 76: THE LISTENING POST IN THE GALLERY. PHOTOGRAPH: MUSEUM OF ARCHAEOLOGY AND ANTHROPOLOGY.

with the inclusion of voices responding to the work. Instead, the tracks were made available at listening stations in the exhibition space (fig. 76) and online as downloads. Nevertheless, it has in many ways fulfilled our intentions – acting as a marketing device to attract people to visit the show, an educational tool that informs and entertains either during a visit to the exhibition or at a later date via the website, a source of information for those unable to attend, and an archival resource giving life to the exhibition beyond the gallery and after its completion. In fact, excerpts from the interviews provided the basis for many of the wall texts in the exhibition, allowing the artists to speak about their work in their own terms. I hope you enjoy listening to these artists of our great Pasifika, which are available online at http://www.pasifikastyles.org.uk. I most certainly did, and thank them for sharing their stories with me.

Notes

1 'Speak to me', in Maori.

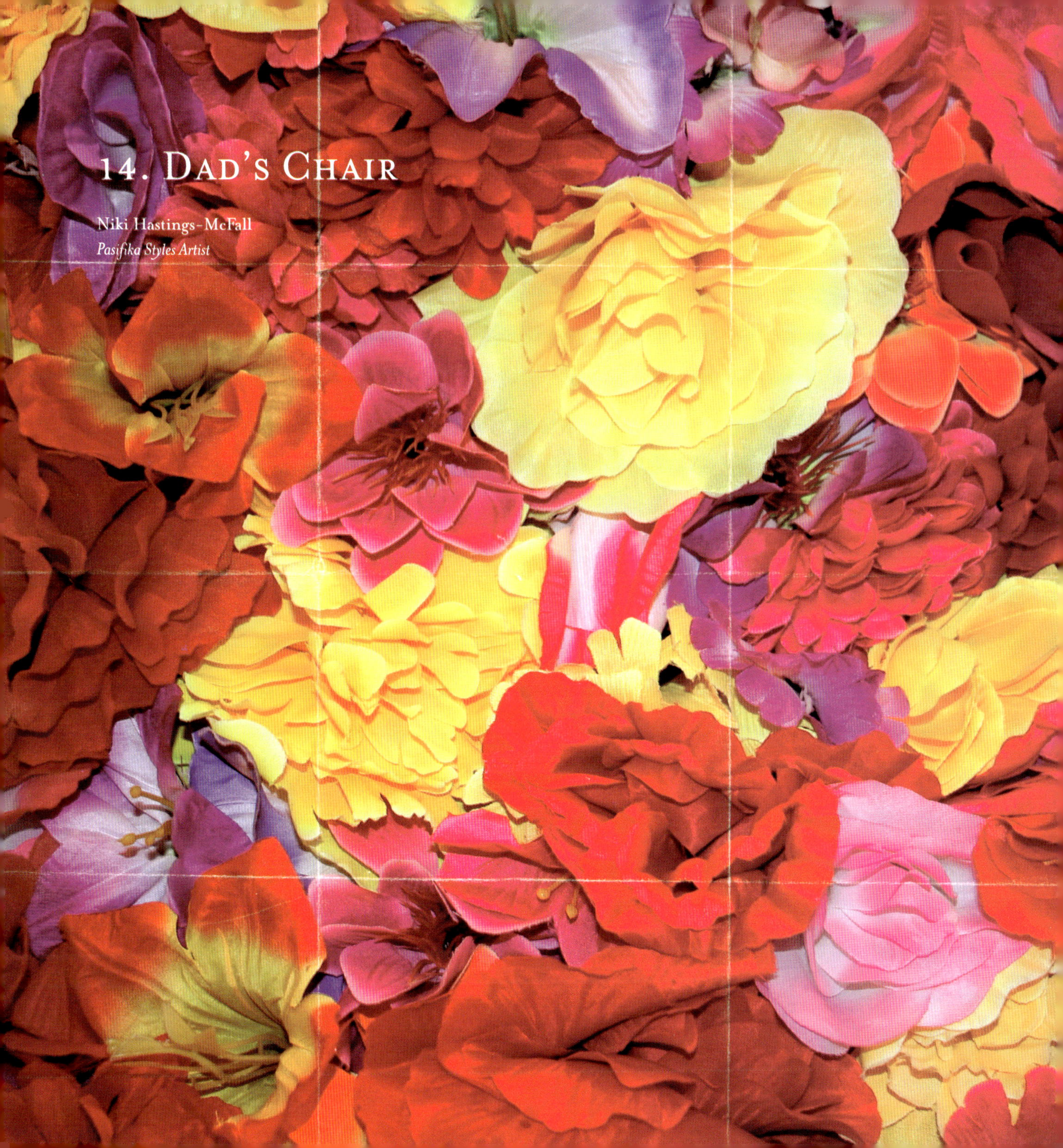

14. Dad's Chair

Niki Hastings-McFall
Pasifika Styles Artist

Detail from *Dad's Chair* (2006) by Niki Hastings-McFall.
Photograph: Amiria Salmond.

14. Dad's Chair

Niki Hastings-McFall
Pasifika Styles Artist

A while ago I heard an interview on National Radio with a Samoan social worker. She was called in to a Polynesian family in South Auckland to assess their situation. The Pakeha[1] social worker who had requested her help felt the children were not cared for adequately. This opinion was founded on the basis that there was very little furniture in the house and they appeared to be living in poverty. The Samoan social worker investigated and found that the children were well cared for. They were well fed, clothed, sent to school regularly and above all they were loved and treasured. They were only poor in the material sense.

On my last trip to Samoa whilst travelling through Upolu and especially Savai`i I frequently noted *fale* (traditional homes without walls) that were clear of furnishings. Save for maybe a wooden pillow or (in one case) a TV on a beer crate, the *fale* were clear of clutter or any Western notion of furniture. Another interesting thing that caught my eye was the 'mile-a-minute' creeper that wound and twisted its way through the forest, smothering, covering and colonising the trees.

I am a Pakeha-Samoan or Afakasi (Samoan transliteration of 'half-caste'). I was born here in Aotearoa and raised by my mother's parents (the *pākeha* or *palagi* side) who were to all intents my mum and dad. I didn't meet my Samoan family until I was over thirty. Through my work I investigate the similarities and differences between the two cultures that constitute my make-up. I make work which speaks of the liminal spaces occupied by people of mixed heritage such as myself.

This series *Polynisation* (with acknowledgment to Jim Vivieaere and Ella Henry for the term) utilises furniture similar to that which I grew up with in the 60s and 70s in Titirangi, West Auckland. Life in the 'burbs'! The synthetic *lei* blooms smother the furniture, inexorably creeping, covering and colonising the Western objects of everyday domestic life. The *lei* (garland necklace) is a symbol of welcome and honour. Here I have returned to the *pākeha* upbringing of my childhood and created a fantasy environment in which the disparate parts of myself have come together in acknowledgment and celebration of both my cultures. Through this work I revisit the past and redress some of the fundamental imbalances that coloured it.

In a wider sense this work also becomes a metaphor for the indomitable spirit of my father's birthplace. The colonised have in turn colonised the colonisers! The Samoan people have generally welcomed the European settlers and their ways (for example Christianity). Rather than being overwhelmed or destroyed they have assimilated some Western ways into their own culture and re-fashioned them until they have become an integral part of the *fa`a Samoa*[2]. While not denying in any way many of the negative results of colonialism's impact, this work celebrates the Samoan culture's vibrancy and it's ability to adapt, evolve and survive within increasingly complex local and global contexts.

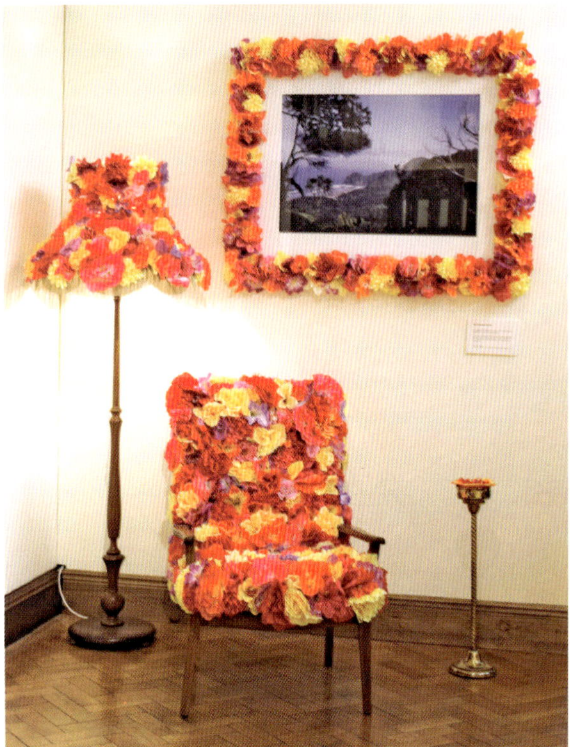

FIG. 77: *DAD'S CHAIR* (2006) BY NIKI HASTINGS-MCFALL. PHOTOGRAPH: KERRY BROWN.

This particular work, *Dad's chair* (2006) (fig. 77) recreates my grandfather's 'spot' in the lounge where he spent long hours relaxing, reading, listening to music and smoking his pipe. The photograph is from his much-loved slide collection, which I have inherited. Dad was a keen amateur photographer and spent many hours tramping round our neck of the woods in the scenic Waitakere ranges west of Auckland, photographing the beauty he saw around him. This particular image is taken from the Anawhata-Piha track looking out over North Piha, which is one of the West Coast's most spectacular places. The floral *lei* have been dismantled and placed around the image in much the same way as my Samoan family adorns and honours their photos.

It seemed so right that this work, with its acknowledgment of both sides of my family, should be sent to sojourn in Cambridge University, or 'Back Home', as mum and dad would say. There is a circular narrative at work here, beginning when my English grandparents migrated to New Zealand in the 1950s, and finally completed fifty years later when I have been able to return some part of my dad in the form of this work to his native land. Following the close of the *Pasifika Styles* exhibition, the image will be handed over to members of our English family who have undertaken to be the *kaitiaki* (caretakers) of this piece of the Pacific.

Notes

1 This term describes a New Zealander of European descent.

2 A traditional term meaning 'the Samoan Way'.

15. *Pasifika Styles*: A visual essay

Kerry Brown

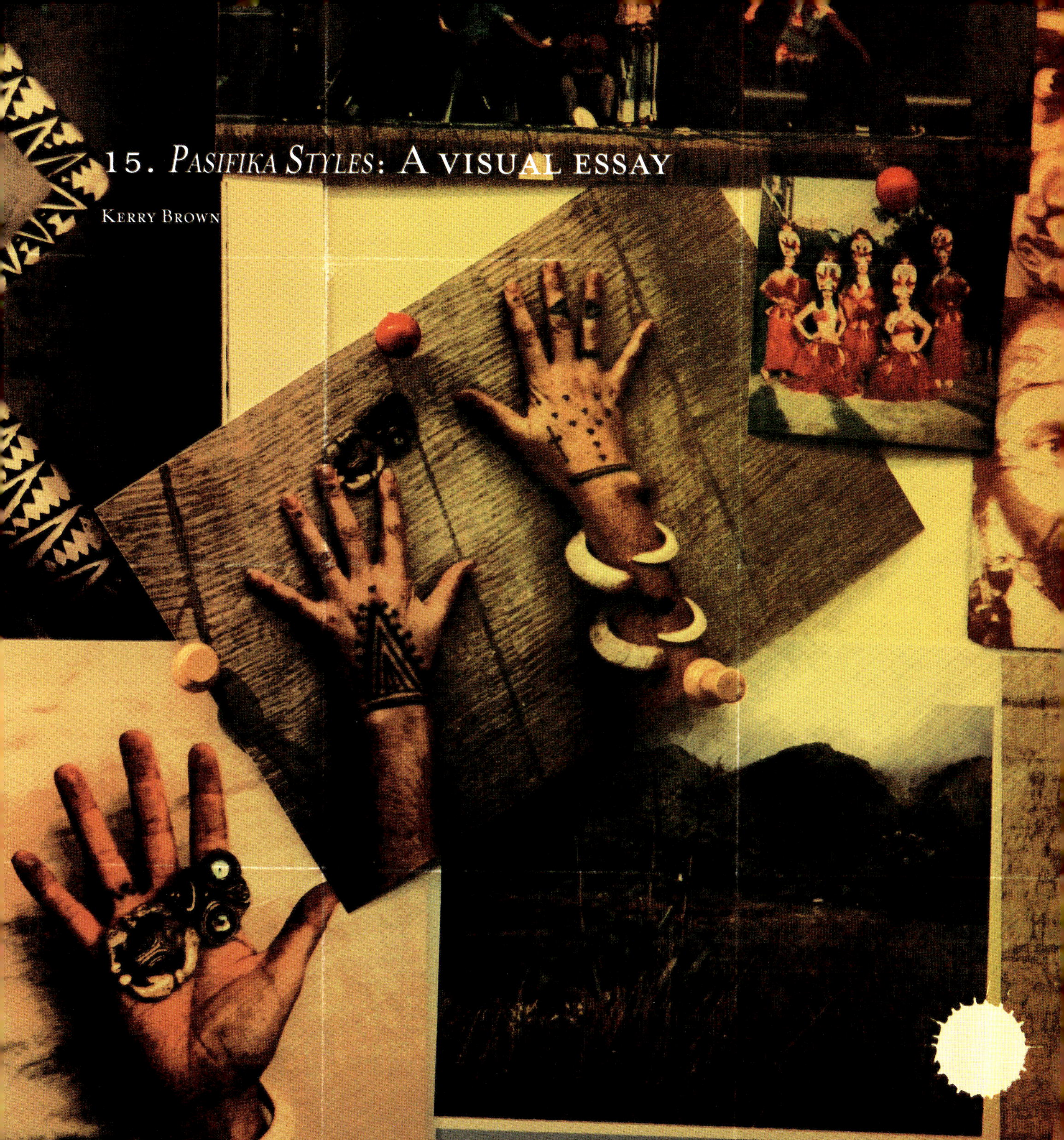

Detail from the installation *Eye land Part II: Welcome 2 da K'lub* (2006) by Rosanna Raymond. Photograph: Kerry Brown.

15. *Pasifika Styles*: A visual essay

Kerry Brown

"This is Pasifika Styles *through my eyes. I was there to capture the new, though it was my sense of the old that showed me where to look".*

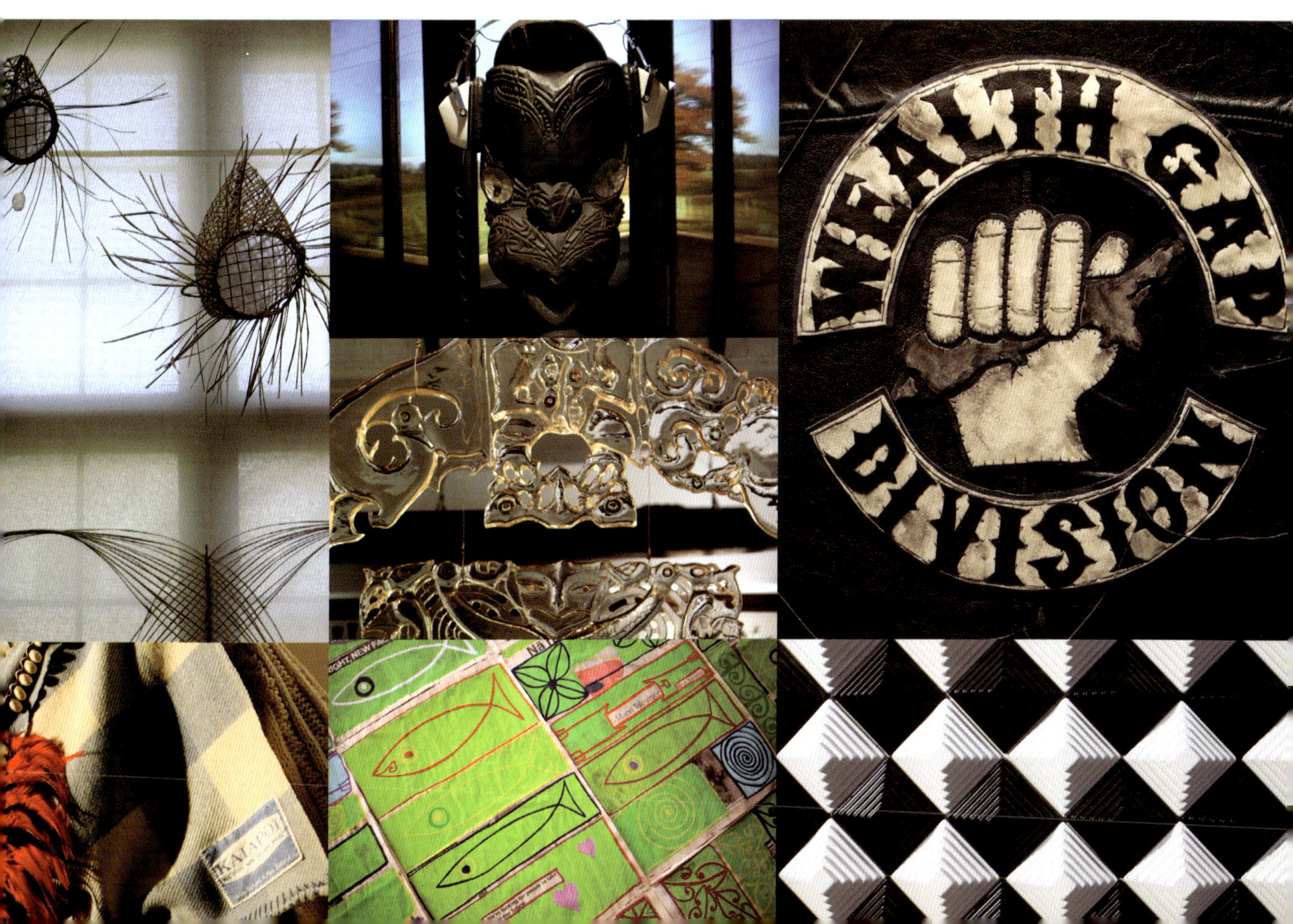

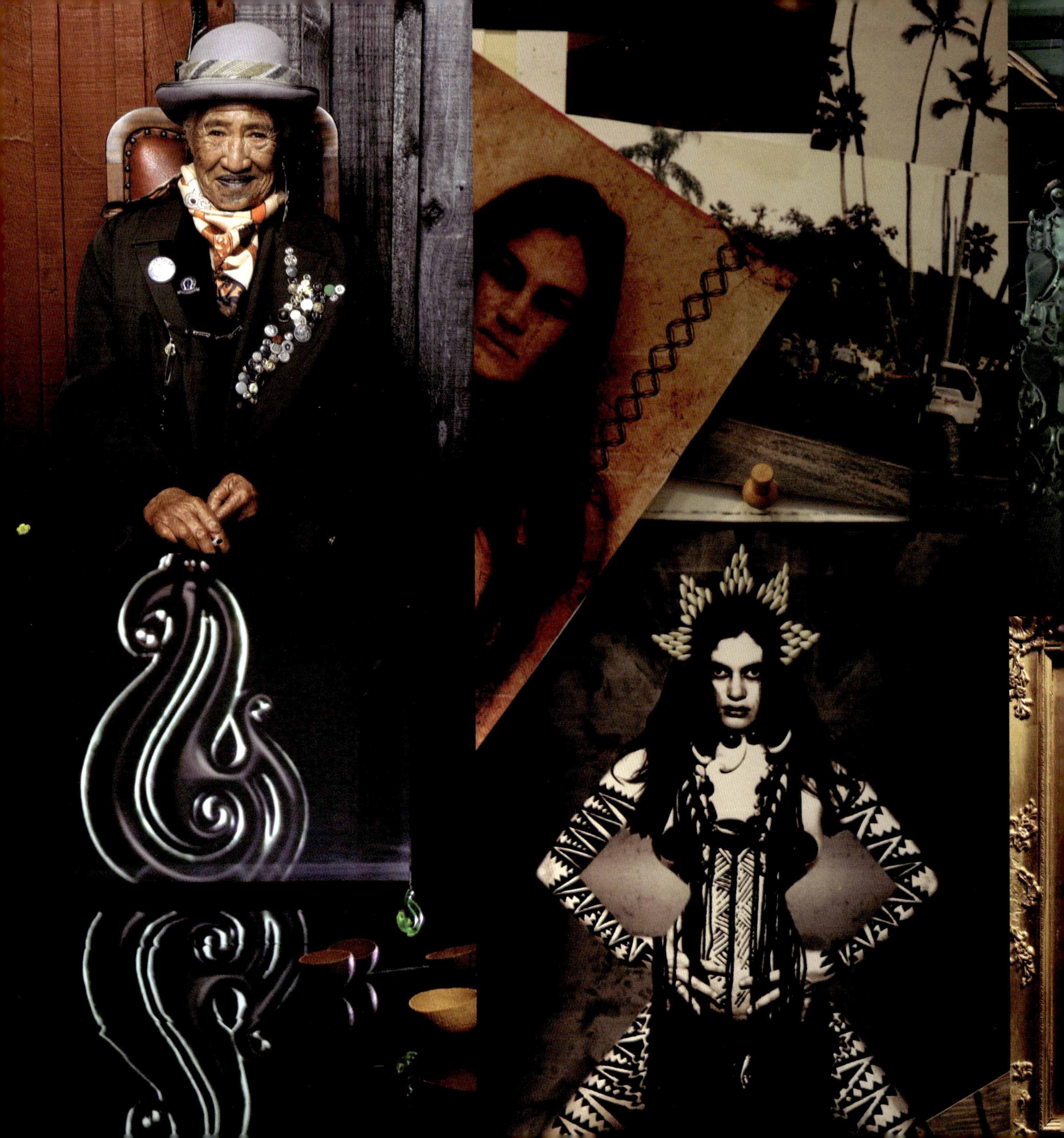

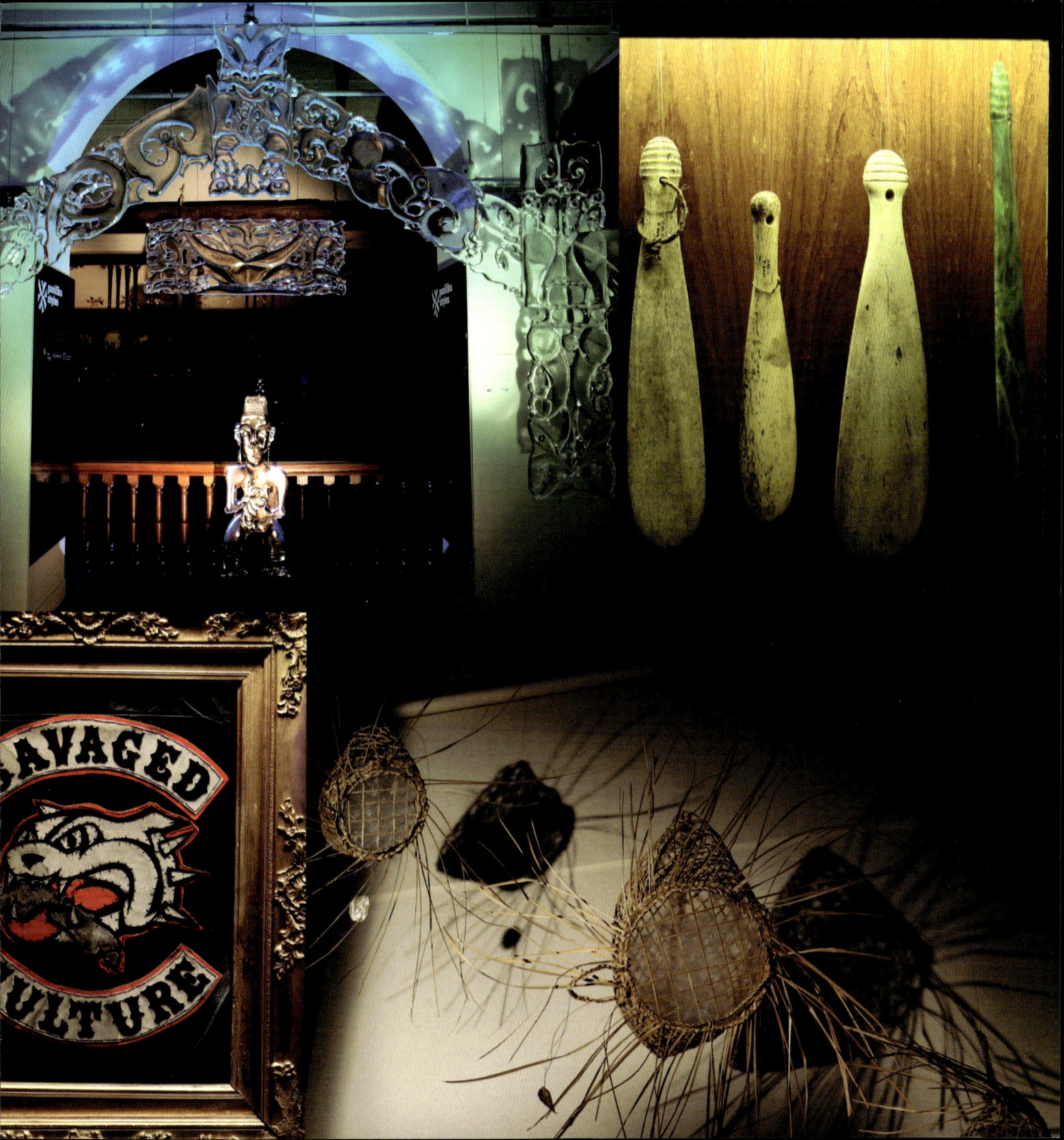
SAVAGED
ULTURE

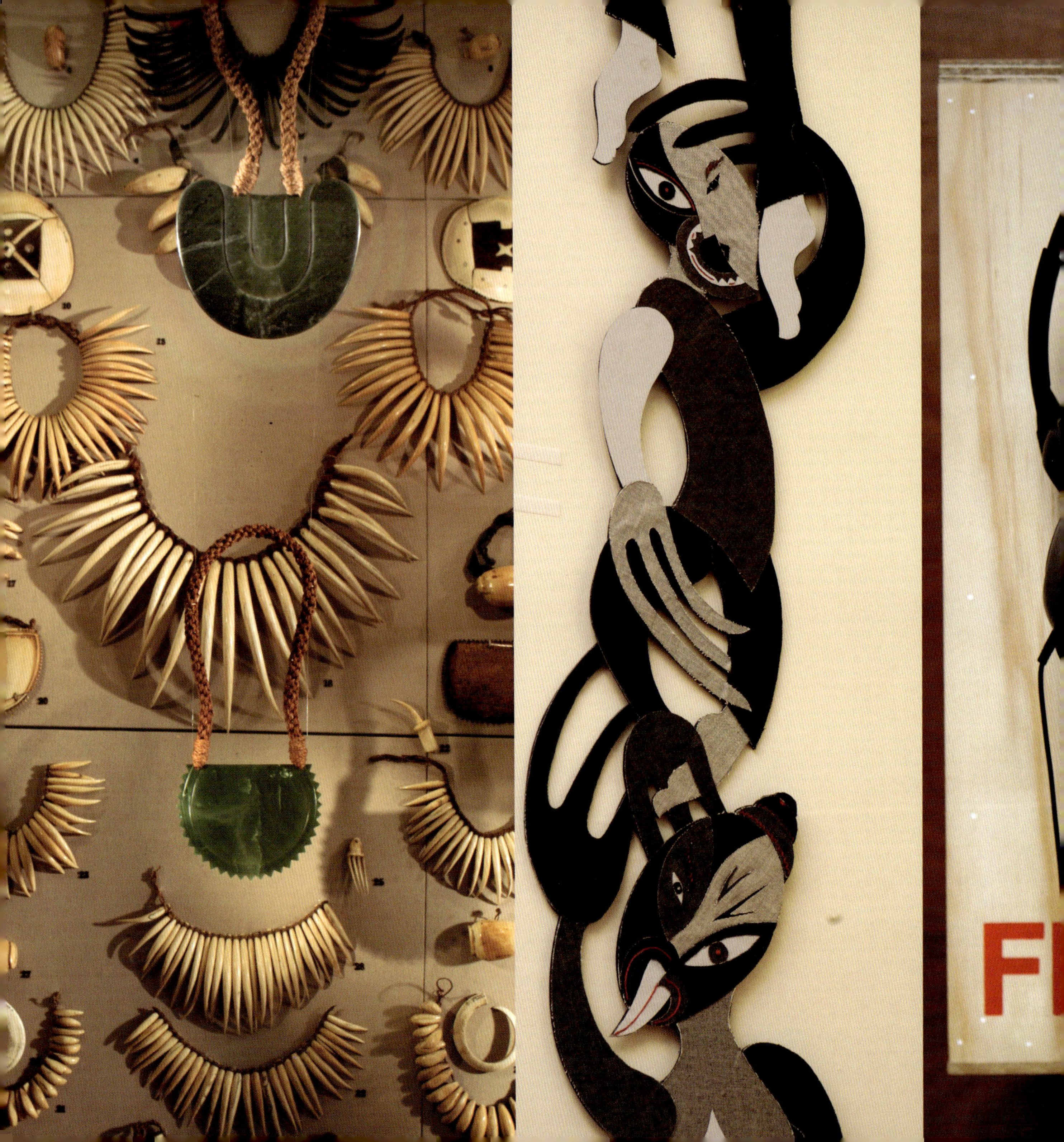

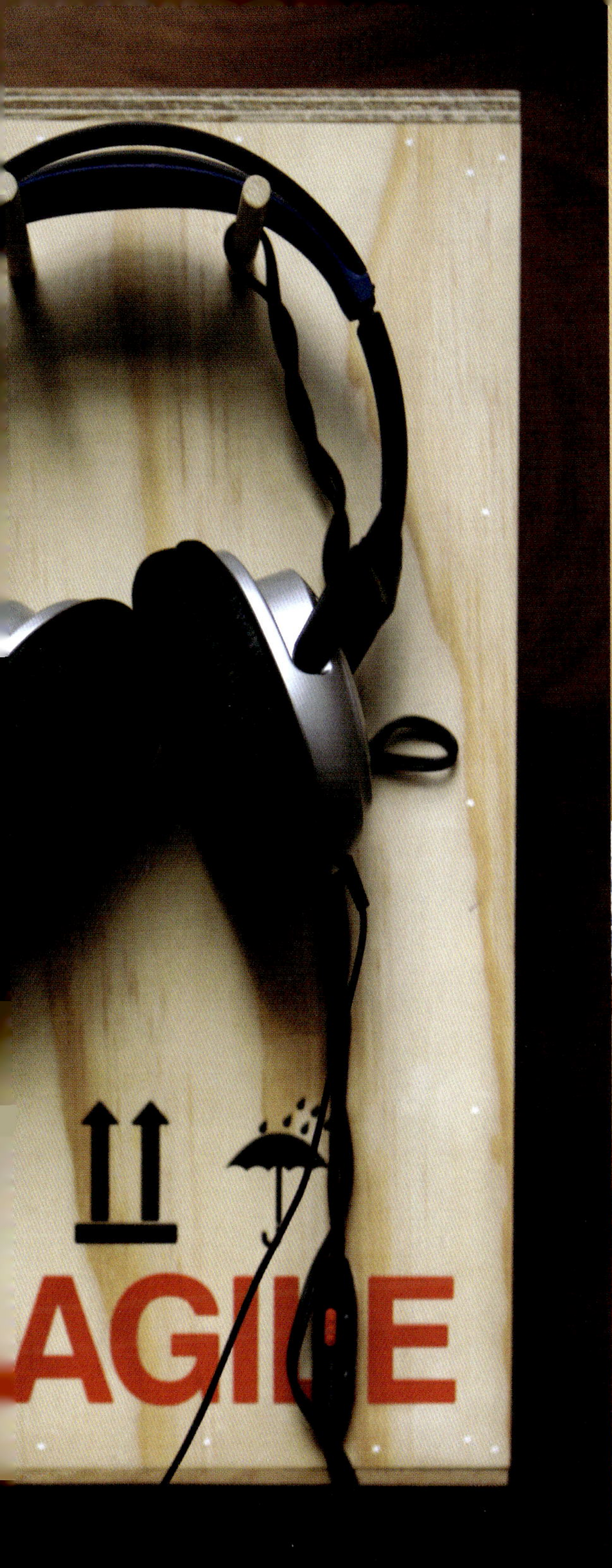

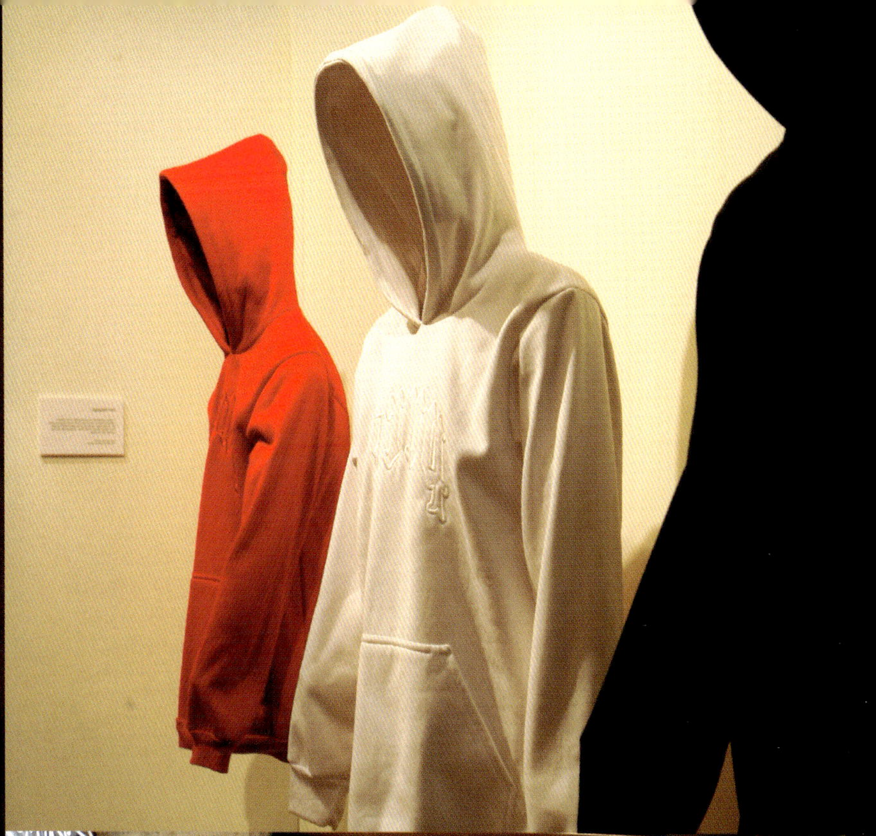

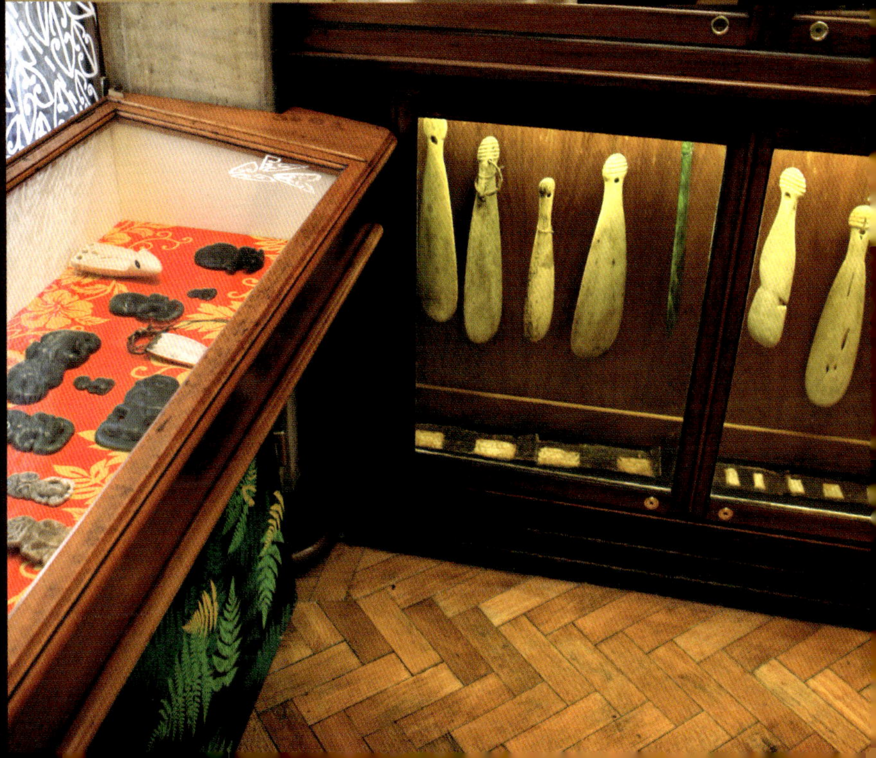

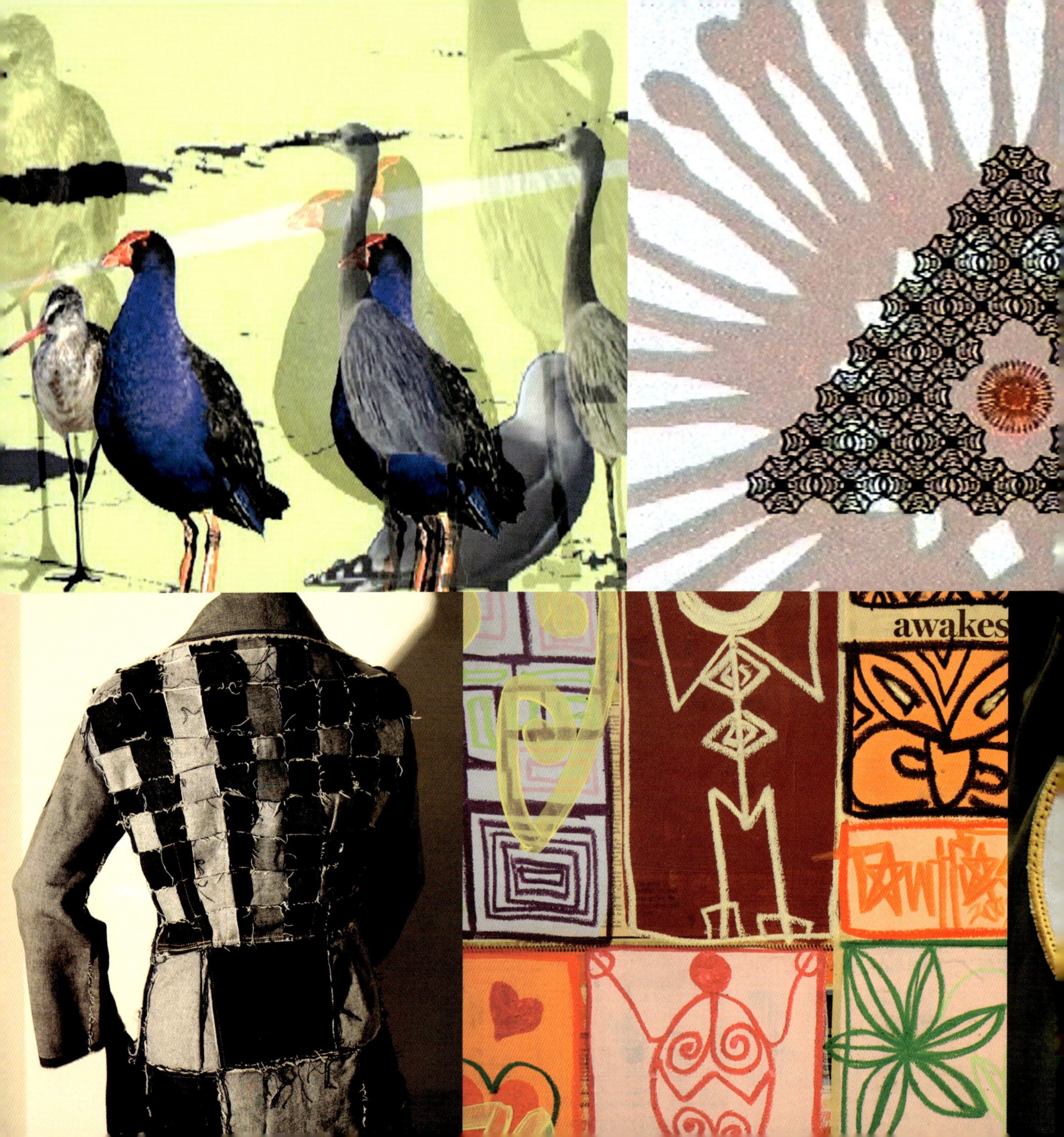
awakes

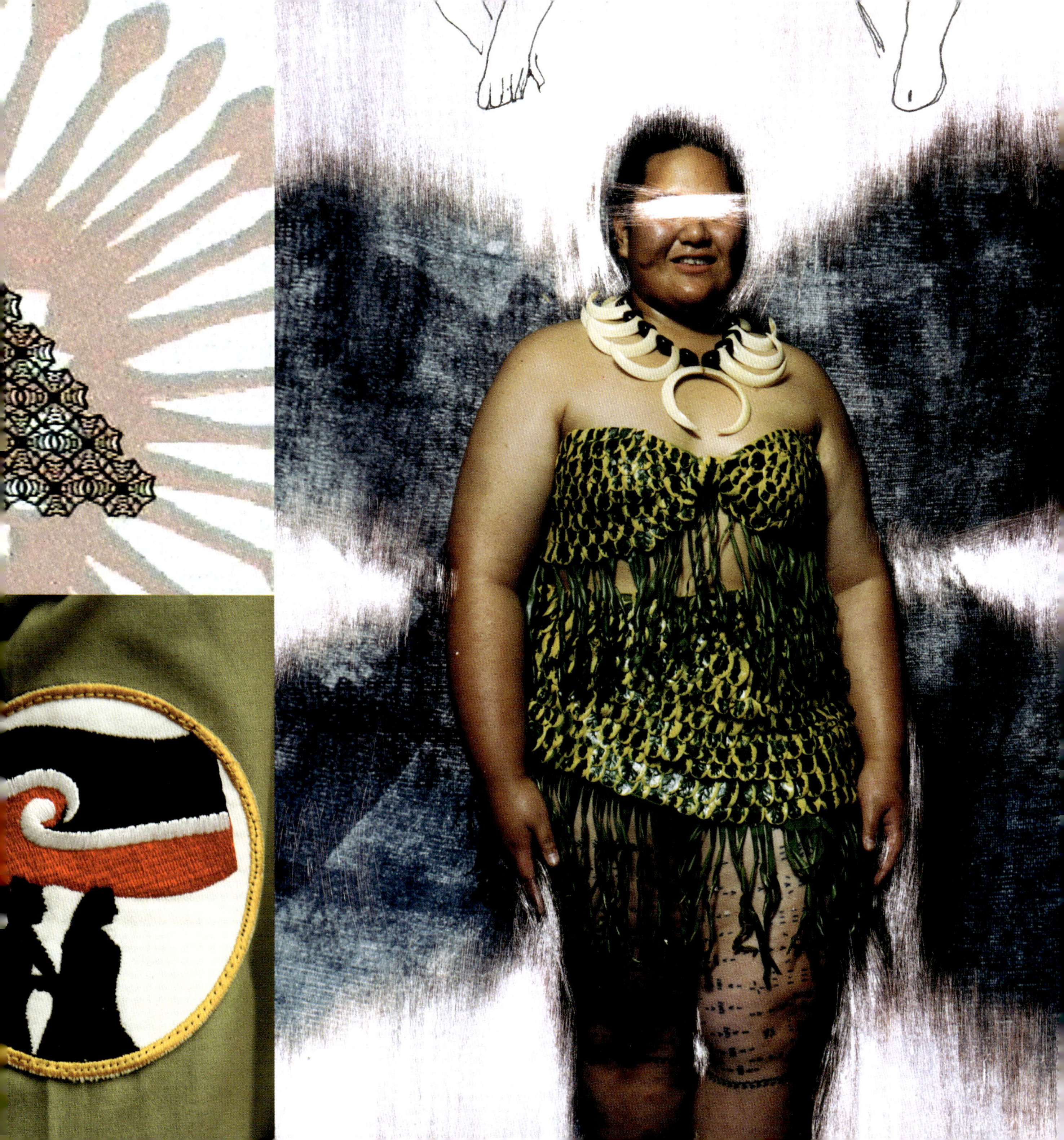

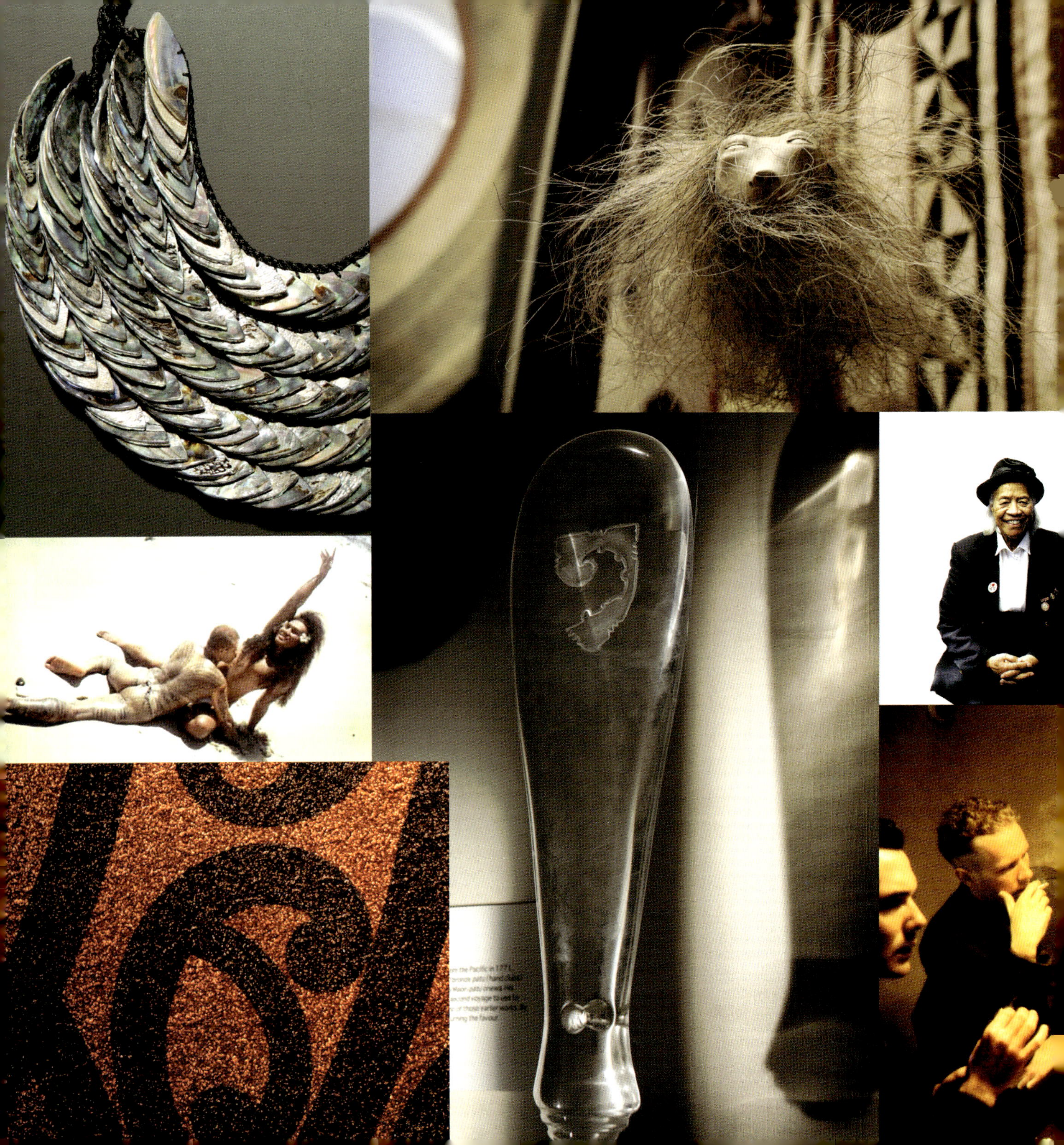

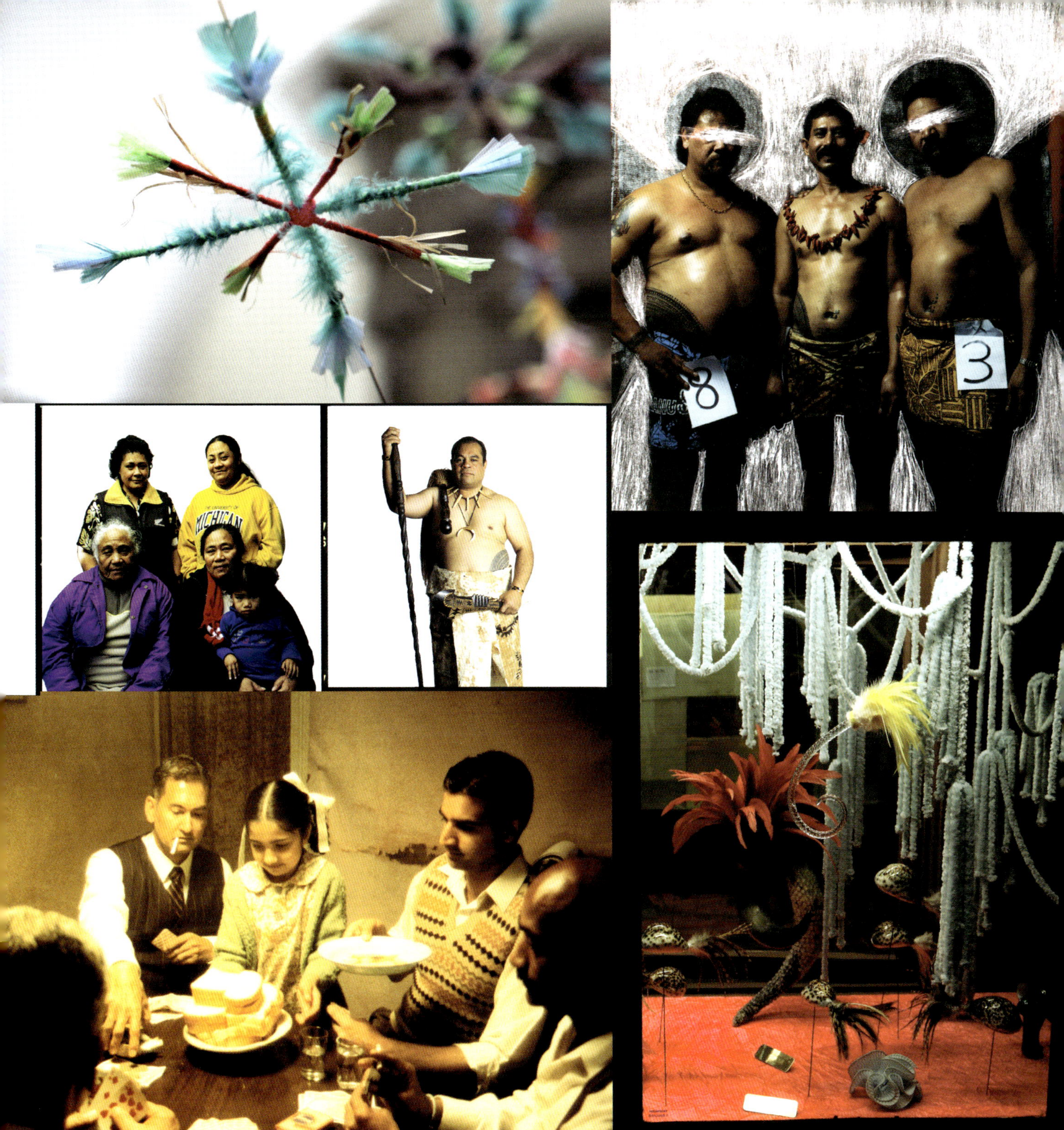
8
3
MICHIGAN

pp. 127

(Clockwise from top left) detail of *Airy-Theory Artefacts* (2006) by Maureen Lander; detail of *he tautoko* (2006) by Lisa Reihana; detail of *Wealth gap division* (2004) by Nick McFarlane; detail of *Tupu`anga (ancestor, origin or source)* (2005) by Filipe Tohi; detail of handpainted wallpaper by Tracey Tawhiao in *The Living Room* (2006); detail of *Bi-cultural Rap Re-mix* (2006) by Suzanne Tamaki; (centre) detail of *Outer Space Marae* (2006) by George Nuku.

pp. 128-129

(Clockwise from top left) *Aotearoa: Land of the wrong white crowd* (2005) by Suzanne Tamaki (photographed by Greg Semu); detail from *Eye land Part II: Welcome 2 da K'lub* (2006) by Rosanna Raymond; *Outer Space Marae* (2006) by George Nuku, detail from *The Living Room* (2006) by Ani O'Neill and Tracey Tawhiao; *Airy-Theory Artefacts* (2006) by Maureen Lander; *Savaged culture* (2004) by Nick McFarlane; still from the video work *Rerenga Pounamu* (2004-05) a collaborative work by Rachel and Otene Rakena.

pp. 130-131

(Left to right) *Kouma* (2005) and *Savageware* (2005) by Chris Charteris, on display among historic Fijian whale ivories; detail of *pART mAOri* (2006) by Bethany Edmunds; *Jack (haki) in the box 1* (2006) by Wayne Youle; detail of *Urge, Purge Pure* (2004) by Hemi Macgregor (top); detail from *The Living Room* (2006) by Ani O'Neill and Tracey Tawhiao (bottom).

pp. 132-133

(Clockwise from top left) Still from the video work *Manukau: place of wading birds* by Sheyne Tuffery; still from the video work *Red* (2002) by Lonnie Hutchinson; Untitled (2006) by Greg Semu; detail of *Fulltime Revolutionary* (2005) by Kewana Duncan; detail of *Heart Infection* (2006) by Tracey Tawhiao; detail of *Rarangarangatahi* (2004) by Jeanine Clarkin.

pp. 134-135

(Clockwise from top left) detail of *Rakiura Southseas necklace* (2006) by Chris Charteris; detail of Sports Heads (2005) by Francis Upritchard; detail of *`etu iti* (2006) by Ani O'Neill; Untitled (2006) by Greg Semu; detail of *fluffy fings* (1998 / 2006) by Lisa Reihana; still from the film Laxmi (2000) by Mandrika Rupa; *Patoo patoo Pasifika* (2006) by George Nuku; detail from *Me at Home* (2006) by Reuben Paterson; still from the film *Sinalela* (2002) by Dan Taulapapa-McMullin; (centre) stills from the video work *South: a portrait of Otara* (2003) by James Pinker and Mark McClean.

Pasifika Styles EXHIBITION:
LIST OF ARTISTS AND WORKS

Donna Campbell

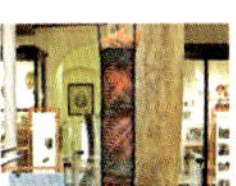

Pacific Totem (2002)
dyed New Zealand flax (*Phormium tenax*), dowel rods, copper wire

Chris Charteris

Wasekaseka (2005)
clear Perspex and linen

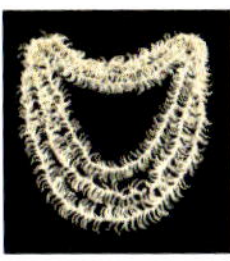

Wedding Lei (2004)
totorere "large ostrich foot" shells, nylon

Wasekaseka (2005)
Black Perspex and cotton

Kouma (2005)
pounamu (greenstone) and coconut fibre

Savageware (2005)
pounamu (greenstone) and coconut fibre

Rakiura Southseas necklace (2006)
paua shell, nylon

Jeanine Clarkin

Papatuanuku Skirt (2004)
denim and fabric ink

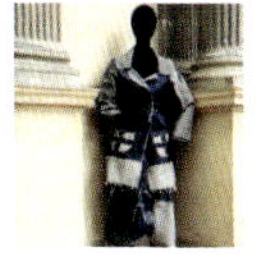

Rarangarangatahi Jacket (2004)
denim

Kewana Duncan

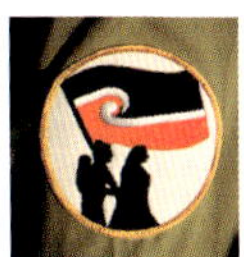

Fulltime Revolutionary (outfit of clothing) (2005)
denim and cotton

Bethany Edmunds

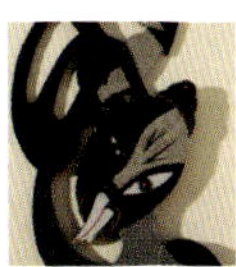

pART mAOri (2006)
denim on hardboard

Jason Hall

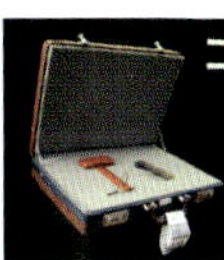

The do-it-yourself repatriation kit (2006)
club hammer, red oxide, brief case

Niki Hastings-McFall

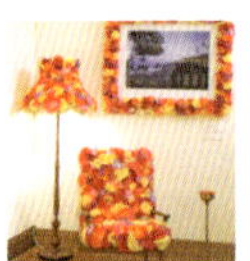

Dad's Chair (2006)

synthetic lei flowers, armchair, ashtray, lamp and printed slide image

Lonnie Hutchinson

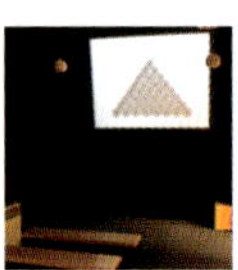

Red (2002)

DVD with soundtrack, 5 mins

Shigeyuki Kihara

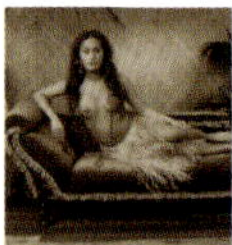

Fa'a fafine: in a manner of a woman (2005)

photographic triptych; C-type photographic prints and mixed media

Maureen Lander

Tane Raises his Eyebrows (2006)

pingao (*Desmoschoenus spiralis*)

Crown grab bag (2006)

pingao (*Desmoschoenus spiralis*), shells

This is not a kete (1994 / 2006)

harakeke or New Zealand flax (*Phormium tenax*)

Mrs Cook's Kete (2002)

(selected items) mixed media

Airy-Theory Artefacts (2006)

harakeke or New Zealand flax (*Phormium tenax*)

Kiwi Identikete (2006)

silver fern, plastic

Nick McFarlane

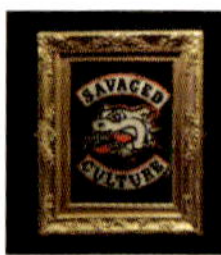

Savaged culture (2004)

hand-stitched leather, broken glass, frame

Domestic violence cycles (2004)

hand-stitched leather, frame

Wealth gap division (2004)

hand-stitched leather, broken glass, frame

Hemi Macgregor

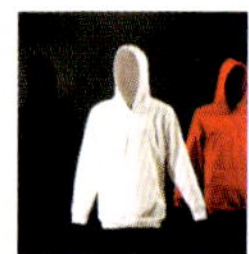

Urge, Purge Pure (2004)

embroidered hooded sweatshirts

George Nuku

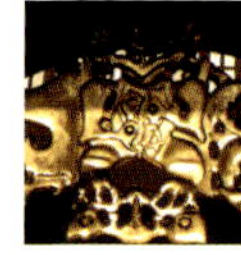

Outer Space Marae (2006)

carved acrylic plastic

Patoo patoo Pasifika (2006)

carved acrylic plastic

Pou whenua (2006)

carved acrylic plastic

Wahaika (2006)

carved acrylic plastic

Tewhatewha (2006)

carved acrylic plastic

Ani O'Neill

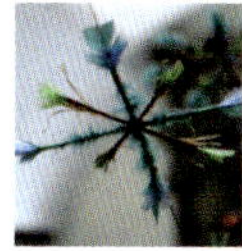

`etu iti (2006)

mixed media: *kikau* (Coconut midrib), feathers, raffia, shells, seeds, beads, sequins, videotape, re-cycled plastic, wool

Ani O'Neill and Tracey Tawhiao

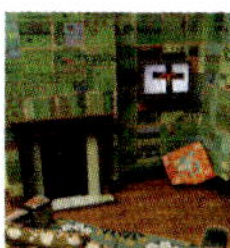

The Living Room (2006)

mixed media installation

Reuben Paterson

Everywhere you go, always take the weather with you (2004-05)

glitter on canvas

Slaughter something innocent (2006

glitter on canvas

Leaving (2006)

glitter on canvas

Me at Home (2006)

glitter on canvas

James Pinker and Mark McClean

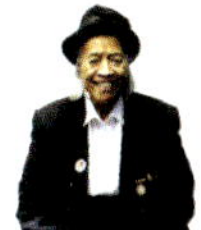

South: a portrait of Otara (2003)

DVD, 75 mins

Louise Potiki-Bryant

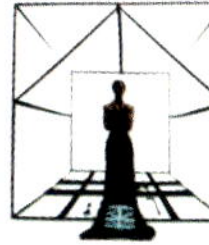

Whakaruruhau (2005)

DVD, 16 mins

Rachel Rakena

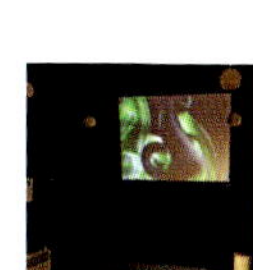

Rerenga Pounamu (2004-05)

a collaborative work with Otene Rakena

single-channel video with sound, 12 mins

Rosanna Raymond

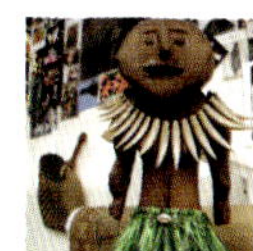

Eye land Part II: Welcome 2 da K'lub (2006)

mixed media

Lisa Reihana

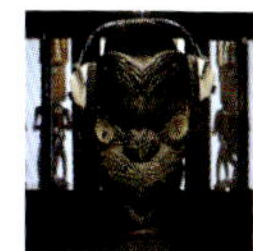

he tautoko (2006)

DVD (35 mins.), headphones, audio (3x10 mins.), and *tekoteko* figure collected by Baron Charles von Hugel, probably at the Bay of Islands, New Zealand (CUMAA 1939.70).

fluffy fings (1998)

horns, dyed chicken feathers, ostrachionte shells, lead crystal, fur, textiles

Hongi Hika BA (Cantab.): "an emblem of wisdom...?" (2006)

College scarves, goat hair, braid

Natalie Robertson and Hemi Macgregor

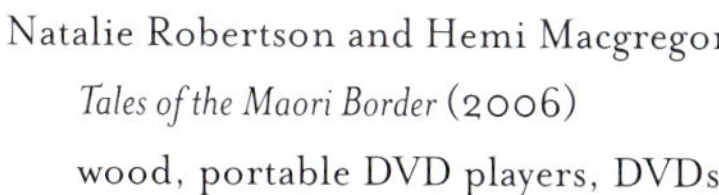

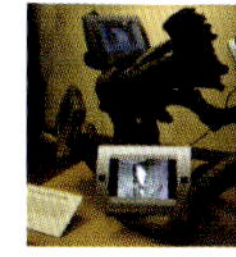

Tales of the Maori Border (2006)

wood, portable DVD players, DVDs

Mandrika Rupa

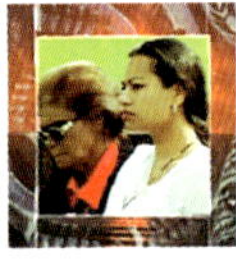

Taamara/Sangam (The joining of two peoples) (2002)

Beta SP, 58 mins

Greg Semu

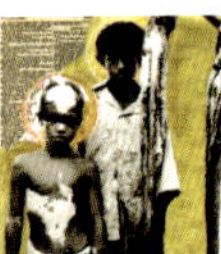

Untitled (2006)

elaborated black & white photographic print

Untitled (2006)

elaborated colour photographic print

Untitled (2006)

elaborated black & white photographic print

Suzanne Tamaki

Aotearoa: Land of the wrong white crowd (2005)

Lambda print, photographed by Greg Semu

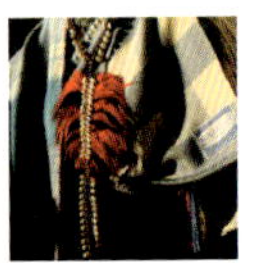

Bi-cultural Rap Re-mix (2006)

recycled and restructured New Zealand blankets with wool blanket stitch trim and pom poms, feather collar, and wool hat with feather trim

Lisa Taouma

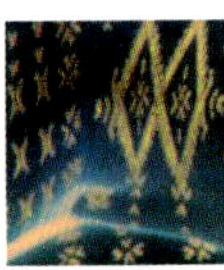

Represent (2006)

DVD documentary, 20 minutes

Dan Taulapapa-McMullin

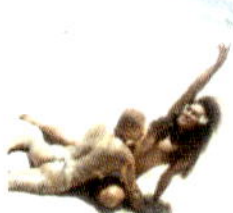

Sinalela (2002)

Short film

Tracey Tawhiao

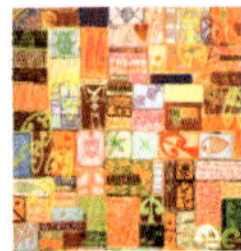

Heart Infection (2006)

mixed media on canvas

Filipe Tohi

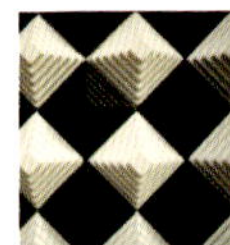

Tupu` anga (ancestor, origin or source) (2005)

plastic

Michel Tuffery

Lau mea ola Laiti (1988)

MDF board sealed with oil-based ink

Insects from Samoa (1988)

MDF board sealed with oil-based ink

Fa'a Samoa Matai (1988)

MDF board sealed with oil-based ink

Halfcasting Samoan Fishingman (1999)

MDF board sealed with oil-based ink

Pili Pili Pili Siva (1999)

MDF board sealed with oil-based ink

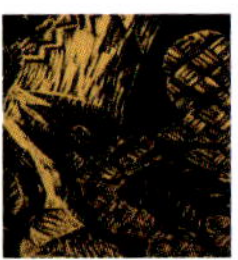

Trading Fish from Samoa (1999)

MDF board sealed with oil-based ink

Sheyne Tuffery

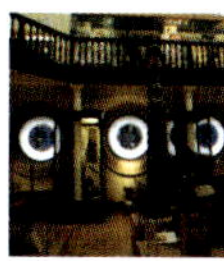

Manu tawhiti tahi (2006)
digital print on vinyl

Manu tawhiti rua (2006)
digital print on vinyl

Sa-Moa (2006)
digital print on vinyl

Manukau: place of wading birds
DVD, 3 mins 30

Francis Upritchard

Jealous Saboteurs (2005)
Modified and elaborated hockey sticks

Sports Heads (2005)
Modified and elaborated sports equipment

Che Wilson

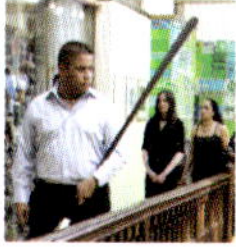

Pasifika Styles (2006)
Waiata (song)

Wayne Youle

Hahea (2006)
light box

Thanks to the magic of religion and television 1 (2006)
pine box with security TV

Thanks to the magic of religion and television 2 (2006)
pine box with DVD player

Te Manawa (2006)
light box

Jack (haki) in the box 1 (2006)
sound box with cd player on continuous loop

Jack (haki) in the box 2 (2006)
sound box with cd player on continuous loop

Glossary of Polynesian* terms

Note on the use of macrons:

Macrons, or horizontal accents above vowels, indicate a long vowel sound in the Maori language. Their use in text is preferred by many Maori speakers, including contributors to this volume. Here they are used on Maori words, but not for words that are proper nouns used in common parlance in English, such as 'Maori' or 'Pakeha' (though they are retained where *pākeha* is used adjectivally).

Ao Maori	the Maori world
aroha	fellow feeling, love, compassion
fale	house (Samoan)
fa`afafine	man who lives as a woman (Samoan)
fa`a Samoa	the Samoan way
hei tiki	neck pendant representing ancestral being
hui	meeting, gathering
kai	food
kaitiaki	guardian
kanohi	face
karakia	prayer, incantation
karanga	a high, haunting call to summon ancestors
kaupapa	guiding purpose
kete	woven bag, basket
kōrero	speak, talk
kōwhaiwhai	curvilinear painted rafter patterns in a meeting-house
kuia	female elder
lei	flower or shell garland, necklace (various, Hawaiian)
mere pounamu	greenstone hand weapon
moko	tattoo
māori	everyday, ordinary; indigenous people of New Zealand
marae	ceremonial meeting ground
pākeha	New Zealander of European descent
pālagi	Person of European descent (Samoan)
pe`a	thigh and buttock tattoo (Samoan)
pounamu	greenstone
pū kāea	trumpet
pūkana	ritual challenge, extending the tongue
rāpaki	woven skirt, kilt
rito	the heart of a flax bush
siapo	bark-cloth (Samoan)
taiaha	fighting staff
tangata, tāngata	person, people
tagata	people (Samoan)
tā moko	the art of tattoo
taonga	ancestral treasure
taonga pūoro	musical instrument

tapa	bark-cloth (Tahitian)
tapu	sacred – ancestral presence and power
tatau	tattoo (Samoan, Tahitian)
tautoko	support
tekoteko	gable figure on a meeting house
tikanga	customary practices
tino rangatiratanga	full chiefly authority
tuahine	sister
tuakana	senior same sex sibling, relative
tukutuku	woven wall panels i-n a meeting house
waharoa	carved entrance
waiata	song, chant
wānanga	ancestral knowledge, session where this is shared
whakairo	carving
whakapapa	genealogy
whakarite	spiritually prepare
whakawātea	spiritually clear, cleanse
whakawhetai	give thanks
wharenui	lit. 'large house;' meeting house
whare wānanga	school of learning

* New Zealand Maori unless otherwise indicated

Bibliography

Ames, Michael 2003. 'How to decorate a house: the renegotiation of cultural representations at the University of British Columbia Museum of Anthropology', in Peers and Brown (eds.), pp. 171-180

Appadurai, Arjun 1986. 'Introduction: commodities and the politics of value', in Appadurai, Arjun (ed.), *The Social Life of Things: Commodities in cultural perspective*. Cambridge: Cambridge University Press, pp. 3-63

Auckland City Art Gallery 1986. Te Maori, *Te Hokinga Mai: The return home*, Auckland: Auckland City Art Gallery / New Zealand Te Maori Management Committee

Bennett, Tony 1995. *The Birth of the Museum: History, Theory, Politics*. London: Routledge

Bevan-Ford, John 1994. *Some thoughts on Maori Carving*. Palmerston North: Massey University Press

Brown, Deidre and Ellis, Ngarino (eds.) 2007. *Te Puna: Maori art from Tai Tokerau Northland*. Auckland: Reed Publishing

Cartwright, Garth 2007. 'The Living and the dead', *New Zealand Listener* 207(3485): 36-40

Clifford, James 1985. 'Histories of the Tribal and the Maori', *Art in America* (April 1985): 164-177

--- 1997. *Routes: Travel and Translation in the Late Twentieth Century*. London: Harvard University Press

Coles, Alex 2000. *Site-Specificity: The Ethnographic Turn*. London: Blackdog publications

Corrin, Lisa G. 1994. 'Mining the Museum: Artists look at museums, museums look at themselves', in Corrin, Lisa G. (ed.). *Mining the Museum: an installation by Fred Wilson*. New York: The New Press, pp. 1-22

Dunn, Michael 2002. *New Zealand Sculpture: A history*. Auckland: Auckland University Press

Edwards, Elizabeth, Gosden, Chris and Phillips, Ruth (eds.) 2006. *Sensible objects: Colonialism, Museums and Material Culture*. Oxford: Berg

Eleey, Peter 2005. 'Time and Place', *Frieze* 95: 115

Faris, James C. 1988. '"ART/artifact": On the Museum and Anthropology'. *Current Anthropology* 29(5): 775-779

Foster, Hal 1995. 'The Artist as Ethnographer', in Marcus and Myers (eds.), pp. 302-309

Gathercole, Peter 2002. '*Te Maori* in the Longer View', in Herle et al. (eds.), pp. 271-279

Gunn, Wendy (ed.) 2005. *Creativity and Practice Research Papers*, Nethergate: Creativity and Practice Research Group Visual Research Centre Dundee Contemporary Arts University of Dundee

--- 2005. 'Learning within the workplaces of artists, anthropologists and architects: making stories for drawings and writings', in Gunn (ed.), pp. 1-11

Henare (Salmond), Amiria 2003. 'Artefacts in Theory: Anthropology and Material Culture', *Cambridge Anthro-*

pology 23(2): 54-66

--- 2005. *Museums, Anthropology and Imperial Exchange*. Cambridge: Cambridge University Press

Henare (Salmond), Amiria, Holbraad, Martin, and Wastell, Sari (eds.), *Thinking through things: theorizing artifacts ethnographically*, Oxford: Routledge

Herle, Anita 1994. 'Museums and Shamans: a cross-cultural collaboration'. *Anthropology Today* 10(1): 2-5

--- 2003. 'Objects, agency and museums: continuing dialogues between the Torres Strait and Cambridge', in Peers and Brown (eds.), pp. 194-207

Herle, Anita et al. (eds.) 2002. *Pacific Art: Persistence, Change and Meaning*. Adelaide: Crawford House Publishing

Hooper-Greenhill, Eilean 1989. 'The Museum in the Disciplinary Society', in Pearce, Susan (ed.), *Museum Studies in Material Culture*, London: Leicester University Press, pp. 61-72

Ingold, Tim 2000. *The Perception of the Environment: Essays in Livelihood, Dwelling and Skill*. London and New York: Routledge

Jacknis, Ira 1985. 'Franz Boas and Exhibits: On the Limitations of the Museum Method of Anthropology', in Stocking (ed.), pp. 75-111

Kent, Rachel 1999. 'Artists and museums: a working partnership'. *Artlink* 19:1: 10-13

Latour, Bruno 2005. 'From Realpolitik to Dingpolitik or How to Make Things Public', in Latour, Bruno and Weibel, Peter (eds.). *Making things public: Atmospheres of Democracy*. Cambridge, Mass.: MIT Press, pp. 14-41

Lavine, Steven D. 1992. 'Audience, Ownership, and Authority: Designing Relations between Museums and Communities', in Karp, Ivan, Kreamer, Christine Mullen, and Lavine, Steven D. (eds.). *Museums and Communities: The Politics of Public Culture*. Washington: Smithsonian Institution

Leach, James 2004. 'Disciplinary specialisation and collaborative endeavour. some challenges presented by sci-art projects', in Gunn (ed.), pp. 11-23

--- 2007. 'Differentiation and Encompassment: A critique of Alfred Gell's theory of the abduction of creativity', in Henare, Holbraad, and Wastell (eds.), pp. 167-188

Lippard, Lucy 1997. *The Lure of the Local: Senses of Place in a Multicentered Society*. New York: The New Press

Macdonald, Sharon 2002. *Behind the Scenes at the Science Museum*. Oxford: Berg

Mallon, Sean and Pereira, Pandora Fulimalo (eds.) 2002. *Pacific Art Niu Sila: The Pacific Dimension of Contemporary New Zealand Arts*. Wellington: Te Papa Press

Mane-Wheoki, Jonathan 1995. 'The Resurgence of Maori Arts: Conflicts and Continuities in the Eighties', *Contemporary Pacific* 7(1): 1-2

Marcus, George and Myers, Fred (eds.) 1995. *The Traffic in Culture*. Berkeley: University of California Press

Mason, Ngahiraka 2005. 'Open for Interpretation', *Art New Zealand* 54: 105

Matthews, Philip 2007. 'Gifts from home'. *New Zealand Listener* 207(3485): 38

Mead, Sidney Moko (ed.) 1984. Te Maori: *Maori Art from New Zealand Collections*, Auckland: Heinemann

Moutu, Andrew 2007. 'A polyphonic collage at the University of Cambridge Museum of Archaeology and Anthropology' (exhibition review), *Anthropology Today* 23(2): 24-25

Myers, Fred R. 2005. '*Paradise Now? Contemporary Art from the Pacific*, Asia Societies Galleries, New York, New York, 18 February - 9 May 2004' (exhibition review), *The Contemporary Pacific* 17(1): 273-277

Ngati Ranana website: www.ngatiranana.org.uk

Pasifika Styles web-log: www.pazifikastyles2006.blogspot.com

Pasifika Styles website, http://wwwpasifikastyles.org.uk

Panoho, Rangihiroa 1990. Te Moemoea No Iotefa, *the Dream of Joseph: A Celebration of Pacific Art and Taonga*. Wanganui: Sarjeant Gallery

Peers, Laura and Alison Brown (eds.) 2003. *Museums and Source Communities: A Routledge Reader.* London: Routledge

Phillips, Ruth 1998. *Trading Identities: The Souvenir in Native North American Art from the Northeast 1700-1900.* Seattle: University of Washington Press, Montreal: McGill-Queen's University Press

Peterson, Giles 2006. 'Pacific New Wave' (exhibition review), *Art Asia Pacific* 52: 66-67

Price, Sally 1991. *Primitive art in civilized places.* Chicago (IL): University of Chicago Press

Raymond, Rosanna 2003. 'Getting Specific: Fashion Activism in Auckland during the 1990s: A Visual Essay', in Colchester, Chlo' (ed.), *Clothing the Pacific.* Oxford: Berg, pp. 193-209

Robley, Horatio 1896. *Moko or Maori Tattooing.* London: Chapman and Hall.

Rosoff, Nancy B. 2003. 'Integrating Native views into museum procerdures: hope and practice at the National Museum of the American Indian', in Peers and Brown (eds.), pp. 72-80

Schneider, Arnd 1996. 'Uneasy Relationships: Contemporary Artists and Anthropology', *Journal of Material Culture 1*: 183-210

Schneider, Arnd and Wright, Christopher (eds.) 2006. *Contemporary Art and Anthropology.* Oxford: Berg

Shand, Peter 2002. 'Scenes from the colonial catwalk: Cultural appropriation, intellectual property rights and fashion'. *Cultural Analysis* 3: 47-88

Simpson, Moira G. 2001. *Making Representations: Museums in the Post-colonial Era*, London: Routledge

Smith, Roberta 2004. 'Art Review *Paradise Now?*: The beauty of the Pacific, enshrined and exploited', *New York Times* 5 March 2004: http://query.nytimes.com

Stanhope, Zara, 1999. 'The mirror in the archive box' (editorial). *Artlink* 19:1: 8-9

Stanley, Nick (ed.) 2007. *The Future of Indigenous Museum: Perspectives from the Southwest Pacific.* Oxford and New York: Berghahn Books

Stevenson, Karen 2002. 'The Island in the Urban: Contemporary Pacific Art in New Zealand', in Herle, et al. (eds.), pp. 404-414.

--- 2004. 'Refashioning the Label, Reconstructing the Cliche: A Decade of Contemporary Pacific Art, 1990-2000', in *Paradise Now? Contemporary Art from the Pacific.* Auckland: David Bateman Ltd, pp. 20-33

Stocking, George W. 1985. *Objects and Others: Essays on Museums and Material Culture.* Madison: The University of Wisconsin Press

Strathern, Marilyn 1990. 'Artefacts of History: Events and the interpretation of images', in Siikala, J. (ed.), *Culture and History in the Pacific* (Transactions No. 27). Helsinki: Finnish Anthropological Society

Te Papa Tongarewa website: http://tpo.tepapa.govt.nz

Thomas, Nicholas 1996a. 'The Dream of Joseph: Practices of Identity in Pacific Art', *The Contemporary Pacific* 8(2): 291-317

--- 1996b. 'From Exhibit to Exhibitionism: Recent Polynesian Presentations of "Otherness"', *The Contemporary Pacific* 8(2): 319-348

---1999. *Possessions: Indigenous Art, Colonial Culture.* London: Thames and Hudson

Vercoe, Caroline 2002. 'Art Niu Sila: Contemporary Pacific Art in New Zealand', in Mallon and Pereira (eds.), pp. 191-208

Vergne, Philippe 2003. 'Globalization from the Rear: "Would you care to dance, Mr. Malevich?"', in Walker Art Centre and DAP, *How Latitudes become Forms: Art in the Global Age* Minnesota: Walker Art Center and DAP, pp. 18-27

Weeks, Jane 2006. 'Style leaders', *Museums Journal* 106(9): 50-51